One of our men opened up on the NVA at about the same time they began firing at us. It was that fast. They were on both sides of us, and the volume of fire was terrific. When they opened up on the team, I was in a kneeling position and immediately began firing back. Suddenly, I felt a round strike me in the chest. It sent me twisting to my left, and as I turned back into my original position, I reached over to grab my knife out of its scabbard, only to discover that I now had half a knife. The bullet that hit me had gone through the day-night flare that was taped to the sheath of the K-bar, which was positioned upside down on my shoulder harness for quick release. The bullet had broken the steel blade of my knife in two. The NVA were still firing at me, and I remember wondering how in the hell had I broken my K-bar. That was before I realized that all of my teammates had been hit and were dead.

By Maj. Bruce H. Norton, USMC (Ret.)
Published by The Ballantine Publishing Group:

FORCE RECON DIARY, 1969
FORCE RECON DIARY, 1970

With Donald N. Hamblen:
ONE TOUGH MARINE

With Maurice J. Jacques:
SERGEANT MAJOR, U.S. MARINES

With Len Maffioli:
GROWN GRAY IN WAR

STINGRAY

Edited by
Maj. Bruce H. Norton,
USMC (Ret.)

BALLANTINE BOOKS • NEW YORK

To Darice, Bruce, and Elizabeth

A Ballantine Book
Published by The Ballantine Publishing Group
Copyright © 2000 by Norton and Son

All rights reserved under International and Pan-American Copyright Conventions. Published in the United States by The Ballantine Publishing Group, a division of Random House, Inc., New York, and simultaneously in Canada by Random House of Canada Limited, Toronto.

Most of the material in this publication is comprised of documents found in *U.S. Marines in Vietnam*, a series of books compiled by the History and Museums Division Headquarters of the United States Marine Corps.

Ballantine and colophon are registered trademarks of Random House, Inc.

www.randomhouse.com/BB/

Library of Congress Catalog Card Number: 00-105083

ISBN 0-8041-1026-3

Manufactured in the United States of America

First Edition: August 2000

10 9 8 7 6 5 4 3 2 1

Contents

"Successful Stingray operations require a complex blend of dedicated assets, which consist of thoroughly knowledgeable planners, commanders, support personnel, and, most important, highly trained reconnaissance elements capable of operating in a fast-reaction target acquisition and destruction mode. Communications and rapid response must be totally reliable and immediate. Anything less is to court disaster."

LT. COL. C. C. COFFMAN JR., USMC (Ret. 1998)

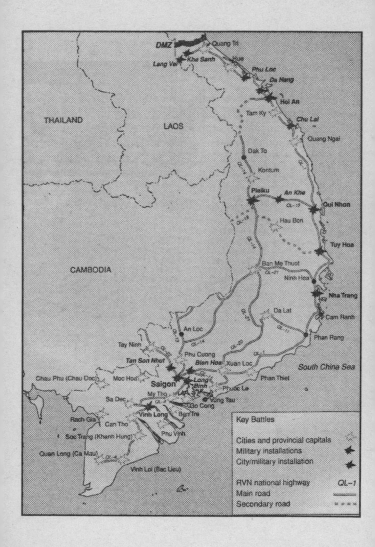

THAILAND

LAOS

CAMBODIA

DMZ

Quang Tri
Lang Vei
Khe Sanh
Hue
Phu Loc
Da Nang
Hoi An
Tam Ky
Chu Lai
Quang Ngai
Dak To
Kontum
Plaiku
An Khe
QL-19
Qui Nhon
Hau Bon
Tuy Hoa
Ban Me Thuot
QL-21
Ninh Hoa
Nha Trang
Da Lat
Cam Ranh
Phan Rang
An Loc
QL-14
Tay Ninh
QL-20
Phu Cuong
Xuan Loc
Tan Son Nhut
Bien Hoa
South China Sea
Chau Phu (Chau Doc)
Moc Hoa
Saigon
Long Binh
Phan Thiet
Phuoc Le
Sa Dec
My Tho
Go Cong
Vung Tau
Vinh Long
Ben Tre
Rach Gia
Can Tho
Phu Vinh
Soc Trang (Khanh Hung)
Quan Long (Ca Mau)
QL-4
Vinh Loi (Bac Lieu)

Key Battles

Cities and provincial capitals
Military installations
City/military installation

RVN national highway   QL-1
Main road
Secondary road

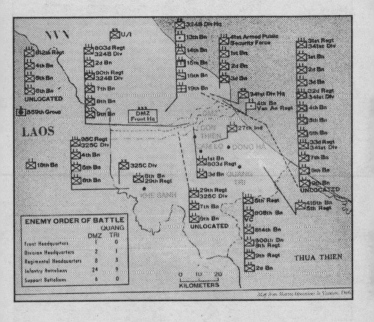

ENEMY ORDER OF BATTLE

	QUANG	
	DMZ	TRI
Front Headquarters	1	0
Division Headquarters	2	1
Regimental Headquarters	8	3
Infantry Battalions	24	9
Support Battalions	6	0

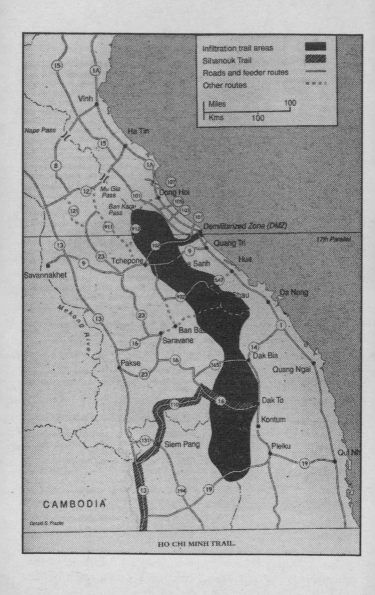

Vinh

Nape Pass

Ha Tin

Dong Hoi

Mu Gia Pass

Ban Karai Pass

Demilitarized Zone (DMZ)

17th Parallel

Quang Tri

Tchepone

Khe Sanh

Hue

Savannakhet

A Shau

Da Nang

Mekong River

Ban Bak

Saravane

Pakse

Dak Bia

Quang Ngai

Dak To

Kontum

Siem Pang

Pleiku

Qui Nhon

CAMBODIA

Daniel S. Frazier

HO CHI MINH TRAIL.

Introduction

Noted Marine Corps historian and author, Allan R. Millet, defined reconnaissance and its importance:

> From time immemorial military commanders have been concerned with the availability of timely, useful information during a campaign, especially when they are operating in foreign lands and distant waters. *Reconnaissance,* the French military term for information gathering, entered the English military vocabulary in the seventeenth century. This standing function of the exercise of command has been performed as long as armies and navies have existed.

Reconnaissance activities generally focus upon two categories of information: data on terrain and weather, and data about the enemy order of battle and activities. For environmental information, reconnaissance units would gather data on road conditions, bridges, tunnels, passes, civilian and military structures of all types, soil trafficability, economical resources, potable water, obstacles, and significant terrain features such as lakes, mountains, forests, and deserts. Data for naval operations included wind and tide information, weather conditions, and the location of harbors and anchorages, as well as shoal waters and all types of landfall information.

Skilled reconnaissance should also offer details about the enemy, provided that enemy forces are within reach of the means of information gathering. An enemy's observable units and their activities can furnish data on strength, force structure, general weapons and equipment, logistical arrangements, patterns of activity in camp or on the march, deployment for battle, and security operations. The one thing reconnaissance observation cannot produce with confidence is insight concerning enemy intentions and plans—unless a reconnaissance unit captures knowledgeable prisoners or enemy documents and maps.

The instruments of reconnaissance have changed, even if its purposes have not. Stealth and established observation posts (usually found on hills) favored the foot observer; coverage of wide areas and the rapid delivery of information required mounted scouts or "rangers." Skilled armies combined both types of reconnaissance units. By the nineteenth century, however, light cavalry, accompanied by staff officers, performed the core reconnaissance functions. The maritime equivalent of light cavalry was the patrol boat and light or "scout" cruiser, built for range and speed, not fighting ability.

The revolution in transportation and communications technology in the twentieth century expanded the capabilities of reconnaissance forces in geographic coverage, the recording of information, and the transmission of data to intelligence staffs. By the time of World War II, Army reconnaissance units could be deployed in motorcycles, scout cars, and light-armored fighting vehicles; light aircraft put observers above and beyond the battlefield. Radios allowed observers to report data without returning to command centers. Aerial photography made its debut in World War I. Allied and German photoreconnaissance aircraft produced overhead and oblique aerial photographs of ever-increasing resolution, and photo interpretation entered the repertoire of the intelligence staff. Electronic reconnaissance became possible first by producing sound-gathering devices that provided range and direction information about enemy artillery, and then by recording the direction and content of enemy radio communications. Nowadays, whole families of satellites can take and transmit photographs, record electronic transmissions, and map the world with radar and infrared sensors and the digital reconstruction of elevations and depressions. The vast menu of technical means of data collection has almost swamped the ability of military staffs to analyze information, which, in turn, places an ever-increasing demand upon computerized data storage, analysis, and retrieval. In the field, reconnaissance elements have the advantage of night-vision devices, sensors, and satellite-linked radios that can be integrated with maps and global positioning systems to determine one's position anywhere on earth in terms of latitude and longitude.

The range, accuracy, and timeliness of reconnaissance information have reshaped concepts of operations for air, naval, and land warfare. Ground commanders employ the concept of "reconnaissance pull" (attributed to the German army of World War II), in which highly mobile mechanized forces rush to exploit reconnaissance reports of enemy weakness. Such forces may enjoy overwhelming artillery support from guns and rocket launchers linked to fire-support teams employed with reconnaissance units. Airborne reconnaissance aircraft can summon up fighter-attack aircraft, armed helicopters to destroy targets of opportunity, or quick-reaction infantry. The destructive power of submarines, another twentieth-century innovation in gathering information, is so great that a submarine can not only attack enemy ships with torpedoes, but also strike land targets with cruise and ballistic missiles. At the same time, all modern armed forces have learned to place emphasis on the destruction of an enemy's reconnaissance assets.

Reconnaissance units have traditionally considered themselves a military elite. European light cavalry regiments claimed special freedoms, usually relief from standard discipline and drills, and this elitism did not disappear with horses. Mechanized cavalry regiments, airborne reconnaissance units, special boat and swimmer units, and helicopter-borne scouts have laid claim to special training, discriminating personnel selection, and a richness in equipment and weapons that often stirs resentment within their own armies and navies. Reconnaissance experts believe that they are unusually skilled and physically gifted—as they often are. The danger to a commander comes when his reconnaissance units substitute bravado for substance, a peril all armed forces have faced in the history of warfare.

Stingray is a book that describes a unique concept/philosophy that was used with telling success by reconnaissance Marines during the course of the Vietnam War. The Stingray concept was, in today's terms, "an enabler"—a force multiplier that was refined year after year.

As early as 1965, the III MAF (Marine Amphibious Force) commander, Maj. Gen. Lewis W. Walt, realized that reconnaissance units, properly utilized, were well equipped to locate an enemy who had already established a reputation for blending into the surroundings, a phantom army which was seldom seen armed and concentrated. Even when Viet Cong (VC) concentrations were sighted, they were usually on the move, fleeting targets at best.

Regular Marine ground units were considered too clumsy for this mission; the VC they found generally wanted to be found. General Walt decided that since reconnaissance patrols could find the VC, then the patrols should be provided with a means to destroy the enemy. Accordingly, he allowed patrols to call in air and artillery strikes. Slow clearance procedures hindered this application in the Da Nang tactical area of responsibility (TAOR), but the system proved to be successful at Chu Lai. The concept was refined, and in 1966 it was adopted as a standard tactic, then known as STINGRAY.

From June 1967 until January 1969, III MAF was commanded by Lt. Gen. Robert E. Cushman, Jr., and the refinement of the Stingray concept continued and was improved upon. Maj. Gen. Raymond G. Davis, Commanding General of the 3d Marine Division in 1969, held the Stingray concept in high regard. General Davis's concept of mobile operations depended not only on the helicopter but on the extensive exploitation of intelligence, specifically that gathered by small reconnaissance patrols, which he continuously employed throughout his division's area of responsibility and which supplemented both electronic and human-source intelligence (i.e., POWs, informers, agents). "Operating within range of friendly artillery fire were the heavily armed 'Stingray' patrols, whose mission was to find, and destroy the enemy with all available supporting arms, and rapid reinforcement, if necessary." The 3d Marine Division, Davis noted, "never launched an operation without acquiring clear definition of the targets and objectives through intelligence confirmed by recon patrols. High mobility operations [were] too difficult and complex to come up empty or in disaster."

Assuming command of III MAF in March 1969, Lt. Gen. Herman Nickerson Jr. placed 1st and 3d Force Reconnaissance Companies under the direction of the newly created Surveillance and Reconnaissance Center (SRC). Under the SRC, the companies were assigned new missions in III MAF's area of interest. Stingray patrols played an integral role during this time and until the end of the Marine commitment in Vietnam. Here is the story of the Stingray concept by those who created it and used it.

1

Force Recon— By Land, Sea, and Air

by
Lt. Gen. Herman Nickerson Jr., USMC*
Marine Corps Gazette, February 1959

Force Recon—By Land, Sea, and Air, written by then Brig. Gen. Herman Nickerson Jr., in February 1959, and published in the *Marine Corps Gazette*, defines the new company's mission, main tasks, and capabilities. Using an amphibious operation ("Strongback") conducted in the Philippines in 1958, General Nickerson explains, in depth, the concept of how the Force Recon Company performs the task of gaining "timely" information to assist the commander in arriving at decisions and in executing its other vital roles in the landings.

"The job: Reduce the Uncertainty." So wrote Brig. Gen. J. M. Masters Sr. in the June 1958 *Gazette*. "Uncertainty is an ugly three-headed spook, which will haunt the commander. . . . The spook's three heads? The enemy, the weather, and the terrain. . . ."

To this statement of the intelligence officer's job we could add a job description: use available tools skillfully to strip

---

*Credited as "The Godfather of Long-Range Reconnaissance," Lieutenant General Nickerson assumed command of III MAF in March 1969. Immediately realizing the need for reconnaissance information beyond that provided division commanders by their respective recon battalions, he put theory to form when he tasked 1st Force Recon Company to conduct deep patrol operations for the MAF in June, followed by the reconstituted 3d Force Reconnaissance Company in October of that year.—Ed.

the veils from the three-headed spook and provide the commander with the information he needs to make a sound decision. One of the commander's best tools, in my opinion, is the force recon company. By well-conceived employment of this organization, many of the uncertainties can be reduced. Only when the commander has the best available information on the enemy, weather, and terrain can he confidently order "Launch helicopters!" and "Land the landing force!"

Perhaps the greatest difference of opinion on modern amphibious tactics and techniques arises from, first, the debate as to whether or not nuclear munitions will be used; and second, the size and degree of unit separation. No matter what size the separation unit is that lands by helicopter in the amphibious assault, we can all agree that the highest order of intelligence is required for this unit to "stay loose," hit hard, then saddle up and move out rapidly—avoiding, all the while, the unproductive moment of nuclear-weapon target-size concentration. How, then, shall we succeed in unveiling the spook?

Within force troops, in both FMFLant and FMFPac, we have the key to unlock a part of the Houdini apparatus—the force reconnaissance company. The proper utilization of these highly skilled "eyeballs" and "eardrums" is the skeleton key to success in modern amphibious warfare.

The general missions of these companies are to support a landing force by, first, conducting a pre-assault and post-assault amphibious and parachute reconnaissance; and second, conducting pre-assault and post-assault parachute and other pathfinding missions.

A force reconnaissance company is a part of the task organization of the landing force and is employed to extend the ground reconnaissance capability of that force beyond the coverage afforded by the organic reconnaissance battalion of Marine divisions. As noted in the mission, this is accomplished by pre-assault terrestrial reconnaissance using amphibious and parachute means. To conduct post-assault deep reconnaissance, helicopter lift and parachuting are used. The company employs helicopters to establish and displace deep observation posts for battlefield surveillance. The reconnaissance-surveillance portion of the force reconnaissance company's mission must be closely monitored by the landing force G-2 to insure that all efforts are integrated into the overall intelligence collection plan. Only by obtaining and using all available information can the intelligence officer fit together the assorted pieces of the jigsaw puzzle and present the commander with a clear picture.

In addition, the force reconnaissance company is employed to provide parachute pathfinder services in the approach and retirement lanes and helicopter landing zones, in amphibious and subsequent land operations. Pathfinder teams provide pre-assault navigational assistance to helicopters in approach to and along approach-retirement lanes.

Pathfinder teams provide terminal guidance to the helicopter assault waves in the landing zones, in either day or night operations. Final pre-H-hour reports of enemy activity, obstacles, weather, and radiological contamination in the landing zones and near vicinity are made by these pathfinder teams. Pathfinders are capable of limited obstacle clearance, should this work be necessary, and they provide emergency communication support and assembly aid to the helicopter-landed troops.

The main tasks of a force reconnaissance company, then, are: first, to perform pre-D-day reconnaissance as required by the overall intelligence collection plan, using parachute and amphibious means; and second, to provide pathfinder services. In order to do these jobs, the company is functionally organized to plan and execute—with the support of tactical and transport fixed-wing aircraft, helicopters, and naval vessels—the following tactical missions: perform pre-D-day amphibious reconnaissance of any landing beaches required by the landing plan; establish coastwatcher stations or inland observation posts after D-day, if required; execute pre-D-day parachute reconnaissance of helicopter landing zones—of the approach and retirement lanes thereto—and of other key inland installations of interest to the Marine expeditionary force; conduct post-D-day reconnaissance, by helicopter or parachute, of critical areas beyond the range of division reconnaissance means; and finally, render necessary parachute or pathfinder support to assault waves.

These varied tasks are accomplished by fourteen officers and 147 enlisted, organized into a company headquarters of four officers and thirty-three enlisted; a parachute reconnaissance platoon of three officers and twenty-three enlisted; and an amphibious reconnaissance platoon of two officers and twenty-three enlisted. A major (0302) is in command. Twelve officers and ninety-seven enlisted Marines are on parachute jump status.

The company is capable of some organic supply functions: organizational first-echelon maintenance of its gear, and second-echelon organizational maintenance of electronics, motor transport, and ordnance equipment. In garrison, it is authorized to conduct parachute maintenance and repair. Also in garrison, it is capable of maintaining and distributing a thirty-day operational level of replenishment supplies and equipment, including 100 percent replenishment of parachutes. In the field, it can maintain and distribute a five-day level. Thus, this company requires aerial resupply support (including packaging) to deliver supplies to deep observation posts and distant reconnaissance patrols or teams.

Now that we recognize the missions, tasks, and organization of a force reconnaissance company, let's take a specific example of its use in one of the major division-wing-size amphibious exercises conducted this past year. We'll briefly outline the 1st Force Reconnaissance Company's part in Operation Strongback, conducted during February and March 1958 in the Philippines. The employment of the 2d Force Reconnaissance Company in Phibex 1-58, conducted at Camp Lejeune, North Carolina, followed a somewhat different pattern. Omission of a narrative of this East Coast action is premeditated in the interest of stimulating letters to the editor.

First, the concept of Operation Strongback called for a deep helicopter landing, with a surface assault and a subsequent joining of these forces.

The parachute reconnaissance platoon was retained at the Marine expeditionary force level; the amphibious reconnaissance platoon was employed with the advance force; and the pathfinder platoon was attached to the helicopter group, MAG-16. It should be noted here that in Phibex 1-58, no advance force was employed, and the pathfinders were not attached to the helicopter group.

Back to Strongback: the plan, as conceived and executed, supported the intelligence collection effort well. Four of five parachute reconnaissance teams dropped into specific objectives from TF-1 aircraft on the nights of D-6 (D-day minus six) and D-5. A fifth team jumped from four F3D aircraft on the night of D-4. The first four had about eighty-five hours and the last one somewhat less time to complete their assigned reconnaissance missions. All teams performed effectively in clarifying, confirming, amplifying, and correcting previous intelligence.

A two-man radio relay team, which parachuted into a relay point on the night of D-5, employed its "MAY" radio to receive messages from the reconnaissance teams and relay them to high-performance retransmission aircraft. By previous arrangement, reconnaissance teams with their AN/PRC-10 radios (using RC/292 antenna) contacted the radio relay team at appointed times on the nights of D-5, D-4, and D-3, when the high-performance retransmission aircraft also arrived on station.

Four of the five reconnaissance teams were recovered by TF-1 aircraft at varying times on D-2 and D-1 from a pickup site at a small airfield on the objective area. The fifth reconnaissance team and the radio relay team remained in the objective area and later joined up with helicopter-borne assault units. All teams were prepared to remain in the objective area for later join-up had the TF-1 recovery failed for one reason or another.

Injection of parachute reconnaissance teams into the objective area proved successful in gaining valuable and timely information on the enemy, weather, and terrain. Thus, detailed intelligence was available on D-2 and D-1 for dissemination by message, but too late for distribution of overlays, sketches, and photographs of landing zones and other objectives. "Skyhook" technique would help overcome part of this difficulty.

Another answer is to introduce parachute reconnaissance teams into the area during the planning phase, at about D-60 to D-30. Last-minute confirmation of intelligence so gathered could be accomplished by jumping parachute reconnaissance teams during the period of D-4 through D-2. The point we make here is that these para-recon teams jumped in and recovered as planned; and they *did* get their messages out.

The amphibious reconnaissance was conducted by the advance force, employing U.S. and Philippine teams. All teams were dropped and recovered during daylight. An APD ship was used as the transporting vessel because of the nonavailability of a fleet-type submarine. These amphibious reconnaissance teams normally would have been transported by submarines and executed their missions during hours of darkness.

The pathfinder platoon was attached to the helicopter group, MAG-16. The concept of the pathfinder operation was to have four teams parachute into the selected landing areas, and establish and operate two primary and two alternate helicopter landing zones. Each landing zone was to be capable of handling flights of five aircraft at each landing site. A four-man team was to establish an IP (Initial Point) for each landing zone at designated points. All teams were to execute pathfinder missions at L-hour (scheduled time for landing first assault waves of helicopters).

So it was planned. The theory of attaching these pathfinding teams to the helicopter group was based on the premise that pathfinding is an extension of the transport aviation function.

All four teams jumped from TF-1 aircraft, generally on schedule. The two IP teams jumped from an R4D aircraft. All the pathfinders accomplished their assigned missions. The helicopter pilots are reported to have "sworn by them!"

Briefly, the force reconnaissance company employed all three of its major tactical elements in the Strongback exercise in performing its mission of gaining information to assist the commander in arriving at decisions, and in executing the vital pathfinding role in the landings.

The force reconnaissance company, as currently organized and equipped, is not the final answer. It cannot snatch the final veil from the "three-headed spooks," nor can it open all the locks of a Houdini apparatus. The company itself appears to contain "apples and oranges," and experts are quick to point out the need to separate the purely reconnaissance function from the pathfinding function. The least common denominator, for the present, is the parachute jumping qualification authorized and required in all three of the major tactical elements of the force reconnaissance company—amphibious, para-recon, and para-pathfinding. The future may see the pathfinders made organic to helicopter groups. In my opinion, the Strongback method of attachment is a good solution for the present.

In addition, there are other problems: first, qualifying men as dual self-contained underwater breathing apparatus (SCUBA) and parachute-trained reconnaissance agents; second, obtaining far better communications; and third, acquiring a means of fast entry into an area to drop the para-recon teams, to name but a few. If we all understand the present force reconnaissance company's capabilities and limitations, and think about ways and means of improving the above stated concept of employment, we'll not awaken during the battle, surrounded by the fog of war, too late. Any ideas?

— 2 —

The Vietnam War:
An Overview

To understand how the philosophy of Stingray would play such a significant role for Marine reconnaissance units from 1965 to 1971, once the offensive posture was taken by the Commander, U.S. Military Assistance Command, Vietnam (COMUSMACV), the strategy and the objectives of Gen. William C. Westmoreland are presented below.

Reconnaissance activities during the Vietnam War focused primarily on two categories of timely information: data on terrain and weather; data about the enemy order of battle and his activities. While the range, accuracy, and timeliness of reconnaissance information have certainly served to reshape concepts of operations for air, naval, and land warfare, the ground commander must be able to understand and accept the concept of reconnaissance if it is to be used to his advantage.

Strategy

Gen. William C. Westmoreland's Strategy for Vietnam

The first U.S. ground combat forces to be deployed to South Vietnam in March 1965 had a defensive mission, to protect the security of air bases in the South from which operations against North Vietnam were launched. Except for releasing some Republic of Vietnam Armed Forces (RVNAF) units from static security duties for operations against Viet Cong forces, those initial deployments were devoid of any strategic concept that related U.S. ground forces to the larger concerns of counterinsurgency in the South. The lodgments of U.S. Marines at Da Nang and Chu Lai and a U.S. Army brigade at Bien Hoa and Vung Tau between March and early May nevertheless implied a more permanent commitment of U.S. military forces to the war than did the sporadic air strikes against the North, which could be stopped on short notice.

Lyndon B. Johnson, who succeeded to the presidency after Kennedy was assassinated and was elected in his own right one year later, approached the use of ground forces in the South with the same caution that he had used when developing his strategy for the application of airpower in the North. He rejected the recommendations of Army Chief of Staff Gen. Harold K. Johnson to send two U.S. divisions to South Vietnam's Central Highlands or to extend a multidivision force across the Laotian panhandle to interdict the Ho Chi Minh Trail. In April 1965 the president sanctioned a change in the Marines' mission from a strictly defensive one to one that included a phase-in of offensive counterinsurgency operations. The conversion from defensive to offensive operations was to proceed in measured increments, moving outward from the secure perimeters of established coastal enclaves over a period of about three months. Despite the addition of an offensive mission, ground forces remained tied to an operational concept rooted in defensive, albeit expanded, enclaves.

To move U.S. ground forces into a more offensive military posture, Gen. William C. Westmoreland, Commander, U.S. Military Assistance Command, Vietnam (COMUSMACV), obtained permission to use Marine and Army ground forces in South Vietnam as reserve/reaction forces in acute situations anywhere in the South. That "fire brigade" concept, together with the establishment of enclaves, was the dominant U.S. ground war strategy during the initial stages of the buildup. Given the limited number of U.S. ground units in

South Vietnam in the spring and summer of 1965, Westmoreland had little choice but to embrace those operational concepts as essentially economy-of-force measures, and neither concept embodied a truly offensive operational strategy.

The Three-Phase Strategy

President Johnson's decision on 28 July to increase the number of U.S. ground troops in South Vietnam from 75,000 to 175,000 by the end of 1965 prompted COMUSMACV to formulate a comprehensive three-phase strategic concept to defeat Viet Cong and North Vietnamese Army (NVA) forces in South Vietnam. The *strategy* required an infusion of large numbers of U.S. ground forces, a revitalization of South Vietnam's military forces and pacification programs, and the success of the air and naval efforts throughout Southeast Asia to stem infiltration from the North. Phase I, which was already being implemented, entailed the development of coastal enclaves and bases and the use of U.S. units in a reserve/reaction role. Its **objective** was to secure population centers and strategic military bases and to stabilize the military situation by halting the Viet Cong and NVA's string of successes, thus laying the foundation for a further buildup of U.S. military forces and the development of a logistical support base.

In Phase II, as more ground forces arrived, COMUSMACV planned to take the offensive to locate and destroy Viet Cong and NVA main force units and bases and to begin the crucial efforts of separating the insurgents from their bases of support among the rural population, thereby eroding the Viet Cong forces' fighting strength. Driven into sparsely settled hinterlands, Viet Cong units would be attacked by the superior air and ground firepower of U.S. forces. Of equal importance to reducing Viet Cong combat strength was refurbishing the RVNAF so it could take a more active role in support of pacification in areas cleared of the larger Viet Cong units by U.S. forces.

The third phase of Westmoreland's strategy entailed

making concerted attacks to destroy the remnants of main force units forced to seek haven in remote bases, and a nationwide effort to eliminate the Viet Cong shadow government in every hamlet and village. While the former might take ground attacks into Laos or even North Vietnam, the latter would fall largely to the RVNAF, which would gradually assume full responsibility for the defense of South Vietnam.

The three phases overlapped one another, and each was repeated when the strategy was applied in new areas of the South as additional forces became available. Other aspects of the overall strategy—U.S. advisory and support efforts, for example—would persist through all three phases and, indeed, would require strengthening if the Viet Cong infrastructure was to be eliminated. COMUSMACV's strategy was broadly similar to that adopted earlier by the French. Reluctant to attach a firm timetable to the fulfillment of his strategy, General Westmoreland thought that the situation envisioned in Phase III could be attained in three to five years if the ground, air, and naval elements of U.S. strategy were successful and if South Vietnam fully mobilized its counterinsurgency efforts.

Conditions for Success

As initially envisioned, Westmoreland's strategy sought to exploit U.S. military advantages—overwhelming firepower and mobility—to avert the pitfalls of a war of attrition, a protracted conflict, the slow erosion of the Viet Cong and NVA's military strength, and the likelihood of greater American casualties. To avoid those dangers, Westmoreland had to wrest the tactical initiative from the Viet Cong and NVA forces and curb infiltration. Failure to accomplish those goals would reduce the benefits of firepower and mobility by allowing the Viet Cong and NVA forces to regulate their rate of casualties and to replace and increase manpower. Westmoreland's campaign strategy was already handicapped by rules of engagement that prevented U.S. ground forces from pursuing enemy troops into Cambodia, Laos, or North Vietnam, thus providing the Viet Cong and NVA with inviolate sanctuaries where they could hide to reduce casualties and refurbish their units.

Success in the South also depended on the effectiveness of U.S. air and naval operations in North Vietnam and Laos, over which COMUSMACV had no control. The overall U.S. strategy, moreover, labored under the disadvantage of a lack of unity of command, effort, and sometimes purpose. Operation Rolling Thunder, in particular, followed a muddled strategy that wavered between attaining military objectives and inducing negotiations. The expansion of North Vietnam's air defense system to formidable proportions, including the use of radar-guided antiaircraft artillery and Soviet-made surface-to-air missiles (SAMs), raised the cost of interdiction and armed reconnaissance north of the demilitarized zone (DMZ) and necessitated the introduction of new tactics to evade both SAMs and MiG jet interceptors.

Perhaps more important to the realization of Westmoreland's strategy in the South was the speed with which U.S. officials made available additional ground forces. Forgoing even a partial mobilization of reserve forces in the summer of 1965, the Army and Marines were limited to meeting troop requirements for South Vietnam by using already existing forces, resorting to the use of strategic reserves, or activating new units from scratch. While the services met all of Westmoreland's early force requirements, his ground strategy was held hostage to the pace at which they could organize and deploy additional units. Relying solely on active forces, the administration was compelled to adopt an incremental strategy for the prosecution of the ground war, and by its decision not to mobilize the reserves, it sapped both its policy and military strategy of an element of resoluteness and public backing.

The Ground War, 1965–67

As the buildup progressed, two divergent operational strategies emerged for the conduct of the ground war. **Two Operational Strategies:** While all ground forces that deployed to South Vietnam needed secure bases from which to operate, the enclave concept as the core of an operational strategy was embraced most extensively by Marines in the I Corps Tactical Zone (I CTZ). Retired Army general James A. Gavin also championed it. Operating within the enclave and slowly expanding its perimeters entailed close coordination with and participation in the pacification efforts of the RVNAF. Search-and-clear and clear-and-hold operations were preeminent. Their objective was to provide a tactical security shield for areas undergoing pacification, thereby enabling the pacification zone to expand in the manner of a spreading inkblot. To enhance antiguerrilla operations in support of pacification, Marine forces organized combined action platoons consisting of Marine and Popular Forces (local Vietnamese military) elements and engaged in civic action and psychological operations. When required, Marine units ventured beyond the enclaves as a reaction force. The enclave concept, in short, constituted the Marines' concept of a "balanced strategy."

In contrast, many U.S. Army commanders, including Westmoreland, opted for an operational strategy that was less defensive-minded and took advantage of their superiority in firepower and mobility, especially air mobility afforded by the helicopters that the U.S. Army possessed.

To some extent the Marines were constrained from adopting a more offensive strategy because they had fewer helicopters, lacked heavy artillery, and depended upon seaward logistical support. Rather than concentrating U.S. Army forces in populated zones, Army leaders believed that ground units could be used more effectively to locate and engage the Viet Cong and the NVA regular forces in remote, sparsely populated regions as they infiltrated into South Vietnam or emerged from their hidden bases. Although such offensive operations—usually characterized as search-and-destroy or reconnaissance-in-force operations—served indirectly as a shield for areas undergoing pacification, the objective of Army operations was the destruction of Viet Cong and NVA combat power rather than population security, as was the case in the enclave concept. A third strategic concept also had particular appeal within the U.S. Army. It sought to use U.S. ground forces to directly interdict infiltration through the Laotian panhandle. Made impossible by military problems and restrictive rules of engagement based upon political considerations, that approach was not tried until later in the war and then primarily by the RVNAF.

In practice, the two major operational strategies were not mutually exclusive or strictly confined to one or the other service. Marine forces, in Operations Starlite, Utah, and Texas, were called on to operate beyond the confines of their enclaves to pursue the enemy or retake important outposts. The forces in such operations, however, did not stray far from the coastal lowlands. Army units, their bases usually further inland, conducted intensive operations in the vicinity of their bases to improve local security and enhance pacification.

The DMZ

While U.S. Marine units in I Corps expanded their coastal enclaves north and south of Da Nang, North Vietnam intensified its military threat along the DMZ to draw U.S. forces away from populated areas. Increasingly in 1966 and 1967, Marines were compelled to reinforce the DMZ by transferring forces from southern I Corps. In operations such as Hastings and Prairie, the Marines withstood NVA artillery attacks and ground assaults across the DMZ. The NVA's continued presence in the vicinity of the DMZ and Khe Sanh necessitated the construction or reinforcement of a string of fire support bases just south of the DMZ, and the United States eventually created the "McNamara Line," which combined electronic sensors and other detection devices with manned strongpoints. Although its purpose was to reduce the large investment of manpower that the Marines had committed to protect the DMZ, the McNamara Line instead forced the Marines into a somewhat static defense of large tracts of barren territory. By the spring of 1967, North Vietnamese strategy had tied down a major portion of the Marine force in Vietnam in the vulnerable border area along the DMZ and around Khe Sanh. Supported by the massed counterbattery fire of Marine and Army artillery, naval gunfire support, and constant airstrikes—including B-52 bombardment—in such operations as BUFFALO, HICKORY II, KINGFISHER, and KENTUCKY, the Marines repelled repeated NVA attacks in combat that frequently resembled World War I trench warfare more than counterinsurgency. Areas vacated by the Marines in southern I Corps were occupied by U.S. Army and South Korean forces which had been moved from II and III CTZs. Their transfer, however, reduced the military support for pacification programs, especially in coastal II CTZ.

Strategic Stalemate

As 1968 approached, the war in Vietnam had reached a strategic equilibrium. For both sides the war had become a contest of strategies of attrition; neither side faced imminent defeat or victory. Westmoreland's strategy had denied North Vietnamese forces a significant tactical success, but it fell short of attaining the level of attrition needed to diminish North Vietnam's ability to wage its own war of attrition against U.S. forces. In the context of his three-phase campaign strategy, Westmoreland had succeeded in stabilizing the military situation and undertaking offensive operations as called for in Phase II. But, although U.S. forces achieved many tactical victories, Westmoreland was unable to transcend the strategic defense that he was forced to assume due to the constraints placed on U.S. ground and air operations and the incremental buildup of military forces in the South.

Although U.S. forces frequently assumed the tactical offensive, Westmoreland generally was unable to deny the tactical initiative to Viet Cong or NVA forces. Rolling Thunder and other air and naval operations against North Vietnam and the Ho Chi Minh Trail, moreover, neither stopped infiltration nor achieved the strategic goal of changing North Vietnam's policy. In the "other war," South Vietnam's pacification efforts, only marginal progress had been made since 1965, despite the fact that nearly 50 percent of the Army of the

Republic of Vietnam (ARVN) and all paramilitary forces were dedicated to the effort.

Unswerving in their strategic goal of unification, North Vietnam's leaders recognized that the strategy of military confrontation they had pursued in the South for over two years had also failed. To maintain its strategic position in the South, North Vietnam had matched the U.S. military buildup; the number of NVA divisions increased from one, in early 1965, to nine at the start of 1968, and guerrilla forces in the South retained a strong foothold in many rural areas. North Vietnam also retained other important advantages, among them use of cross-border base areas, the ability to continue infiltration under arduous conditions, continued external support from Communist-bloc nations, a society in the North mobilized for war, and a large untapped pool of manpower.

To carry out his campaign strategy, General Westmoreland needed more troops. He had requested additional ground forces in 1967 to reinforce those already in place, to compensate in part for the diversion of units from other corps areas into I Corps, and to extend operations into Laos and possibly North Vietnam. The U.S. government's rejection of his request had serious strategic implications because, in effect, it placed a troop ceiling on U.S. strength in South Vietnam and, for the time being, confined Westmoreland's acknowledged strategic options to South Vietnam. Still confident of success, Westmoreland acknowledged that the realization of Phase III of his initial strategic concept would be set back two to three years without the additional reinforcements.

Vietnamization, 1968–73

Under an overarching policy called Vietnamization, which began in the waning days of the Johnson administration under Clark M. Clifford, who had replaced Robert McNamara as secretary of defense in early 1968, U.S. strategy and operations entered a new phase. The two main objectives of Vietnamization were the withdrawal of U.S. forces and the creation of a stronger, largely self-reliant South Vietnamese military force. While the latter was a long-sought goal of U.S. advisory and support attempts, past efforts to strengthen and modernize the RVNAF had been conducted without the pressure of diminishing U.S. support, the prospect of large-scale conventional combat, or the presence of strong NVA forces in the South.

The military aspect of Vietnamization consisted of three overlapping phases: the redeployment of U.S. units and the RVNAF's assumption of their combat and support roles; measures to improve the RVNAF's combat and support capabilities, especially firepower and mobility, through training and the transfer of equipment; and the retention of a residual U.S. presence in the form of an advisory group. An additional aspect of Vietnamization was the fostering of political, social, and economic reforms to create a vibrant political and social foundation to help bolster the South Vietnamese government's political stature. The success of that aspect was closely tied to progress in the pacification program.

Gen. Creighton Abrams's Strategy

The task of implementing Vietnamization and its supporting military strategy fell to Gen. Creighton Abrams, who replaced General Westmoreland as COMUSMACV in June 1968. Abrams was under significant pressure from U.S. officials to minimize American casualties and conduct operations with an eye toward leaving South Vietnam in the strongest possible military position after U.S. forces withdrew. Adjusting his strategy to a new military situation—the near-complete destruction of the Viet Cong in the Tet campaign of 1968—Abrams took advantage of the weakened condition of Viet Cong forces to promote and accelerate efforts to restore rural security and enhance pacification. He stressed the importance of small-unit tactics and in the context of clear-and-hold operations instead of large-scale search-and-destroy operations. To improve the RVNAF's effectiveness, he encouraged more combined operations. As Viet Cong and NVA forces dispersed across South Vietnam's borders into Laos and Cambodia after the Tet Offensive, Abrams increased military pressure against their logistical support system rather than attempting the attrition of the enemy's combat forces. At the same time, the reduction of air operations over North Vietnam allowed the concentration of the air effort against the Ho Chi Minh Trail in Laos, thus complementing Abrams's logistical offensive.

Abrams envisioned the RVNAF assuming the majority of combat at the completion of Vietnamization, its operations shifting to the border to assume the role of defensive shield, similar to that performed by U.S. forces. In turn, paramilitary forces were to take over the ARVN's role in area-security and pacification support. The newly organized People's Self-Defense Force would assume responsibility for village and hamlet defense. To help the South Vietnamese government carry out its pacification programs, Abrams accorded a high priority to the U.S. advisory effort and initiated new efforts, such as the Phoenix program, to eradicate the Viet Cong infrastructure. Stressing the importance of subsuming and coordinating all operations under a unified strategy, Abrams propounded the concept of "one war" in contrast to the dichotomy of the big-unit war and the "other war," or pacification, that had defined U.S. operational strategies before the Tet Offensive.

General Abrams's strategy, however, retained elements of continuity with Westmoreland's. Operations in War Zones C and D in III CTZ were similar to those launched by U.S. Army units in 1966 and 1967. As part of a post-Tet offensive, Abrams also sought to disrupt and reduce the bases from which communist forces could again threaten the Saigon region. Rather than large sweeps, U.S. Army and RVNAF forces scoured the base areas with numerous small-unit operations, frequently resweeping areas, and established a more effective screen along the Cambodian border to prevent Viet Cong and NVA forces' regaining access to their bases. As an economy-of-force measure, the communist forces resorted to a "high point" strategy that entailed occasional rocket attacks against Saigon and other cities. Such attacks incurred little risk to their forces and were a violent reminder of their presence and of the South Vietnamese government's inability to protect its population. The attacks also distracted U.S. and allied forces from other tasks in order to periodically clear the "rocket belts" that the communist forces established around nearly every urban center in South Vietnam.

Abrams's Strategy in Action

Until all U.S. Army forces withdrew from the Highlands in 1971, the war there changed little under Abrams's tenure. Army units continued a war of attrition, with combat focusing on the defense of border posts and Special Forces camps. Viet Cong and NVA attacks against such targets along the entire border attested to their ability to seize the tactical initiative. Many camps—Ben Het, Thien Phuoc, Thuong Duc, Bu Prang, Dak Saeng, Dak Pek, Katum, Bu Dop, and Tong Le Chon—attacked earlier because of their proximity to communist bases and infiltration routes, were attacked anew. With the departure of U.S. Special Forces in March 1971, and the conversion of CIDG (Civilian Irregular Defense Group) units to Regional Forces, the future of some camps was in doubt. The departure of Special Forces brought an end to any significant U.S. Army role in the Highlands.

Army and Marine operations in the northern provinces were emblematic of Abrams's strategy. While continuing to support pacification along the coast, U.S. and RVNAF units began a series of forays into long-neglected communist base areas. Operations such as Delaware and Dewey Canyon, in the A Shau Valley along the Laotian border, were part of COMUSMACV's logistical offensive. The operation in the A Shau produced some of the bloodiest combat of the war, such as that at Hamburger Hill in May 1969. Like Westmoreland's search-and-destroy operations, the effects of such operations were transient. As U.S. forces dwindled, few of the enemy's major base areas could be reentered or permanently occupied. Military operations on the coast, where the pacification effort had made some modest gains, would likewise feel the effects of diminished support as Marines and Army units withdrew.

With most U.S. combat units slated to leave South Vietnam in 1970 and 1971, time was critical for the success of Vietnamization. Although General Abrams's logistical offensive helped reduce the level of Viet Cong and NVA activity in the South, NVA forces, command centers, logistical depots, training camps, and other facilities remained across the border in Cambodia and Laos. Those forces still posed a threat to Vietnamization and pacification. To reduce that threat and to give the South Vietnamese government more time to consolidate its strength and pacify the country, Abrams proposed large-scale sweeps into base areas in Cambodia and Laos.

The Concept of Reconnaissance

Especially when operating in foreign lands and distant waters, military commanders have always fretted about the availability of useful information during a campaign.

Reconnaissance, the French military term for information gathering, entered the English military vocabulary sometime during the seventeenth or eighteenth century. A standing function of the exercise of command, reconnaissance has been performed as long as armies and navies have existed.

Reconnaissance activities focus on two categories of information: data on terrain and weather, and data about the enemy "order of battle" and activities. For environmental information, reconnaissance units gather data on road conditions, bridges, tunnels, passes, civilian and military structures of all sorts, soil trafficability, economic resources (such as forage), potable water, obstacles, and significant terrain features such as lakes, mountains, forests, and deserts. Data for naval operations would include wind and tide information, weather conditions, the location of harbors, anchorages, and shoal waters, and all sorts of landfall information.

Skilled reconnaissance should also provide information about the enemy, provided that enemy forces are within reach of the means of information gathering. An enemy's observable units and their activities can provide data on strength, force structure, general physical condition and state of morale, nature of weapons and equipment, logistical arrangements, pattern of activity in camp or the march, deployment for battle, and security operations. The one thing reconnaissance observation cannot produce with confidence is insight concerning enemy intentions and plans—unless a reconnaissance unit captures knowledgeable prisoners or enemy documents and maps.

The instruments of reconnaissance have changed, even if its purposes have not. Stealth and established observation posts, usually located on high ground, favored the foot observer; coverage of wide areas and the rapid delivery of information required mounted scouts or "rangers." Skilled armies combined both types of reconnaissance units, but by the nineteenth century, light cavalry accompanied by staff officers performed the core reconnaissance functions. The maritime equivalent of light cavalry was the patrol boat and light or "scout" cruiser, built for range and speed, not fighting ability.

The revolutions in weaponry, transportation, and communications technology in the twentieth century expanded the capabilities of reconnaissance forces in geographic coverage, the recording of information, and the transmission of data to intelligence staffs. Army reconnaissance units by the time of World War II could be deployed in motorcycles, scout cars, and light-armored fighting vehicles; light aircraft put observers above and beyond the battlefield. Radios allowed observers to report data without returning to command centers. Aerial photography made its debut in World War I; Allied and German photoreconnaissance aircraft produced overhead and oblique aerial photographs of ever-increasing resolution, and photo interpretation entered the repertoires of intelligence staffs. Electronic reconnaissance became possible, first by producing sound-gathering devices that provided range and direction information about enemy artillery, and then by recording the direction and content of enemy radio communications. In the 1990s, whole families of satellites took and transmitted photographs, recorded electronic transmissions, and mapped the world with infrared sensors or the digitized reconstruction of elevations and depressions. The vast menu of technical data collection has almost swamped the ability of military staffs to analyze information, which in turn places an ever-increasing demand upon computerized data storage and analysis. In the field, reconnaissance elements have the advantage of night-vision devices, sensors, and satellite-linked radios that can be integrated with maps and electronic methods of precisely determining one's position anywhere on earth in terms of latitude and longitude. Such instrumentation has been common aboard aircraft and ships since World War II.

The range, accuracy, and timeliness of reconnaissance information have reshaped concepts of operations for air, naval, and land warfare. Ground commanders employ the concept of "reconnaissance pull," which is attributed to the German army of World War II, in which highly mobile mechanized forces rush to exploit reconnaissance reports of enemy weaknesses. Such forces may enjoy overwhelming artillery support from guns and rocket launchers linked to fire-support teams deployed with reconnaissance units. Airborne reconnaissance aircraft (light or heavy) can summon up fighter-attack aircraft or armed helicopters to destroy targets of opportunity. The destructive power of submarines, another twentieth-century innovation in gathering information, is so great that a submarine can not only attack enemy ships with torpedoes, but also strike land targets with cruise and ballistic missiles. At the same time, all modern armed forces stress the destruction of an enemy's reconnaissance assets, including aircraft, satellites, and underwater sensor systems.

Reconnaissance units have traditionally considered themselves a military elite. European light cavalry regiments claimed special freedoms, usually relief from standard discipline and drills, and this elitism did not disappear when the horses did. Mechanized cavalry regiments, airborne reconnaissance units, special boat and swimmer units, and helicopter-borne scouts have laid claims to special training, discriminating personnel selection, and a richness in equipment and weapons that often stirs resentment within their armies and navies. Reconnaissance experts believe that they are unusually skilled and physically gifted—and often they are. The danger to a commander comes when his reconnaissance units substitute bravado for substance, a peril all armed forces have faced.

=3=

"In the Beginning . . ."

Operation Shufly: 1962–1965

The Marine Corps' involvement in Vietnam began in 1962, when Lt. Gen. A. W. Shapley, FMFPac, sent one Marine helicopter squadron into the Mekong Delta in support of military advisor operations code-named Operation Shufly. In late 1962, the squadron headed north, to Da Nang, where Marines experienced an environment quite different from that of the Mekong Delta. As the tempo of offensive operations between the Viet Cong and the soldiers of the 2d ARVN Division increased, so did the requirement for additional Marine security.

On 22 November 1962, the sudden death of President John F. Kennedy placed the mantle of the presidency upon the shoulders of Lyndon B. Johnson. And thus began a division of commitment: between those who viewed the conflict in Vietnam as a civil war, and those who saw it as a blatant attempt on the part of the Communists to annex Southeast Asia, nation by nation; an encroachment that had to be resisted.

By December 1964, the Marine security platoon was replaced by a reinforced rifle company from 3/9, stationed on Okinawa. The defense-oriented American involvement was coming to a close as Viet Cong sapper attacks in Saigon and Pleiku killed and wounded dozens of American servicemen. On 6 March 1965, the 9th Marine Expeditionary Brigade, afloat off the shores of Da Nang, received the message to "Land the Landing Force."

In 1962, while the situation in Vietnam was considered "serious and unstable," it was not yet viewed as a war in terms of U.S. involvement. The intent of the American commitment was assistance and defense. Early indications were that additional helicopter strength would be needed to support the Army of the Republic of Vietnam's swift-strike capability. The Chief, Military Advisor and Assistance Group, Gen. Charles J. Timmes, USA, recommended that U.S. Marine helicopter pilots be assigned to temporary familiarization duty with Army helicopter companies already in Vietnam. When asked to study the proposal, Maj. Gen. Carson A. Roberts, commanding general (Air), Fleet Marine Force, Pacific (Air FMFPac), suggested that the commanding general, FMFPac, Lt. Gen. Alan W. Shapley, offer a counterproposal, i.e., that one complete Marine Corps helicopter squadron with support units be committed to a mission similar to that of the Army helicopter companies. That recommendation was approved, and a Marine Corps helicopter squadron with its supporting Marine air base subunit was ordered to Soc Trang, Ba Xuyen Province, in the Mekong Delta, with the understanding that, when the tempo of operations in the northern corps tactical zone permitted, it would exchange places with the Army unit at Da Nang. The decision was approved by the Joint Chiefs of Staff and the Vietnamese government on 9 April 1962, and Operation Shufly was launched.

The personnel of Marine Task Unit 79.3.5, consisting of Marine Medium Helicopter Squadron (HMM) 362, and Subunit 2, Marine Air Base Squadron (MABS) 16, began to arrive at Soc Trang on board KC-130F Hercules transport aircraft from Marine Corps Air Station (MCAS) Futema, Okinawa, on 9 April 1962, and immediately established a functional base. By 16 April the major body of HMM-362 arrived on station off the mouth of the Mekong River. The transfer of men and material from the amphibious assault ship USS *Princeton* (LPH 5) began at once, and by the end of the day the airlift was complete, with elements of Shufly ready to undertake their mission the following morning.

The Marine command was located near an old World War II Japanese airstrip and surrounded by patches of flat sunbaked brown earth laced with occasional glimmering squares of water-filled rice paddies. One building, a tin-roofed hangar of Japanese construction sturdy enough to have withstood spring and fall monsoon rains for nearly twenty years, remained standing but in barely usable condition. The airfield looked as if it had been ravaged by some type of rat: the hangar, and even the runway itself, was full of holes and in a general state of cluttered untidiness and disrepair. During the summer monsoon season, the entire region was under six to eight inches of water. In the months to come, even in the dry months, helicopters sometimes sank to their wheelhubs when not parked on steel runway matting.

In September 1962 the Operation Shufly unit redeployed to the former French airfield at Da Nang in Quang Nam Province, northern I Corps. The city, called Tourane by the French, was a principal port of eastern French Indochina and the second-largest city in South Vietnam. The airfield was southwest of the picturesque city, beginning almost at the apex of the half-moon-shaped bay that served the city as a quiet, deepwater port. The men and equipment of Subunit 2 and HMM-163 were established on the west side of the sprawling airfield. The airstrip was considerably longer than the one at Soc Trang and was already being used by the Vietnamese Air Force. It was a mile and a half long and was operated from a control tower housing radar and other essentials for all-weather, twenty-four-hour operations. Both hangar facilities and barracks were in good repair and required no extensive renovation prior to the Marines moving in.

The airstrip was 375 miles north of Saigon and 84 miles south of the demilitarized zone (DMZ), which, at the 17th parallel, divided South Vietnam from the Communist-controlled Democratic Republic of Vietnam, or North Vietnam. The Marines had become used to flat, canalled, segmented delta land at Soc Trang; the terrain at Da Nang varied vastly. White sandy beaches bordered the coastline, backed by a narrow coastal plain that rose toward jungle-covered mountains with inaccessible peaks of six thousand feet and higher. The terrain was a new experience and a fresh challenge for the men of the task unit.

Because of the difference in terrain, the climate was almost the exact reverse of that at Soc Trang. The monsoon season, which so heavily affected operational capability, occurred in the winter at Da Nang, extending from September to March. In the extreme south it occurred during the summer. High altitude, high temperatures, and high winds coupled with low ceilings, fog, and heavy rains presented operational problems not experienced in the delta.

Weather was not the only problem to irritate the task unit. Security also proved to be awkward. Initially a permanent sergeant of the guard was detailed to maintain a security force of men from Subunit 2 and HMM-163. Posts were manned around the flight line, the hangar, the motor pool, the communications area, and the billeting compound. This arrangement was workable but caused problems in effectiveness and morale. Marines who served all night as security guards often were expected to put in a full working day at their regular jobs. Realizing the problem, the command initiated a request via COMUSMACV to FMFPac for a permanent security force. That resulted in the assignment to Vietnam of a security platoon from the 3d Marine Division on Okinawa. As enemy harassment continued, the platoon was increased in size to a reinforced company.

Operation Shufly's mission at Da Nang was essentially similar to that at Soc Trang, but there were important differences produced by the terrain, weather, and general plan on military activities in the I Corps Tactical Zone. In the northern provinces, landing zones for the most part had to be hacked out of the jungle, so surprise was difficult to maintain when moving to strike the enemy. When flat-bottomed, walled valleys with dangerous wind currents had to be used as landing areas, it was not uncommon for landing zones to be too far from the point of need, so effective employment of retaliatory troops was difficult.

The resupply of U.S. Army Special Forces outposts produced the single most important shift in HMM-163's mission, a mission it had not had in the Soc Trang area. It was clear that strategic hamlet defense would have to depend largely upon Special Forces units permanently positioned in the mountains and in the jungles, whose primary duty was to halt [enemy] infiltration. A second major change to the operational mission occasioned by the Da Nang deployment was the relocation of some important hamlets that could not be successfully defended. This meant transporting people, belongings, equipment, livestock, food, and fuel to areas more secure.

On 6 October 1963 the Marines of the Shufly mission received a grim reminder that they were in a genuine conflict filled with all of the dangers accompanying warfare. A search-and-rescue helicopter crashed and burned fifteen miles west of Tam Ky while participating in a twenty-plane helolift of 2d ARVN Division units. Seven died in the crash: five Marines, a Navy doctor, and his corpsman assistant. They were the first casualties suffered by the Marine task unit since its arrival in Vietnam, and they were felt deeply.

The mood was subtly changing during those months in Vietnam, and nothing contributed more to the feeling of foreboding than an event that took place thirteen thousand miles from Vietnam, in Dallas, Texas. On 22 November 1963 the United States was dealt a stunning blow when its president, John F. Kennedy, was shot by an assassin and died shortly thereafter.

". . . To Preserve the Freedom and Independence of South Vietnam"

Seven months prior to the terrible events of 22 November, the opinions of officials in the Defense Department were buoyant and positive. Predictions that the Vietnam conflict would soon end could be heard. "The corner has definitely been turned toward victory," a government spokesman said.

But such was not the case, and deterioration was swift.

Buddhists, objecting to Roman Catholic domination of the Diem government, rioted, and some, while the world watched incredulously through media eyes, immolated themselves. The activities of two thousand or so Buddhists were interpreted to represent the attitude of the entire country, and the United States believed that all Vietnam was aflame. In November 1963 a military coup assassinated President Diem and overthrew his government.

Having received the mantle of the United States presidency, Lyndon Johnson immediately was faced with burdensome decisions concerning Vietnam. Some Americans had begun to see the conflict as a civil war in which America had no honorable involvement. Others saw it as a blatant attempt on the part of Communism to annex the whole of Southeast Asia nation by nation, an encroachment that had to be resisted. The troops in Vietnam seemed largely to favor the latter view and found themselves adopting increasingly belligerent attitudes as they saw, though most Americans did not, the terror and maiming carried on by the Viet Cong against innocents, as well as atrocities conducted against missionaries.

The darkening mood of the American serviceman in Vietnam was fed by confusion concerning the direction of the war and increased activity on the part of the Viet Cong.

The tempo of the Viet Cong activity stepped up. Ambushes increased around the perimeter of the base. Snipers began to fire upon guard posts. Vietnam became an issue in the presidential election of 1964. There were charges of poor supplies and old equipment. Suddenly everything coming to Vietnam took on a high priority. Vietnam entered the spotlight, and everything tightened up. War was no longer romantic.

As the war intensified, and security tightened in response to stepped-up Viet Cong activity, my ministry moved into another sphere. There were memorial services; there were more troops in the area, and thus more formed, and the religious life of the camp took on a new vitality, a quality of honest devotion I had never before experienced in a group of men.

The last month I was with the subunit, we had full alerts perhaps five to eight times. We knew without a doubt that something big was up. We were all frustrated because no one seemed to be making decisions as to our involvement.

It was apparent that the United States stood at a crossroads. To leave Vietnam then would make the investment of the previous two years appear futile; to remain would entail stronger, more aggressive responses to the provocation and belligerency of the Communists. The tension was felt by Americans in the States, but not nearly as intensely as among the Marines in Vietnam. Chaplain John G. Harrison gives a small picture of the character of the tension within some of his Marines:

On the day that I left, the C-130, which was the only real link with the outside world, was full of Marines returning to Japan after completion of their tour. We were flying over the Tonkin Gulf [August 1964], when word was passed through the plane, "We're at war with North Vietnam." For some reason everyone broke out in a tremendous cheer. As it turned out, the North Vietnamese had attacked some of our ships with armed torpedo boats, and we retaliated. Somehow it indicated a new direction in our struggle to preserve the freedom and independence of South Vietnam, and it made sense. It made sense because we had witnessed at first hand the increasing infiltration of the North Vietnamese. We had visited villages where the leaders had been murdered because they had cooperated with the government. We had seen schools, which we helped to build, burned. We had seen our friends in the Special Forces wounded or killed by communist insurgents. We had buried shipmates who had been killed because they could not fire until we had been fired upon, even though we knew the enemy was there.

* * *

In December 1964 the security platoon, which had deployed to Da Nang from the 3d Marine Division in March, was replaced by a reinforced company from the 3d Battalion, 9th Marines. The threat from the Viet Cong was growing. After dark, travel was curtailed, as were routine people-to-people visits to the countryside. Terrorist activities in the villages just outside the Da Nang airbase compound and sniper fire at guard posts made the increasing hazards of Shufly duty a clear reality. Shortly thereafter a Marine light antiaircraft missile battery arrived to defend the airfield against possible air attacks from the North. By March 1965 the situation had clearly changed, and Operation Shufly was officially terminated when the helicopter squadron and subunit were reassimilated by the arriving Marine Aircraft Group 16.

The defense-oriented American involvement was coming to a close. In response to communist activities such as the Tonkin Gulf incident and the Viet Cong attack on the U.S. bachelor officers' quarters in Saigon on Christmas Eve, 1964, which killed two Americans and wounded 109, President Johnson ordered retaliatory air strikes on North Vietnam. The VC continued their attacks by mortaring the U.S. compound at Pleiku on 7 February 1965. By the twenty-seventh, the president decided to commit a brigade-size force (nine hundred Marines and personnel) to Da Nang with the mission of protecting that major base.

On 6 March 1965 the signal was sent to elements of the 9th Marine Expeditionary Brigade (MEB) off Vietnam shores: "Land at once at Da Nang MEB command and control elements, a surface battalion landing team. . . ." The miniwar was no more.

4

Marine Reconnaissance in Vietnam: 1965

The initial deployments of two Marine reconnaissance units in Vietnam were designed to serve the needs of the Marine Expeditionary Brigade Commander (9th MEB) and the 3d Marine Division. The 1st Force Reconnaissance Company and 3d Reconnaissance Battalion were designated, respectively, to conduct reconnaissance operations within the tactical areas of responsibility (TAORs) around the Da Nang, Chu Lai, and the Hue/Phu Bai areas. Numerous operational difficulties were experienced, including problems associated with unreliable communications, logistical snafus, and a lack of military vehicles committed to reconnaissance operations. Soon, three separate reconnaissance elements—the addition of 1st Reconnaissance Battalion in August 1965—were required to support combat operations in and around I Corps. By mid-1965, force and division reconnaissance units were experiencing utilization problems which ranged from assignments in total disregard of existing doctrine to assignments that had nothing to do with reconnaissance.

With the approval of Maj. Gen. Lewis W. Walt, then commanding general of III MAF and the 3d Marine Division, both force and division reconnaissance assets were relocated and three separate RAOR (reconnaissance areas of responsibility) enclaves were established to cover the Marines' TAOR in I Corps. The introduction of radio relay stations also helped to solve the radio range problem. It would take the merging of force and division recon assets, and a decisive battle at a place called Ba To, before Marine recon units enjoyed improved coordination, cooperation, and defined capabilities.

All Marine units were exposed to severe doctrinal tests in 1965; for "Recon" Marines the year was one of change and adjustment. The two committed reconnaissance units—the 3d Reconnaissance Battalion, an integral 3d Marine Division battalion, and the 1st Force Reconnaissance Company, a Force Troops unit—both experienced great difficulty in responding to demands imposed by the three growing TAORs at Da Nang, Chu Lai, and Hue/Phu Bai. The two ground reconnaissance units were different in many respects, which caused many reevaluations, as well as revelations, during the opening months of Marine ground action in Vietnam.

Reconnaissance missions were clearly defined by tables of organization. A division reconnaissance battalion, in this case the 3d, was charged with the primary mission of conducting "reconnaissance in support of a Marine Division and its subordinate elements." A force-level company, on the other hand, was to "conduct pre-assault and distant post-assault reconnaissance in support of a landing force."

1st Force Reconnaissance Company, The Early Days

Early beach reconnaissance efforts of Capt. David Whittingham's Subunit 1, 1st Force Reconnaissance Company, were textbook examples of proper employment of the company. On 23–27 February, Subunit 1, in conjunction with Underwater Demolition Team 12, operating from the USS *Cook* (APD 130), accomplished the reconnaissance of Red Beaches 1 and 2 at Da Nang. As a result, Red Beach 2 was selected as the landing beach for BLT (battalion landing team) 3/9, the first element of the 9th MEB to land in Vietnam.

The period of 15–20 March was devoted to reconnaissance of the beaches and terrain near Phu Bai. Subunit 1's reports resulted in 3d MEB's decision to send its first BLT to Phu Bai by way of the river approach to Hue and then overland to Phu Bai; the proposed landing beaches were backed by impassable lagoons that made exit almost impossible. For Subunit 1, that was its first real test. The VC were active in the area, but the mission was accomplished without loss and with excellent results.

Eight days later, Subunit 1 undertook the reconnaissance of the beach that was to be the site of the 3d MEB landing, Chu Lai. Its reconnaissance was finished on 30 March, again with excellent results.

On 20 April, eighteen days before the Chu Lai landing, the force reconnaissance Marines started a survey of a beach south of the Tra Bong River, ten kilometers southeast of the proposed 3d MEB landing beach. On 22 April the reconnaissance party encountered light resistance, but the next day five Marines on the beach were caught in the crossfire of twenty-five VC. Cpl. Lowell H. Merrell was wounded twice and two sailors in the beach party's LCVP (landing craft, vehicle/personnel) also were hit. All three subsequently died. The 1st Force Reconnaissance Company had lost its first Marine to VC fire. In memory, the new force reconnaissance camp would be named Camp Merrell.

In May, Subunit 1 teams were sent to Special Forces camps to serve as patrol leaders for CIDG (Civilian Irregular Defense Group) patrols. Other teams were assigned to reconnaissance-in-force patrols composed of U.S. and Australian-led Nungs,* which operated from Da Nang. A third mission was to provide quick response patrols to act as

*Nungs are ethnic Chinese, originally residents of Guangxi Province, but an appreciable number lived in northern North Vietnam. They are noted for their martial skills. Many served, willingly, under the French, and for that reason emigrated to South Vietnam in 1954 when the country was partitioned. At one time after the formation of the republic, the South Vietnamese Army included a division of Nungs, but it was broken up because of its potential threat to the

security for downed Marine helicopters. Initially all force reconnaissance reports and debriefings were coordinated by the III Marine Amphibious Force (MAF) G-2, Lt. Col. Robert E. Gruenler.

On 10 July another platoon reinforced Subunit 1, and during July and August the two-platoon subunit operated from the 4th Marines' Chu Lai base. Another force recon platoon was conducting beach surveys for the commander, Task Force 76; still another platoon was assigned to the SLF (special landing force). The rest of the company was still at Camp Pendleton.

On 11 August, Maj. Malcolm C. Gaffen, the company commander, arrived and relieved Captain Whittingham as subunit commander. During Operation Starlite, in August, Subunit 1 was attached to the 2d Battalion, 4th Marines, and the 3d Platoon, attached to the SLF, landed with BLT 3/7. At the conclusion of Starlite, Subunit 1 returned to Da Nang.

The company headquarters and a fourth platoon arrived on 24 October while the subunit was participating in Operation Red Snapper with the 2d Battalion, 3d Marines north of Da Nang. The China Beach site had been selected because of its ready access to the ocean for amphibious training and because it provided room for parachute requalification.

The arrival at Camp Merrell of two-thirds of the company and the fact that the 5th and 6th Platoons had moved west to Okinawa from Camp Pendleton suggested that soon the company would be operating as an independent force unit carrying out the "distant post-assault reconnaissance" specified in its table of organization.

During the summer and fall, company units had experienced a variety of operational difficulties. Communications problems were rampant. The force platoon with BLT 2/1 during Dagger Thrust II in September had to be extracted be-

incumbent government. Nungs, hired on as mercenaries, eventually came under the domain of U.S. Special Forces and other agencies involved in unconventional warfare.

cause radio contact could not be established. Another unit was landed from a Coast Guard patrol boat on the relatively secure coast near the Hai Van Pass north of Da Nang to test communications and control, and that operation, too, was a bust. The company's vehicles were "down"; supply problems were rampant; and the partially developed MAF staff was not designed to deal with such difficulties.

Maj. Gen. Lewis W. Walt's solution was to transfer Subunit 1 to the operational control of the 3d Marine Division which, in turn, transferred the unit to "opcon" (operational control of) 3d Reconnaissance Battalion. The transfer was effective 30 October; two days later Subunit 1, 1st Force Reconnaissance Company, became 1st Force Reconnaissance (-) with a strength of nine officers and 103 enlisted men.

In effect, the force company became a sixth, smaller, company of the reinforced 3d Reconnaissance Battalion. Although the "in country" elements of "1st Force" were assembled at last, the assimilation by "division recon" was not an entirely satisfactory solution; some knotty problems arose.

3d Reconnaissance Battalion, Opening Moves

When the 9th MEB landed at Da Nang on 8 March, a platoon from Company A, 3d Reconnaissance Battalion, attached to BLT 3/9, became the first division reconnaissance element to be resident in Vietnam. Other platoons arrived as attachments to BLTs, a platoon from Company B with BLT 3/4, a platoon from Company D with BLT 1/3, and a second Company D platoon with BLT 2/3. Platoon attachments lasted until 13 April, at which time the four "in country" reconnaissance platoons were regrouped as a new Company D, 3d Reconnaissance Battalion. Capt. Patrick G. Collins's Company D operated as the brigade reconnaissance company of the 9th MEB until 7 May, when Lt. Col. Don H. "Doc" Blanchard, his battalion staff, and the rest of the battalion landed at Chu Lai with the 3d MAB. "Doc" Blanchard did not stay at Chu Lai very long; on the twelfth, he, his staff, battalion headquarters, and Companies A and C moved to Da Nang, where they were reunited with Company D. Company B remained at Chu Lai. In the process, Companies A and B were brought up to strength by integrating the Company D platoons that had arrived with the battalion at Chu Lai, i.e., there were no longer two Company D elements. Company C was detached from Da Nang to the 3d Battalion, 4th Marines at Hue/Phu Bai on 26 May.

On 13 September, Company C moved again, returning to Da Nang, leaving its 3d Platoon at Hue/Phu Bai still attached to the 3d Battalion, 4th Marines. Battalion integrity was improved somewhat on 19 September by a directive from General Walt, which stated that the reconnaissance battalion should be used in general support of the 3d Marine Division. Although that measure simplified command and control, the division was still operating from three separate enclaves, and three separate reconnaissance elements were required. On the nineteenth, reinforcement of division reconnaissance was accomplished by attaching Company C, 1st Reconnaissance Battalion, which had arrived in August, as an attachment to the 7th Marines.

The new battalion commander since 1 September, Lt. Col. Roy R. Van Cleve, ordered some adjustments on 20 September in order to comply with III MAF's general support order. The new dispositions were: Headquarters, Companies A, C(-), and D at Da Nang; one Company C platoon at Hue/Phu Bai; and newly designated Reconnaissance Group ALPHA, composed of Company B and attached Company C, 1st Reconnaissance Battalion, at Chu Lai. During that period the reconnaissance battalion was faced with the question "Reconnaissance of what?" The Hue/Phu Bai, Da Nang, and Chu Lai enclaves were essentially defensive positions. By virtue of III MAF's mission, all reconnaissance efforts were defensive patrols, but the restrictions imposed by the TAORs limited the patrols to "their own front yard," and there were many people in the "yard."

Geography solved part of the problem. The physical characteristics of the Hue/Phu Bai lodgment provided the Marines with excellent observation. This resulted in the reduction of the reconnaissance force there to only one platoon in September.

At the other two enclaves, RAORs evolved slowly. On 19 June, at the recommendation of Lieutenant Colonel Blanchard, General Walt had approved the formation of a RAOR that extended from four to ten kilometers forward of the Da Nang defensive positions. At Chu Lai, the RAORs were as required by the two regiments there, the 4th and 7th Marines. Even with the formation of Reconnaissance Group ALPHA in September, the two Chu Lai–based reconnaissance companies continued to function as direct support companies for the respective regiments.

Another factor that limited the range and duration of reconnaissance patrols was the radio equipment then in use. The PRC-47 radio was too big and too heavy for small teams, but it did have sufficient range. The smaller, lighter PRC-10 did not have the range required for deep patrols. Both sets used batteries at a high rate, and battery consumption was accelerated by the tropical climate, which reduced battery life by more than half. Of all the patrol equipment, only water had a higher supply priority than batteries, and both were heavy. Patrols were caught up in the simple equation that restricted patrol duration to the number of batteries that could be carried, which, in turn, was limited further by the amount of other equipment and supplies that had to be carried.

Radio relay stations helped solve the radio range problem to some degree, but the arrival in November of the PRC-25 radio with its long-life BA 386 battery finally enabled reconnaissance Marines to carry out deeper, long-duration patrols. Although communications were vastly improved, reconnaissance units were continually faced with the grim reality of heavier loads for longer patrols.

The size of reconnaissance patrols, especially in the Da Nang TAOR, became a matter of great concern. Although the Marines were operating from fixed bases in relatively secure areas, [recon] patrols had to be large enough to fight their way out of any entrapment and deal with the possibility of ambush. Sgt. Richard A. Van Deusen of Company D, 3d Reconnaissance Battalion, recalled this uneasy situation:

It's very hard in an alien country to hide yourself. I mean, you're going along, and people are all over the place, and they know you're out there, so this right away compromises any chance of "recon." It all depends on the area you're in. Now if you're in the mountains, you can live there for days before they ever realize you're up there. Sometimes they never know you're up there. But if you're south—and each tree line has a village on it—the only good chance you have is moving at night.

By mid-1965, both force and division reconnaissance formations began experiencing utilization problems that ranged from assignments in total disregard of existing doctrine to assignments that had nothing to do with reconnaissance.

Reflecting on this situation, the 3d Reconnaissance Battalion commander, Lieutenant Colonel Van Cleve, recalled:

They [recon Marines] were being used for any mission that might come up. If you didn't have somebody else to do it, why, give it to recon. They ended up on some raider-type missions; they ended up as CP [command post] security frequently on operations. As a result of this General Walt decided that the reconnaissance effort should be controlled at the reconnaissance battalion level, and that any request for reconnaissance-type missions would come through the division staff, the division reconnaissance officer, G-3/G-2, advising, "Yes, this is a reconnaissance-type mission," or "No, this is not a reconnaissance-type mission." Division would task reconnaissance battalion to provide to whatever organization was asking for the necessary forces. People were realizing there was a lot of talent in the recon battalion that was not being used for strictly recon purposes, and the divisions and MAF were losing a lot of potentially valuable information.

Were reconnaissance Marines "fighters" or "finders"? When the first revision of the provisional M-Series table of organization was published on 20 February 1958, it stated that "The [Division] Reconnaissance Battalion may be employed as a unit to screen the advance of the Division or execute counter reconnaissance missions." Those were clearly defined fighting missions. The publication of the approved M-1428 (Division Reconnaissance Battalion) Table of Organization, 5 March 1961, reversed that concept, stating "The Reconnaissance Battalion . . . will be employed to gain intelligence," and "It is not equipped for decisive or sustained combat . . . it is not capable of screening or counterreconnaissance missions," but, the table of organization went on to explain, commanders supported by division reconnaissance could, in the event that the reconnaissance element was in danger of being "overwhelmed," "reinforce the reconnaissance force, directing that force to destroy the enemy."

Revision 1 of 23 September 1963, still in effect in 1965, carried the transition a step further by deleting the "not equipped for decisive or sustained combat" restriction, but some damage had been done. Misinterpretation of mission and the natural aggressiveness engendered by the demanding physical conditioning program required by reconnaissance units produced a strange amalgam of "fighting" and "finding" reconnaissance Marines.

Many senior Marines had been members of special units during World War II, notably the raider and parachute battalions, and all Marines were familiar with the legendary exploits of those units. Of the senior commanders in Vietnam in 1965, four were raider battalion veterans: Major General Walt and three of his regimental commanders, Colonels Wheeler, Dupras, and Oscar Peatross. There was bound to be some "raider" thinking, but the commanding general, FMFPac, Lt. Gen. Victor Krulak, resolutely insisted that "Combat assault operations, including amphibious raids, are missions to be conducted by rifle companies, rather than reconnaissance units." Nevertheless, during the summer and fall of 1964, Company C, 3d Reconnaissance Battalion, had actually trained as the battalion's "raid" company. The die was cast.

By 12 March 1965, Company D, 3d Reconnaissance Battalion, had been reconstituted in Vietnam. It was the 9th MEB's reconnaissance company, and, as such, in April it claimed more VC "kills" than all of the "in country" infantry units, even though patrolling beyond the Da Nang and Chu Lai TAORS was not authorized until 20 April. The company commander, Capt. Patrick G. Collins, recalled, ". . . surveillance and observation missions quite frequently turned into contact with the Viet Cong and having some quite spirited actions. . . ." More specifically, Col. Frank E. Garretson, the 9th Marines' commander, told Captain Collins: "You find [them]; we'll bail you out."

As a result, early reconnaissance patrols were large, usually between twelve and twenty-two Marines; a number were even company strength. Large patrols did not guarantee absolute safety. On 12 July, an eighteen-man patrol from Company A operating near Dai Loc, eighteen kilometers southwest of Da Nang, tangled with a VC company. One officer was killed and three men were wounded. The dead officer, 1st Lt. Frank S. Reasoner, was posthumously awarded the Medal of Honor for his actions on 12 July, the first Marine action in Vietnam to merit the nation's highest honor. The 3d Reconnaissance Battalion's camp at Da Nang was named Camp Reasoner, but the lieutenant's heroic death did little to solve the problem of patrol security. (See chapter 3.) The problem of proper mission was only solved later, when TAORs were enlarged to include the rugged, sparsely inhabited terrain to the west, and when reconnaissance efforts were concentrated on the business of finding the enemy.

According to *U.S. Marines in 1965*, the III MAF commander, General Walt, realized that reconnaissance units, properly utilized, were well equipped to locate an enemy who had already established a reputation for blending into the surroundings, a phantom army seldom seen armed and concentrated. "Even when VC concentrations were sighted, they were usually on the move, and presented fleeting targets at best. Regular Marine ground formations were too clumsy for the mission of finding them; the VC they did find generally wanted to be found. General Walt decided that since reconnaissance patrols could find the VC, the patrols should be provided with a means to destroy the enemy. Accordingly, he allowed patrols to call in air strikes and artillery strikes. Slow clearance procedures hindered that application in the Da Nang TAOR, but the system proved to be successful at Chu Lai. The concept was refined, and in 1966 it was adopted as a standard tactic, then known as STINGRAY."

Any doubts about the mission of reconnaissance Marines were resolved by General Walt's September directive that restored the division reconnaissance battalion to its general support role. Lieutenant Colonel Van Cleve's appreciation of his mission essentially put an end to the "raider" days, although some experimentation persisted.

On 18 October 1966, two 3d Reconnaissance Battalion companies hiked into Happy Valley for Operation Trailblazer. Their mission was to determine the size of enemy concentrations in the hills west of the Da Nang TAOR. For six days, 18–24 October, the reconnaissance force prowled the hills. Two VC were killed, but five separate enemy base areas were discovered and a vast amount of trail network information was accumulated. Trailblazer was the last of the reconnaissance-in-force operations conducted by the 3d Reconnaissance Battalion. A new trend was in motion. By December the battalion was concentrating on patrolling, sending out more and smaller patrols; company-size patrols became the exception.

Force and Division Reconnaissance Merged

The force reconnaissance Marines viewed their attachment to division "recon" with trepidation, and the first weeks of the new arrangement were not without some trying moments. During November, 1st Force Reconnaissance Company executed division reconnaissance-type patrols in the Da Nang area, but the III MAF planners had not forgotten the force company's capabilities. As a result, on 27 November the 2d Platoon was returned to III MAF operational control and sent to Special Forces Camp A-106 at Ba To, forty-two kilometers south-southwest of Quang Ngai. On 7 December, III MAF reassigned another force recon platoon, the 3d, to Camp A-107, Tra Bong, twenty-seven kilometers southwest of Chu Lai, on the upper reaches of the Tra Bong River. The mission, code-named Birdwatcher, was ". . . to test the feasibility of *deep* recon patrols." At last, force "recon" was going deep, but the 2d Platoon at Ba To was in for a tough school session.

At 0530, 15 December, three reconnaissance teams (twenty Marines and CIDG troops) plus a sixty-one-man base defense reaction force moved out "to determine the location, identity, strength, movement, and armament of VC/PAVN units." More than seventy enemy soldiers were sighted during the next two days, but the U.S./Vietnamese reconnaissance force made a serious mistake. The patrol base was not moved for two nights. The only redeeming feature of the situation was that the base was on a hill, the best defensive terrain in the area.

By 1730, 16 December, all teams had returned to the patrol base, but the planned move back to Ba To was canceled when dense fog settled over the camp. The force of eighty-one Marine, Special Forces, CIDG, and Nung troops was stuck in the same campsite for the third consecutive night.

At 1900 the Viet Cong began walking mortar rounds across the patrol base. The Vietnamese lieutenant in charge of the patrol was mortally wounded and a U.S. Special Forces sergeant was hit. Enemy automatic-weapons fire swept the hill position as the mortar bombardment continued. Then the assault started. Between 150 and 200 Viet Cong attacked. Confusion swept through the mixed force of defenders; they broke up into small groups. The Marines, led by G.Sgt. (Gunnery Sergeant) Maurice J. Jacques, withdrew into a small perimeter, but of the thirteen Marines assigned to the patrol, five were already missing. In the perimeter a Marine was hit, their corpsman was seriously wounded, and a second Marine was wounded. Jacques's Marines moved off the hill into the darkness. They hid in a clump of banana trees, formed a defensive perimeter, and waited for the dawn, hoping that aerial observers would spot them in the morning. Of the thirteen Marines, four were still missing and one was known to be dead.

Dawn came, but the fog persisted. There was no possibility of being seen from the air. The Marines tried again to regain the trail to Ba To, but enemy troops firing at what were probably other stragglers drove them back into the bush. After moving about four kilometers, they found thicker cover and started moving up a ridgeline; they knew the trail to Ba To was on top of the ridge. At that time they were joined by two CIDG survivors, but the two Vietnamese were almost killed; a Vietnamese with the Marines saved them by causing the Marines to hold fire as they came out of the bushes.

The Marines reached the Ba To trail, but again faced a tough decision. It is a bad practice to use trails in enemy territory, but the Marines had to get away quickly, and fog still blanketed the area. Fortunately, the wind picked up, and it was loud enough to cover noise the patrol made, so Jacques decided to "head for home." Putting the two Vietnamese stragglers out as the point on the trail, the Marines moved out and reached Ba To without incident.

An hour after Gunnery Sergeant Jacques's party arrived at the base, another Marine survivor, wounded L.Cpl. (Lance Corporal) Donald M. Woo, was brought in. Determined to survive, Lance Corporal Woo had been captured and escaped twice, and, in turn, captured two NVA soldiers and forced them, at knifepoint, to carry him to Ba To.

On 21 December the two missing Marines were found, dead. A patrol found fourteen bodies; three Marines, the Special Forces sergeant, the Vietnamese lieutenant patrol leader, and nine CIDG troops.

As a result of the Ba To experience and some other misadventures, a long-standing force reconnaissance operational procedure was suspended. Previous training had dictated that when a force reconnaissance patrol was discovered it was to split up, each member evading on his own. After Ba To, force patrols went in together and came out together.

The 2d and 3d Platoons were returned to 3d Reconnaissance Battalion control on 24 December. On the twenty-eighth, Capt. William C. Shaver relieved the recently promoted Lieutenant Colonel Gaffen, who was transferred upon his promotion.

As the year ended, both force and division reconnaissance units could state that their respective situations were much improved. Although "force" was not pleased with the prospect of remaining under the paternal hand of the 3d Reconnaissance Battalion, the force company was, at last, able to conduct deep missions, and the company's supply situation was vastly improved. Division reconnaissance was still spread among three enclaves, but it also was vastly improved. Coordination, cooperation, and understanding of reconnaissance capabilities and limitations were getting better. "Recon" had a clear view of the future.

=== 5 ===

The Creation of Stingray

In the summer of 1975, Lt. Comdr. Ray W. Stubbe, Chaplain Corps, USN, spent several weeks interviewing several of us who had served in 3d Force Reconnaissance Company during the Vietnam War. At the time of the interviews, I was a platoon leader in India Company, 3d Battalion, 1st Marines (Camp Horno, at Camp Pendleton, California) and our battalion commander was Lt. Col. Alex Lee, former commanding officer of 3d Force Recon Company (August 1969 to March 1970). Also interviewed during that time was S.Sgt. (Staff Sergeant) Byron Tapp, who had served with distinction in 3d Force Recon as a platoon sergeant. Lieutenant Commander Stubbe was gathering information from primary sources as part of his "efforts to research and write the history of Marine Corps force-level reconnaissance units and activities," from 1900 to 1974.

Ray Stubbe's draft, originally titled *AARUGHA!*, was published in 1989 by Owen A. Lock, at Ivy Books, as *Inside Force Recon*. With the assistance of author Lt. Col. Michael Lee Lanning, USA (Ret.), Ray's years of research, interviews, and writing started the "historical ball" rolling regarding the history of Marine reconnaissance, with particular emphasis on the Vietnam War. Singular credit and much thanks are due to Ray W. Stubbe from those of us who later became authors and felt that we, too, had important histories to write, describing personal experiences and those many lessons learned during the Vietnam War that would benefit Marines past and present.

With the permission of Ray W. Stubbe and Michael Lee Lanning, the original draft as it pertained to Ray Stubbe's significant research in Stingray operations from primary sources during the early use of Stingray, in 1965–66, is presented here as written by Ray in 1974:

> The concept of employing small groups of men to harass, destroy, and create confusion in the enemy's rear was certainly not novel. What was new was the speed of reaction in destroying fairly large units without actually being in contact with them, by firepower directed by very small units in a FO (forward observer) role. Smallness of the patrol, ensuring swift, silent movement, no longer implied avoidance of offensive action. The key was to engage the enemy silently and destroy him without endangering themselves in the process. Action was not the same as contact.
>
> The peculiar nature of the war in Vietnam, where the enemy generally moved in very small, fragmented groups, necessitated destroying him wherever and whenever detected. Use of infantry to close in on enemy forces so dispersed was impractical. Furthermore, by the time we could react, the enemy would be far distant. One officer noted that it took usually three to four days to prepare operation orders; men would spend twelve hours a day with SITREPS (Situation Reports) just to ensure correct grammar.
>
> Inability of [Marine] infantry to capitalize on lucrative targets due to such dilatory procedures compelled reconnaissance to assume a new posture. Once [the enemy was] spotted, artillery and air could react much quicker in destroying the enemy infantry. The S-2 (intelligence) chief of 1st Force Recon Company, 1965–66, noted: "Small unit aggressive actions are the best means to combat known VC forces. In my experience, in my unit, this is the type of action we have fought against the VC."

Not everyone agreed with this evolving role. FMFM (Fleet Marine Field Manual) 2-2 clearly dictated a supportive, not combat, role for reconnaissance units. With regard to the force recon company, FMFM 2-2 specified "The company has no offensive capability and is not employed as a tactical unit: that is . . . it is not assigned tactical missions, objectives, or tactical areas of responsibility." The doctrine did, however, allow for some apparent offensive employment of reconnaissance units. FMFM 6-2, *Marine Infantry Regiment,* and FMFM 6-1, *Marine Division,* specified not a "reconnaissance in force" role as well as a mission of ". . . control and adjustment of long-range fires." FMFM 8-1, *Special Operations,* notes parachute and subsurface entry in connection with raiding, and since in the Marines those methods are peculiar to force reconnaissance companies, it directly sanctioned force recon teams to be utilized as raiders. FMFM 8-2, *Counterinsurgency Operations,* while noting that reconnaissance units with their mobility provided a commander with a most important asset by gathering information to conduct operations against guerrillas, also noted that such reconnaissance personnel could be employed to attack small isolated forces and, in antiguerrilla operations, conduct limited tactical operations against located guerrilla bands.

Reflecting on his experiences with the CIA's Naval Advisory Detachment in Da Nang, Maj. "Reb" Bearce proposed that force recon Marines be granted at least limited combat roles and that FMFM 2-2 be revised to reflect that role. His study argued that the type of person normally found in force recon is a "highly trained, highly motivated Marine indurated with unrelenting resolve to discharge assigned duties who is trained in infantry skills and has an inherent capability to conduct small unit operations independently and clandestinely. Second, teams from Force Recon are responsible to the CATF (Commander Amphibious Task Force) while individuals within the team can take command of the team as required, thus making the command and control of the teams particularly suitable for rear area operations. Third, Force Recon Marines are already trained in specialized insertion techniques, such as submerged submarine, parachute, and stay-behind, which provide them with a great psychological advantage, not normally found within line units, to enter enemy rear areas and operate in a clandestine manner within a hostile environment. Fourth, Marines in Force Recon have been trained to call in Air/Naval Gunfire/Artillery strikes to assist them in breaking contact, have utilized electronic sensors to pinpoint enemy locations without revealing their own locations, have employed sophisticated equipment such as the Noise Suppression (MAW XM-21) Sniper Rifle, so that none of the enemy know from where the fire is coming and therefore can take no evasive action as they see each other being eliminated. Finally, there are appropriate missions which could be assigned such as limited sabotage and demolitions operations in the enemy rear which would produce a tremendous demoralizing influence on the enemy."*

Some teams from 1st Force Recon Company used supporting arms on the enemy from the beginning. On force recon platoon OPCON (under operational control) to an infantry battalion in Operation Deckhouse, I observed a village before the infantry swept through and, after the infantry departed, noticed the Viet Cong return to the village. "When they started moving back, we'd catch the Cong outside the village and call mortar fire. We'd call in and . . . they'd send a platoon right back up. They ended up apprehending about twenty more suspects from the village." This particular platoon also employed artillery if available and even took the enemy under fire itself: "If they were a small group and we could get close enough, we'd take them under fire ourselves."

Sgt. Orest Bishko's patrol from 1st Force Recon Company of 28 July 1966 was the determining event. Accompanying the patrol, Capt. Francis J. West Jr., a tactical specialist, observed, analyzed, and reported in such a manner that Stingray was officially born. The team had been ". . . given a simple mission: get into the bush, find the enemy, and destroy him. . . .

*Michael Lee Lanning and Ray William Stubbe, *Inside Force Recon* (New York: Ivy Books, 1989).

For two days we moved through the thick undergrowth, staying well hidden, occasionally hearing the enemy chopping wood or shouting. . . . By the third morning we knew where their battalion bivouac area was, and called in artillery fire. . . . Chased by a NVA platoon, we left the scene at top speed and before we could be overtaken . . . jet fighters were scrambled. . . ." Following the debrief, General Walt and his G-3 (operations officer), Col. John C. Chaisson Jr., decided that such missions merited a special section in the reporting system and chose for the teams the operational code name of "Stingray."

The concept of Stingray was officially adopted the month after Sergeant Bishko's patrol, in July 1966, and by December 1966, 601 enemy were killed at a cost of nine Stingray outpost Marines.

On 12 January 1967, Lieutenant McDonald's Team Hong Kong, from 2d Platoon, 1st Force Recon Company, was operating from an OP (observation post) on Hill 257 (BS414775) when it spotted groups of five and ten VC moving on a trail. Previously plotted artillery concentrations were called in on the enemy. Then, as twilight approached, the enemy began to emerge along a stream so that they looked like one long line of black-dressed VC with rifles and gear. Before it became dark over 557 were counted. Again a fire mission was called as well as air. To mark the spot, Sergeant Arnold stood in front of the lieutenant with a poncho as he used a strobe light, which would be visible from above. Secondary explosions followed as two 175mm rounds crashed into the area every five minutes. Sergeant Arnold later stated, "We stayed there at that OP site because we knew we hadn't finished our job there at all; there was still a lot of VC in the area."

In another instance, a team from 1st Force Recon Company operating in support of Operation Union II, on 26 May 1967, noticed various groups of enemy forces, one man approximately six feet tall, about 250 pounds, walking in a military manner not characteristic of Vietnamese, probably a mainland Chinese advisor, as well as groups of Vietnamese carrying rifles and packs. In each instance the team called in effective artillery-fire missions to destroy the enemy right then and there:

". . . at one time, early in the morning, at 0900 we saw five VC step off a trail for the high ground—approximately 50 meters high—set down their packs and weapons, and [they] appeared to be observing the trail on which they had just come. I called in artillery, had excellent coverage of the area, and we noted one VC limping away. Again, I called in artillery and brought it on top of the man . . . 25 minutes later I observed two VC stopped by a large dike full of water . . . I called an artillery mission in on them. One confirmed KIA—I saw his body lying on the dike—and one probable. At 0940 of the same day there was observed five VC moving up the hill toward our position carrying packs and weapons. Called a fire mission, had excellent coverage on the target."

The next morning, when the team received some sniper fire, they called artillery in on the sniper, moved, and continued calling artillery on every enemy they spotted throughout the patrol.

Stingray patrols were generally lightly armed and equipped teams, inserted by helicopter at points near their objective, who then moved by stealth to their OP, where they remained for several days, causing heavy enemy casualties at a low cost to themselves. It was officially noted that from May 1966 through December 1967, Stingray patrols accounted for 1,845 enemy confirmed killed while sustaining 69 Marines killed as a result of these operations, a ratio of 27:1 in favor of the Marine recon units. Rather than engage the enemy themselves with their organic weapons, the team engaged the enemy indirectly through supporting arms: "five men with one radio had the firepower of a regiment at their disposal."

HQMC (Headquarters Marine Corps) established the Stingray Project (30-67-05) in June 1967 to study the new tactic to improve effectiveness of operations then in progress in Vietnam, and to examine the long-term effects of the recon teams on the long-term plans of the Marine Corps. To avoid duplication of effort with the Small Independent Action Forces (SIAF) Project conducted by Advanced Research Projects Agency (ARPA) of the Office of the Secretary of Defense (OSD), the Stingray project was terminated in May 1971.

In 1968, 101 patrols fired 369 artillery missions and 39 air strikes, which resulted in 275 confirmed enemy KIAs and five friendly KIAs. Less than 3 percent of the recon extractions were under fire, indicating that the mission did not compromise the position or presence of the team. The following other statistics were significant:

Kill ratio for Marine infantry, 7.6:1; for recon, 34:1.

Tons of ordnance per kill: seven for infantry, two for recon.

Men days per kill: 480 for infantry, 171 for recon.

Mortality rate (for a year-long assignment): 20 percent for infantry, 6 percent for recon.

Contacts originated by enemy vs. contacts originated by Marines: for infantry, 80 percent of contacts were enemy-originated, for recon, 5 percent of contacts were enemy-originated.

In more than eight thousand Stingray patrols, only one patrol was totally annihilated, not one patrol was ever captured, and no patrol ever disappeared. "This appears to counter the theory of the vulnerability of small teams operating in enemy territory." *The 8,317 Stingray recon patrols had 15,680 sightings of over 138,252 enemy; they called in 6,463 fire missions and 1,328 air strikes, resulting in 9,566 confirmed killed, 85 enemy captured, and over 300 weapons captured.*

Gen. Raymond G. Davis credited the Stingray patrol, coupled with rapid reinforcement and exploitation, with the destruction of enemy activity in the 3d Marine Division AO (area of operations) while he was the commanding general. Not infantry sweeps, but small, highly mobile units were key to success, an old lesson recognized by the British in the Boer Wars, "that it was not elaborate maneuvers, but rapid movement and attack wherever the enemy could be found, which paid."

Not only did Stingray tactics save the lives of Marine participants, but frequently such patrols annihilated sizable enemy units closing in to attack friendly bases. One such patrol probably foiled a major attack in June 1967. 1st Lt. Robert F. Drake assembled his eight-man Team Hateful on 11 June 1967 to issue the patrol order. The mission was to conduct an area reconnaissance in the Elephant Valley and the Garden of Eden just outside Da Nang to discover infiltration routes and staging areas for VC. Intelligence reflected that it should be a quiet patrol; not many sightings of the enemy had been made in that area.

The team was inserted at 0900 on 12 June 1967, on a road, and immediately moved into foliage. From the sound of firing aimed at their insertion helicopters as they departed, it was apparent that the enemy was in their area. The patrol moved to high ground to establish communications with a radio relay located at Dong Din. While moving up the hill the patrol paused to change radios and the radioman, from H&S (Headquarters and Service) Company, having to relieve himself, moved outside the team's perimeter. All at once *bam-bam-boom!*—two rounds and an explosion, and the radioman was crying for help. He had been hit by fragments from an M-26 grenade. While the lieutenant and corpsman were working on him, the lieutenant looked up, saw the VC moving back into a bush, and shot him eight times across the back. The doc looked up and saw one more enemy above the group, fired, and drove him away. The dead VC had several M-26 grenades on his body. Everyone pulled back and the lieutenant called in a medevac chopper, which arrived shortly and evacuated the radioman, who had been badly cut up. In all the rush, the team neglected to secure the radioman's gear and was subsequently forced to carry it during the next three days, considerably impeding their movement.

The enemy force, estimated at ten to twenty soldiers, continued moving around Team Hateful during the radioman's hoist extraction into the CH-34 helicopter. The team then slithered away while Lieutenant Drake walked artillery concentrations behind the team as it proceeded. That night the enemy was still moving around the team, so Lieutenant Drake called in artillery right up to Hateful's harbor site (nighttime position), "very, very close, in fact, we had shrapnel flying all over us, cutting trees and everything, but it protected us; that was the main thing."*

Artillery completely saturated the area the next morning, and during the next two days the team moved without contacts or sightings until its extraction on the fifteenth. The only enemy encountered at that time was the exceedingly dense vegetation, which in some places made it necessary to crawl two hundred meters on hands and arms, and the plethora of wiggling, squirming leeches that always posed special problems for clandestine movement. Leeches were particularly attracted to arms and legs, and at times even crawled into the penis. Once they've attached themselves, just smashing the itching, bloodsucking parasites results in infection because part of the leech is left in the subcutaneous tissue. And they can't be gently pulled off. The only effective method is to squirt mosquito repellent on them until they drop off. But the scent of the repellent will also betray the team's presence.

Lieutenant Drake radioed to confirm the extraction before proceeding downhill. At about 1630, he again called, since the team's extraction was scheduled for 1700. He was then told, "There's a chance now that the extraction will not go, on account the birds are down—mechanical failures with the helicopters, the CH-46s." Almost immediately voices were heard by the team, and the patrol, located in deep grass alongside the road, hit the deck and retracted into the bush except for the lieutenant and the new radioman. The two proceeded cautiously toward the road and observed ten very heavily armed VC walking by. They were wearing Bermuda shorts with large pockets, carrying AK-47s, M-1s, and other small arms. Each one carried a big bush in his hands for camouflage. After the information was called in to the COC (combat operations center), an artillery mission was called on the area through the night.

At about 2100 the patrol heard a very large group pass by them, approximately a hundred soldiers, a suspected VC

*Inside Force Recon.

company moving westward toward Laos. They were running, wet, tired, and dragging their weapons. Lieutenant Drake, who could understand some Vietnamese, heard one of the men say that he didn't like this at all and wasn't going to make it. Later, several other large groups moved past the recon team toward Da Nang. It was not thought advisable to call in artillery because the enemy force might move right into the hidden patrol, which was only about five feet from the road.

Battalion dispatched a "Spooky" C-47 gunship with miniguns, but Lieutenant Drake didn't want to use them either since they would have to use flares, which might disclose his own position. He suggested they proceed up the valley and work from the relay point, with Patrol Consulate under Sergeant Livingston, to annihilate the enemy in the valley.

Two companies of enemy soldiers passed by, moving toward Da Nang. Battalion recon coordinated TPQ-10 artillery and air strikes on those retreating westward, while from 2100 to 2400 three Spookys took turns firing all of their ammunition on the groups moving toward Da Nang. Sampans on the river, laden with rockets, were also sunk by the Spookys.

Fixed-wing aircraft completely saturated the area the next morning. At 0900 a CH-46 Sea Knight suddenly landed on the road and Team Hateful was extracted. It had probably foiled at least a major rocket attack.

=== 6 ===

First One In—Last One Out

Following is a January 1997 interview with Sgt. Maj. Maurice J. Jacques, USMC (Ret.), who served with Force Recon and 1st Recon Battalion for forty-three months during the Vietnam War (June 1965 to August 1970). On Sunday, 11 May 1997, Sergeant Major Jacques died of a heart attack while driving home after a hot several rounds of trap and skeet at Camp Pendleton with his best friend, 1st Sgt. Don "Woody" Hamblen, USMC (Ret.).

Since my biography *Sergeant Major, U.S. Marines* was published in 1995, I have been asked many times by young Marines to discuss the changes in our reconnaissance training and tactics during the Vietnam War, particularly concerning the effective use of the Stingray concept, which I observed and in some ways helped create during my forty-three months of combat in Vietnam.

As a gunnery sergeant aboard the USS *Diachenko* (APD 123) in June of 1965, I was one of two Force Recon platoon leaders tasked with conducting the first hydrographic beach surveys on a spit of land east of Saigon called Vung Tau. This was the first utilization of recon Marines in Vietnam, with the exception of those Marines assigned duties in 1964 with MACV-SOG (Special Observation Group).

Initially armed with the inaccurate M–3A1 [.45-caliber] "Grease Gun," we soon came to realize the limitations of this, our T/O weapon, and gladly replaced it with heavier M-1 Garands and several BARs. That was probably one of our first lessons learned—"don't bring a butter knife to a gunfight."

There were sixteen recon Marines in my team, led by 1st Lt. J. C. Lenker, and we felt that we were a well-trained and professional group ready for the rigors of close combat if necessary. I say this because, at first, we did fight as we had trained for combat, and that was perhaps the second, and most important, lesson learned. Our training for several years at Camp Pendleton and later on Okinawa did very little to properly prepare us for the realities of combat in the jungles of South Vietnam. In fact, our training, and the thinking that went into it, was probably responsible for the subsequent wounding and deaths of many of the first Marines to fight in Vietnam.

While a few skeptics may raise their eyebrows at such a statement, I seriously doubt that any of them could state with any degree of accuracy that they served with Force Recon for one year prior to going to Vietnam, and then spent the better part of four years in Vietnam—most of it in the bush. I did. My first tour in Vietnam lasted nineteen months.

During the early 1960s, 1st Force Recon Company had, in my opinion, suffered under the delusional leadership of some operations and training officers who thought that parachuting and scuba diving were to be the definitive marks of a "recon Marine." Some of them had never served in combat, never heard a shot fired in anger, and spent little or no time in the field observing or helping to change our training. The coming of Marine Corps' involvement in Southeast Asia was obvious in 1963. And because almost no Marines had seen combat since July of 1953 in Korea, most had absolutely no credibility when it came to expressing opinions *based upon combat experience*. These "textbook captains" did more damage than they would be willing to admit.

1964–66

As a staff sergeant, my initial introduction to 1st Force Reconnaissance Company, in January 1964, began with a very tough series of physically demanding exercises designed to weed out those "wannabe" volunteers who could not meet the basic physical requirements of all Marines in the company. While my basic knowledge of infantry skills was tested to the satisfaction of the company's assistant training officer, it was still a matter of "brawn over brain" to get into the company. I think that too much emphasis was placed on each Marine's ability to do push-ups, run, swim, become a qualified scuba diver, and jump out of airplanes as a qualified parachutist.

Before I listen to the howling of indignation by some former Force Recon Marines, I must say that to have been selected to serve in 1st Force Recon Company, for two of my three tours in Vietnam, was a personal milestone for me. To have been entrusted to lead many of those recon Marines on numerous reconnaissance patrols, deep in enemy-held territory, was the culmination of everything I had done in the Corps from the time I joined in July of 1948.

After completing our mission of beach surveys along the coast of South Vietnam, our platoon joined up with the rest of the company, then located on the beach at Camp Merrell, just south of Marble Mountain. While we had spent the better part of two months in the water, the rest of the company had been conducting reconnaissance patrols in support of Operation Starlight and Operation Jackstay. It wasn't long before we received word that we would begin patrolling around the Da Nang area, in support of Marine infantry operations. My very first patrol caused a significant change in the way we made contact with the Viet Cong.

Prior to coming to Vietnam, it had been a doctrinal policy that reconnaissance Marines were to avoid all possible contact with the enemy. If contact was made, it was to be broken off immediately, and we practiced what we referred to as "quail tactics," meaning that we would take flight, run off in every direction, and plan to meet up later, probably at our last known and easily recognized rallying point. This was a recipe for disaster.

I had led a six-man patrol onto an island north of Da Nang, and our mission was to locate a known group of VC who had been sniping at passing boats and ships. We were given three days to find them and then pass on the location to the infantry so they could ferret them out later. After we completed our mission we were to swim away from the island for a rendezvous with the Swift boat that had brought us to it. By the second day we hadn't seen anyone, but that changed when we came under VC fire, splitting up the team. Following orders, we did not return fire, but we had to disengage, then wait until nightfall before we could link up. We swam out to our pickup point on the third night of the mission, and only by the grace of God, and some frantic waving on our part, did we avoid being shot in the water by a U.S. Navy patrol boat.

The next morning our patrol was debriefed by then Major Paul Xavier Kelly (later the twenty-sixth commandant of the Marine Corps). Being responsible for the success or failure of the mission, I told Major Kelly that our orders had prevented us from firing at the VC, and having to break contact during a firefight created the problem of the team's being divided for nearly a day. I didn't mince my words when talking to Major Kelly. I told him that we felt we had come there to fight, not run. He agreed with me, and must have taken my words all the way up to the III MAF commander, because the following day we received word that from that day on we were not forced to break contact with the VC. Common sense dictated that six recon Marines, lightly armed, were in no position to take on a platoon of VC, but the morale of the Marines in the company rose significantly upon learning that we did not have to run away upon receiving fire.

The number of patrols the Marines in 1st Force and 3rd Recon Battalion ran in 1965 was significant for several reasons. Not only did we have to change our own tactics to survive in the jungle, we had to become familiar with the tactics of the Viet Cong, and later, the North Vietnamese Army.

The increase in reconnaissance patrols using helicopters as our primary means of insertion soon made these into smooth and professional operations. Being able to talk with the pilots, take advantage of visual overflights prior to a patrol, and having two dedicated A-4 Skyhawk jets to provide close air support was a dramatic improvement over being taken close to a proposed recon zone by truck. The CH-34, and later the Huey, could easily carry a recon team, and by using false inserts to confuse any watching VC or NVA, our tactics improved, as did our morale.

On 26 November 1965 my recon platoon was called to the company mess hall to meet with Maj. Gen. Lewis W. Walt, then commanding general of III MAF. The general, an enlisted Marine machine gunner on Guadalcanal during the Second World War, was well known and highly respected by the Marines who were the "eyes and ears" of his amphibious force. Having twice been awarded the Navy Cross and a Silver Star, he was no stranger to the intricacies of reconnaissance work. Now he was sending us to a U.S. Army Special Forces camp known as A-106, located near the village of Ba To, and planned to send a second recon platoon from the company to Special Forces Camp A-107 near the village of Tra Bong, thirty kilometers southwest of Chu Lai. We were going there to "test the feasibility of deep reconnaissance patrols" on a mission code-named Birdwatcher.

I'd had the privilege of serving with General Walt during the Korean War, when he was regimental commander of the 5th Marines. He was, in my opinion, one of the few senior officers who realized that his reconnaissance teams, when properly trained, equipped, and utilized, could be depended on to locate an enemy who had already established a reputation for blending into his surroundings well. Regular Marine infantrymen, General Walt believed, were too slow for this mission. The general had decided that because reconnaissance teams had demonstrated their ability to find the VC, they should be provided with a way to destroy them. Accordingly, he allowed our teams to call in artillery and close air support directly. The often slow and frustrating clearance procedures that had hindered our being able to bring fire to bear on the enemy in the Da Nang TAOR did not exist at Chu Lai. The general wanted to make these capabilities available to his reconnaissance teams wherever and whenever they were operating in enemy territory. This concept was continuously being refined with the introduction of better radios, longer-reaching and dedicated artillery, and the rapid response of close air support, night and day. By 1966 this tactical concept would be adopted as a standard reconnaissance tactic known as a Stingray mission.

I don't think it's necessary for me to again detail all that happened at the battle of Ba To, but a short version of that action might help to set the stage, as the lessons learned from that event were certainly significant.

Our mission was to go to Ba To and patrol until we found the enemy. General Walt's G-2 section believed that the local VC and NVA were preparing to attack the 7th Marine Regiment, and we were specifically detailed to locate their avenues of approach and egress, if possible, and try and locate their staging area and an underground field hospital believed to be in our TAOR.

On 16 December 1965 a force of sixteen recon Marines from 1st Force Recon, one U.S. Army Special Forces staff sergeant named West, and sixty-one South Vietnamese CIDG (Civilian Irregular Defense Group) troops left the village of Ba To, in Quang Ngai Province, and moved eight kilometers to the west to overlook the village of Vuc Liem. We set up on our objective area, and on the afternoon of our first day out I sent three four-man recon teams out to move at night and radio back any significant information they might have. Each team reported back with the discovery of several large hootches and the location of enemy observation posts and listening posts. Several large groups of well-armed and equipped North Vietnamese soldiers were also sighted. This information caused quite a stir at III MAF headquarters.

The three recon teams had planned to return to our hilltop on the sixteenth of December. However, rugged and heavily vegetated terrain and a slow, cautious pace caused the teams to return late in the afternoon, and the South Vietnamese lieutenant in command of the CIDG force insisted that it would be too dangerous to move off the hilltop with nightfall coming on. I tried several times to get him to change his mind, but he refused, waving me off. In retrospect, I should have shot the bastard.

We were set up on a kidney-shaped piece of high ground with a small stream running below the face of the hill. The hillside was covered in knee-deep grass, and at the extreme edge of the two fingers that ran off the hillside we had two two-man listening posts.

At exactly 1900 hours that night we were attacked by the NVA, and their assault began with two well-placed 60mm mortar rounds impacting on our hill. That was followed by more than one hundred incoming rounds of mortar fire during the next two hours of fighting. The first casualty was the South Vietnamese lieutenant who had insisted that we remain in place on the hill. He was literally ripped to pieces by one mortar round, but with him went our primary radio, a far more important asset than the lieutenant.

The size of the attack group was estimated to be between 150 and 200 NVA regulars using heavy and light automatic weapons, hand grenades, and infantry small arms. The dense vegetation allowed both the NVA and us to remain hidden, but "fire discipline," the hallmark of all Marine infantrymen, was totally unknown to the CIDG forces. They fired at every sight and sound as they scattered to the winds in what can only be described as the classic "every man for himself" drill. To add to the confusion, it began to rain very hard. With the recon teams split in different directions, there was absolutely no control over them, nor the CIDG soldiers. While every man knew the center location of our patrol base, no one would try to make his way there and run the risk of being shot out in the open. And, while I tried desperately to set up a hasty defense, there was just too much confusion and a growing number of wounded to deal with.

There was no countermortar fire from the South Vietnamese, who had our mortars, and without that suppressive fire there was no way to silence the NVA's heavy or light machine guns.

L.Cpl. William P. Moore was wounded as he tried to unwrap some 60mm mortar rounds. Then our corpsman,

Doc Haston, was seriously wounded in the chest by a huge piece of shrapnel. Within seconds Corporal Joy was wounded in the head, and despite Haston's attempt to stop his best friend's bleeding, nothing could save him. I knew that if we continued to remain in our present positions we would all die. The NVA knew where we were, and with mortar rounds and machine guns they increased their volume of fire.

I was finally joined by Sergeants Blanton and Akioka and Corporal Lynch, and we tried to cover the withdrawal of several CIDG troops and my interpreter, Truong. I decided that our only hope was to get my wounded men down from the hilltop and into a hiding position that might let us escape from the NVA, who were rolling up our flanks. Sergeant Akioka had also been wounded, but he helped lead the way off the hill, under fire. While Blanton and I covered the withdrawal of the rest of the group, they moved over the crest of the hill and down into a large banana grove. As Sergeant Blanton and I moved in trace, I was shot in the neck and knocked backwards. Because it was dark and raining heavily I had no way to know how badly I had been hit, but I was spitting up a good deal of blood and despite a constant burning sensation I knew I must keep moving if I wanted to live. Using the fingers of my left hand to keep my tiger-striped shirt pressed hard against my neck, I grabbed my M-2 [.30 caliber, fully automatic] carbine and crawled off in the direction of the banana grove.

At the first opportunity to take care of myself I discovered just how lucky I had been. As I tried to open up my first-aid pouch, which I kept fastened on my suspender-strap harness, I noticed that the bullet had bounced off my first-aid pouch before ricocheting into my neck. If I had taken that AK-47 round directly, I wouldn't be here to tell you this story.

One of my team members, a Lance Corporal Brown, had been wounded during the initial moments of the NVA assault and lay unconscious until two NVA soldiers came upon him. They stripped his uniform and equipment from him, but their attention was diverted by the moans of a dying Corporal Joy, who was nearby. They moved to him, stood over him, and shot him to death.

Returning to Brown, they picked him up and began carrying him off the hill. Brown, realizing that immediate escape would be his only chance for survival, waited until the moving column of NVA reached a narrow part of the trail, then dove head-first into the dense vegetation. Several NVA fired in his direction but apparently none dared to follow. Brown landed only several yards from where we were hiding. We grabbed him, pulled him into our group, and waited.

Suddenly the night sky was lit up by a powerful searchlight that the NVA had mounted on a tripod. As quickly as they could shine their light on a wounded South Vietnamese soldier or Marine they would shoot to kill. Hidden in the banana grove, we remained motionless, hoping that spotter planes would be able to find us in the morning and coordinate an emergency extraction plan.

When morning came we knew that our hopes for any type of extraction were in vain. A thick blanket of fog covered the ground, making aerial observation impossible.

Since our only way to escape was to avoid the NVA and move in the direction of Ba To, we began our journey. Nearly four kilometers away from where we had been hit we were met by Sergeant Baker and Corporal Young, who I thought had been killed the night before. With two CIDG soldiers in the lead, we moved back to Ba To.

At 1400 on the seventeenth of December, nine of us finally walked through the Ba To perimeter wire. We were met by Major Gaffen, our company commander, and those of us who required medical attention were taken by medevac helicopter to B Company, 3rd Medical Battalion, for treatment.

On the twenty-first of December, a Marine combat patrol left Ba To and recovered the bodies at the scene of the battle: Marines Joy, Constance, Sessions, and Moore; Special Forces sergeant West; the young South Vietnamese lieutenant patrol leader; and ten CIDG soldiers. Nine other CIDG were never found. Each dead Marine had been mutilated by the NVA.

As a direct result of what happened at Ba To, one of our long-standing operational procedures was completely terminated. After Ba To, all Force Recon patrols trained together, went in together, stayed together, and were extracted together. The use of CIDG personnel was practically eliminated, because so many of them were sympathetic to the local VC or NVA. Dependency on South Vietnamese military interpreters was also greatly reduced; they were replaced by Marine graduates of Vietnamese language schools in the States and in country.

After the experience at Ba To, I hoped the new year could only be better. We had learned a great deal from our success, and our failure, but as the war in Vietnam expanded so did our commitment and responsibilities.

In support of Operation Double Eagle, which lasted until 16 February 1966, I participated in four reconnaissance missions, all beginning from Ba To. Our four platoons conducted a total of thirty-five team-size and five platoon-size patrols, thirty-one of those patrols making contact with the enemy. To our credit we suffered just one Marine killed in action and one wounded, but we also lost one recon Marine to capture by the enemy. L.Cpl. D. S. Dowling, who was assigned to Lieutenant Lenker's recon team, had positioned himself in a tree as he watched for NVA. For whatever reason, he began to move around, movement detected by an approaching NVA patrol. They shot and killed Dowling and wounded his teammate, Cpl. G. P. Solovskoy, hitting him in both legs. But the more somber incident occurred with the capture of L.Cpl. Edwin R. Grissett. He was point man on a patrol led by 1st Lt. R. F. Parker. During a rest period Grissett had distanced himself ahead of his team. When the team was ambushed by the NVA, Grissett was too far from the main body, was captured, and was last seen being led away by NVA captors. (Years later, I learned that Grissett had been forced to walk north all the way to Hanoi, where he was held as a prisoner of war until 1968, when he died of malnutrition at the hands of NVA prison guards.) Again, obvious lessons were to be learned from these incidents.

In early May my recon platoon was inserted into a recon zone northwest of Quang Ngai, about thirty-five miles from Chu Lai, in support of Operation Montgomery. Our mission was to provide reconnaissance information in support of a regiment-size landing by the 7th Marine Regiment. My platoon had been inserted by helicopter four days before the landing to try and locate any NVA positions, and to remain in place as a blocking force in the event that the regiment's landing flushed the enemy from his positions.

This, in my opinion, was another poor idea, but one frequently tested. To use lightly armed reconnaissance teams numbering only seven strong as blocking forces was not a good idea. If we proved successful in that role, it would be repeated again and again until a recon team was heavily mauled or annihilated by a superior NVA force.

Nonetheless, after landing in our LZ without coming under enemy fire, sometime close to 1730, we headed off in a westerly direction and moved quietly into heavy vegetation, which provided us with a good place for our harbor site. We set up in a tight 360-degree defense and went on a 70 percent alert for the remainder of the night. With Sgt. Johann Haferkamp as my assistant platoon sergeant, I felt very comfortable that we could handle any problems.

Six of us were armed with the new M-14 rifles, and Lance Corporal Rossi, our team's grenadier, carried the M-79 grenade launcher, which was capable of accurately firing 40mm high explosive (HE) rounds out to a distance of three hundred meters. Each of us carried twenty magazines of 7.62mm rounds as well as six M-26 or M-33 hand grenades.

Just before first light we moved out of our harbor site and into an OP site that offered us a commanding view toward the west and the south-southeast. Before long we reported cooking fires in the valley nearly a half mile to our west and observed uniformed NVA soldiers getting water and washing their cooking pots in a stream. Our sighting of a concentration of NVA soldiers was considered so significant that we soon received word that the position we were observing had been assigned as a target for a B-52 Arc Light mission. This high-altitude carpet bombing was planned for 1200 that same day.

We remained in our position to observe. At 1203, though we never heard or saw any aircraft, the ground beneath us began to shake, rattle, and roll. The tremendous thundering roar from dozens of five-hundred-pound bombs simultaneously detonating on target was so overwhelming that one of our new men, a young private, was overcome, fouling his camouflage trousers. Fearful we'd all be killed, he began to shout, but before he could give away our position Sergeant Haferkamp jumped up, slapped his hands over the private's mouth, and held him until he calmed down and returned to his senses.

During the next several days we had to carefully watch the new man's every move for fear of a repeat performance. To us he was, potentially, as dangerous as the NVA. Believing him to be a mental time bomb, we called back to the COC and requested an extraction for the man. The word came back that a helicopter would extract the entire team and take him to the nearest medical battalion for observation and the remainder of us to a new OP.

While waiting for our extraction bird we were able to watch a Marine rifle company being helilifted into an area about two klicks (kilometers) to the southeast. To put an entire Marine rifle company into a tight landing zone, numerous helicopters were required, and we had rarely seen so many in place at one time. Even more impressive than the number of CH-34s were the Marine infantrymen scrambling out of the helicopters and moving quickly toward a tree line in front of them. Before they reached the cover of the trees, their own 60mm mortar section had been set up and was covering the area with white smoke rounds to help obscure their movement. I told Sergeant Haferkamp that I had never witnessed 60mm mortar fire being delivered so quickly or accurately. The sight remained with me as a good idea, one to be used later.

* * *

I have already told my story about being the jumpmaster for the first true combat jump in Marine Corps history, which took place near the village of Tra Bong on 14 June 1966, but there is more to that story that I think should be mentioned. Here, another lesson *failed to be learned* as a result of what happened to us at the battle of Ba To, and was significant in the continuing development of the Stingray concept.

Following the helicopter insertion of S.Sgt. Jimmie L. Howard's eighteen-man reconnaissance patrol near Nui Vu on 13 June 1966, he moved to a fifteen-hundred-foot-high hill mass to set up a radio-relay position and, for two days, maintained a commanding OP (observation post). Supported by a South Vietnamese Army 105mm battery located at the Thien Phuoc Special Forces Camp nearly five miles west of Nui Vu, his recon team began to call artillery fire on numerous targets of opportunity.

But with the chance to accurately hit the North Vietnamese Army also came the possibility that the NVA would retaliate. The NVA weren't stupid, and despite Howard's taking the precaution to call his fire missions only when our spotter planes were in the area, it didn't take the NVA very long to figure out where the fire was being directed from. On the night of the fifteenth a patrol from the Special Forces camp at Thien Phuoc reported an enemy battalion moving toward Nui Vu from the southeast.

Between 2130 and 2330, Howard called for artillery support as the Marines heard North Vietnamese troops massing at the bottom of the hill. Shortly after midnight the Communists probed the Marine defenses and then followed with a three-sided all-out attack. According to the Navy corpsman with the Marines, the enemy forces ". . . were within twenty feet of us. Suddenly there were grenades all over. The people started hollering. It seemed everybody got hit at the same time." Despite the intensity of the enemy assault, which was supported by heavy machine gun fire, the Marine perimeter held. Howard radioed Lt. Col. Arthur J. Sullivan, his battalion commander, "You've gotta get us out of here. . . . There are too many of them for my people." Lieutenant Colonel Sullivan attempted to reassure the patrol leader and told him that assistance would be on the way.

About 0200, supporting air arrived overhead, including Marine and Air Force flare planes, helicopters, and attack aircraft. Under the light of the flares Marine jets and Huey gunships attacked the enemy forces massing at the bottom of the hill. At times VMO-6 gunships strafed to within twenty meters of the patrol's perimeter, and fixed-wing aircraft dropped bombs and napalm as close as one hundred meters. At 0300 enemy ground fire drove off a flight of MAG-36 helicopters coming to pick up the patrol. Lieutenant Colonel Sullivan told Howard that the patrol could not expect any reinforcements until dawn and to hold as best he could.

The action on and around the hill was reduced to small, scattered individual firefights. Wary of U.S. aircraft orbiting overhead, the Communist forces decided against another mass assault but continued to fire at the Marines throughout the night. Running short of ammunition, Howard and his men fired single shots, even throwing rocks at suspected enemy positions, hoping the NVA would mistake the rocks for grenades. The fighting was exacting a heavy toll on the reconnaissance patrol—each man had been wounded at least once, and six of the eighteen Marines were dead. Staff Sergeant Howard was struck in the back by a ricochet, temporarily paralyzing his legs. Unable to use his lower limbs, Howard pulled himself from hole to hole, encouraging his men and directing their fire.

At dawn on 16 June, MAG-36 UH-34s escorted by Huey gunships safely landed Company C, 1st Battalion, 5th Marines, near the base of Nui Vu. One of the gunships, piloted by Maj. William J. Goodsell, commanding officer of VMO-6, was hit by enemy fire and crash landed. Major Goodsell and his copilot were evacuated, but Goodsell later died of his wounds.

The Marine company on the ground met some resistance as it advanced up Nui Vu to relieve Howard's patrol. When the relief force finally reached the top of the hill, Howard greeted them with the warning, "Get down . . . There are snipers right in front of us!" 1st Lt. Marshall B. Darling, Company C commander, remembered that he found Howard's men armed mostly with AK-47s taken from dead North Vietnamese. The North Vietnamese, later identified as a battalion from the 3d NVA Regiment, continued to battle the Marines for control of the hill until noon and then disengaged. They left behind forty-two dead and nineteen weapons. Company C suffered two Marines dead and two wounded.

For this action, fifteen men of Staff Sergeant Howard's recon platoon were awarded the Silver Star and two more the Navy Cross. S.Sgt. Jimmie L. Howard was awarded the Medal of Honor.

I had known Jimmie Howard for several years before he came into the company. After Vietnam we talked about the similarities in our experiences. Jimmie was a fine Marine, had even been the manager of the Marine Corps Recruit Depot, San Diego, baseball team, and had a reputation for looking out for his men. But his mission was almost a carbon copy of what had happened to us at Ba To just six months earlier. To take to the high ground, unsupported by artillery because hilltops are so damned difficult to hit, and remain in the same position for more than a few hours was just asking for trouble. I know; it happened to my platoon, too. Additionally, despite our protests about sending large numbers of recon Marines into the bush as one unit, no one was listening. In my opinion, one shared by many team leaders, eight recon Marines was the maximum number for a team. And by 1969 that number was reduced to six-man teams that had better training, better equipment, and better supporting arms response time. But sadly, in 1966 it took a dramatic life-or-death firefight, the deaths of eight more Marines, and the wounding of nearly two dozen others before the Stingray concept was to see significant change. If recon OPs were to be established, they would have to be well defended. Later, they were. The changes seemed obvious: keep our recon teams small, six to eight men; keep them quiet; and stay on the move, making them more difficult targets to locate.

* * *

In our mess hall not long after this incident I was joined by a staff sergeant and a sergeant from F Company, 2d Battalion, 7th Marines, who were assigned to provide for an ammunition dump located on the opposite side of a hill near our company compound. The staff sergeant, Pete Connors, was from South Boston, Massachusetts. During our meal he mentioned that he had participated in Operation Montgomery, and then I realized that it was Connors's company I had observed assaulting the tree line near the village. I told him that I had watched their progress that day and was particularly impressed by how rapidly they put their 60mm WP (white phosphorus) rounds into the tree line.

Staff Sergeant Connors laughed and said that what I had witnessed was not 60mm mortar fire, but rifle grenades used in a unique manner. Connors told me he assigned one M-14 grenade launcher to each squad. Since new men had a problem spotting the location of enemy firing, he gave the rifle grenade launcher to his most experienced men. The M-14 rifle needed to have the spindle valve turned to the "off" position to fire the rifle grenade. Connors said he required his grenadier to have one WP grenade attached to the rifle and a crimped cartridge in the rifle's chamber. The grenadier also had a full magazine of 7.62mm rounds locked in his rifle's magazine well. As soon as he fired the WP grenade, the rifleman/grenadier turned the spindle valve to the "on" position, pulled back the operating rod, and loaded a live round into his weapon. He followed the burst of his WP grenade with a stream of accurate rifle fire, often using tracer rounds to help mark the position. Knowing where the enemy was located, the rest of the squad could key in on the bursting white phosphorous grenade and deliver much more accurate fire.

The very next day I assembled my recon platoon on the beach, where we test-fired our M-14 grenade launchers and practiced Pete Connors's idea until we had it down pat. On several later recon patrols we were able to break contact with the NVA and live to fight again because of Pete's "better idea." Later in my extended tour with 1st Force Recon, I was saddened to learn that Staff Sergeant Pete Connors, F Company 2/7, was killed in action trying to save one of his men who lay wounded in a rice paddy.

1967–68

My second tour of duty in Vietnam began in November of 1967, with orders to 1st Recon Battalion, located at Camp Reasoner in Da Nang. As a first sergeant my assignment was managed by the division sergeant major, who had originally slated me for duty with 1st Medical Battalion. Some gentle protestation on my part fortunately allowed for the change in my assignment. Sgt. Maj. Billy Lyday thought I would be happy serving with 1st Force Recon Company again, but Lt. Col. Craig R. Steinmetz, the battalion commander, wanted me to go to a new company forming within his battalion, E Company. The colonel and I had a discussion about the training program I had worked on while working with 5th Force Recon Company back in the States, and he wanted it to continue in his battalion.

The company commander was Capt. J. P. Cahill, assisted by 1st Lt. Andy Finlayson, who had made a name for himself as the leader of Team Killer Kane. Every Marine in the company in the grade of lance corporal and below had come to us from the reconnaissance school co-located at Camp Pendleton's Infantry Training Regiment (ITR) and had been given the MOS (Military Occupational Specialty) of 8651, Basic Reconnaissance Marine. It was obvious that the Marine Corps was taking the professional training of recon Marines quite seriously.

These new men were motivated and eager to learn from those of us in the company who had experience in combat. Additionally, all of the noncommissioned officers (corporals and sergeants) who had recon MOSs had come to E Company from infantry regiments of the 1st Marine Division. The majority came to us with combat experience and all were volunteers. The staff noncommissioned officers had also come from infantry regiments in country, and many had previously served in reconnaissance companies during their careers. Some of the best SNCOs from within the battalion, those who were considered "short-timers," came to the company as instructors before returning home. And, with the exception of three newly joined lieutenants who had come directly from the Basic School at Quantico, all of our officers had considerable reconnaissance experience.

Echo Company was organized into five platoons: one headquarters platoon consisting of an administrative section, a supply section, and a communications section; and four operational platoons of three squads each, with nine men per squad. We totaled eleven officers and 133 enlisted men, including five Navy corpsmen.

Initially we were told that our company was going to be used in a Stingray-type role, but that changed due to the increased requirement for reconnaissance teams in the field to support infantry operations. We operated as a regular recon company, and it wasn't long before we had more recon teams in the bush than any other company in the battalion, including 1st Force Recon Company, which at the time was still located with 1st Recon Battalion.

During the first week of January 1968 the entire company was flown to Okinawa as part of our training program. The difference in training from what I had received and had given in 1965 was remarkable. Our first two weeks of training at the NTA (Northern Training Area) were dedicated to the basics: individual and team training with emphasis on patrolling techniques. SNCO instructors accompanied every patrol, acting as "lane graders" for particular events. In addition to the patrolling package we concentrated on live-fire exercises at the range and along jungle trails prepared with pop-up targets, which added to the realism.

In my opinion the time we spent on those quick-kill/quick-fire ranges was invaluable to our recon teams' ability to counter the everpresent ambush threat posed by the NVA. To prepare for what was to come, we also adjusted our schedule to insure that 70 percent of all training was conducted at night. If we "trained the way we would fight," the nights in Vietnam would no longer belong to the enemy. As our training transitioned to the platoon level, special emphasis was not placed on platoon-size patrols—they were things of the past. Instead, recon platoons would be employed to raid suspected POW camps, and attacking mock-up camps and staging POW recovery operations were great for boosting morale within the company.

We returned to Vietnam during the celebration of the lunar new year there, known as Tet. In less than a week's time we had eight recon teams in the bush, and six of these made contact with the NVA without the loss of a single Marine. We also had an operational responsibility to man four combat outposts assigned to the battalion. This responsibility was rotated among the five recon companies, and it had a dual mission: calling in artillery fire and close air support on observed enemy concentrations, and acting as radio-relay sites for recon teams patrolling at the extreme edge of our radio communications range. New and better equipment and closer liaison with supporting artillery and air assets combined to make our OPs extremely effective.

Each OP required at least a squad, if not a platoon, to provide adequate security. Here, at least, was one lesson written in blood and learned from our experiences at Ba To and on Howard's Hill.

One such outpost, Dong Din, sat on a large hilltop about twenty miles northwest of Da Nang, and because of its altitude it was usually covered by low-level clouds. To be sent out to occupy and defend this OP was considered an unofficial R&R within the company. Our second outpost was simply referred to as Hill 427, and it was located along a major NVA infiltration route. It had three well-constructed bunkers and several M-60 machine gun emplacements for added security. Our third OP was built around the ruins of a French hotel known as Ben Na. Usually defended by no less than twenty recon Marines, it, too, was well known to the NVA and VC who operated within our TAOR. The fourth, and undoubtedly most dangerous, OP was located on Hill 200, and it was here that we suffered our heaviest casualties in support of Stingray missions for the 1st Marine Division.

In May of 1968, Captain Cahill's replacement, First Lieutenant Badger, was replaced by Capt. William "Doc" White, who brought his own ideas to the company from his previous time spent with the grunts. In June, as enemy activity began to increase, Captain White organized and trained a company reaction force that was to go to the immediate assistance of any recon team or OP that found itself in serious trouble. Training of each of our company's teams began as soon as they returned from the bush, and within a few weeks we thought we were prepared for this new additional duty. Soon we were put to the test.

In July, nineteen Marines from Echo Company out on Hill 200 were attacked just after midnight by a very large force, estimated to be more than two hundred NVA soldiers. As word of the assault came to the COC, we began to ready the reaction force. Ammunition was drawn, equipment checked, and we assembled at the battalion LZ for a briefing prior to flying out before the first light.

In my opinion it is important to recognize that there was no "down time" on our part, nor any on the part of the helicopter pilots and their crews, and for us to have this new mission and the capability of executing it—being ready and "airborne" within several hours of receiving the call—was a marked improvement in our abilities to coordinate such efforts.

Coming in to our LZ, still nearly two klicks from Hill 200, flying tracers showed that the fight was still going on around the OP. Once we got on the ground we radioed our position and direction of movement toward the OP. With our arrival the NVA began to break contact and moved off toward the east. And, once inside the perimeter wire, we were greeted by quite a scene.

Every defensive bunker had been destroyed by explosive charges or direct hits from rocket-propelled grenades (RPGs). Five Marines were dead and everyone else was wounded. Leaving our corpsmen to tend to the wounded, along with a section of the reaction force on the hill, a group of us moved in trace of the NVA and found more than twenty of them dead, hidden in the brush. I did find one NVA soldier alive and carried him on my shoulder to the top of the OP, where one of our corpsmen came to help, but the soldier had taken a fatal round in the head and died a few minutes later.

The medevac helicopters began to arrive and within a short time we had loaded all our dead and wounded aboard for the flight back to 1st Medical Battalion. As the last of the birds departed, Captain White issued orders to clear the hill of unexploded ordnance. One bunker the NVA hit had contained extra ordnance, which was scattered all over the hill from the impact of an RPG round.

We learned that during the nighttime attack, one of our E Company Marines had distinguished himself by his courage and tenacity in trying to protect his fellow Marines from the NVA assault. L.Cpl. Kenneth Jones, inside one of the destroyed bunkers, kept standing up with his M-79 grenade launcher and firing into the ranks of the oncoming NVA. He fired so many rounds from the grenade launcher that he wore down the lands and grooves in the barrel before he was killed. He was recommended by Captain White for the Navy Cross.

1969–70

My third tour in Vietnam began with my assignment to M Company, 3d Battalion, 1st Marine Regiment, but because of a serious personnel problem in 1st Force Recon Company, I was directed to report there and replace the first sergeant, who had been involved in illegal financial dealings. Our company commander was Maj. Bill Bond. At the same time I reported for duty, I was joined by Capt. Norman Centers, the replacement for the company's executive officer, who was involved in the same scandal as the first sergeant. The CO, XO, and I had a major mission in trying to restore the morale of the company while it was actively carrying out its primary mission, reconnaissance.

In my opinion the tactical situation for Marine reconnaissance troops in Vietnam in the spring of 1970 was totally different from the operations I had participated in from 1965 to 1969. The Marines who were actually "in the field" paid small attention to political policy. In the early years we believed that we had come to Vietnam to stop the VC, engage the NVA, and, at some time, hand the country back over to the ARVN so they could eventually fight, and win, their own war. We had never lost a battle to the NVA. Sure, we had some bad situations and lost several teams during a five-year period. But the record of casualties we inflicted on the VC and the NVA while conducting Stingray and Keyhole missions speaks volumes for our success against the enemy.

Several Stingray missions conducted during 1970 stick out in my memory as primary examples of our success. Perhaps the mission led by Sgt. James R. Christopher, in early May, is representative of the refinement of our capabilities during the previous five years.

On 9 May, knowing they were being followed by the NVA, Christopher's nine-man team was quickly moving across the saddle between Hills 510 and 487 in the Thuong Duc river valley. As the team continued on, the point man, L.Cpl. Samuel Bayles, encountered a second group of enemy soldiers. He opened fire, killing two of them, but the rest of the NVA squad scattered for cover. Christopher directed his M-79 grenadier forward to provide fire support to the front as the team withdrew from its initial contact. Within seconds they were taken under fire by an NVA machine gun team and by a group of perhaps fifteen NVA regulars. Christopher demonstrated exceptional coolness and directed the fire of his recon team as the Marines maneuvered to get away from and suppress the enemy's automatic weapons fire. Well outside the safety of the closest friendly artillery fan, the team was engaged in what was to become a forty-five-minute firefight. Using close air support, Sergeant Christopher directed Marine helicopter gunships and fixed-wing aircraft to the target and watched as they delivered their ordnance in and around the enemy positions. The team was extracted under heavy enemy fire but without sustaining a single casualty, and it accounted for at least six enemy soldiers killed.

While it takes less than a minute for me to describe the events, it took the Marine Corps several years to learn how to go deep into enemy-held territory, conduct Stingray patrols, and, even though under fire, have the training and confidence to fight it out while waiting for artillery or close air support. That was progress.

The Escalating Role of the NVA

Not only were Americans fighting an unseen enemy in Vietnam, they were also fighting an unknown quantity. No one could ever accurately estimate the number of North Vietnamese combat forces leading and assisting the Viet Cong in their struggle, nor how many more were being prepared for future action. A lack of detailed knowledge meant that whatever the success of individual operations, it was often difficult to tell who was actually winning the war. Confusion was not exclusively the lot of soldiers on the firing line.

More accurate estimates are now available. North Vietnamese infiltration into the South began as far back as 1959, and by 1964, 30,000 military personnel had begun to reinforce the Viet Cong as a fighting force. In the latter months of 1964 the buildup of North Vietnamese Army troops intensified as three additional NVA regiments moved south.

Although NVA forces accounted for only a fraction of communist troops (79,000 out of a total of some 325,000 in the winter of 1967, for example), all operations were masterminded by Hanoi general Vo Nguyen Giap. It was Giap who had organized the expansion of the NVA to fifteen divisions plus regimental units and the massive channel of arms and supplies that flooded down the Ho Chi Minh Trail.

As the war developed, General Giap devised two distinct kinds of tactics—small-scale guerrilla attacks designed to have a cumulative effect, and large ground assaults on vulnerable regions which would limit the maneuverability of enemy reinforcements.

General Giap's strategy depended upon a close interplay of NVA and Viet Cong units, with the VC leading the guerrilla warfare and their northern allies mounting most of the main-force assaults. In spite of the massive buildup of U.S. forces, Giap's astute maneuvers helped the North maintain the initiative.

Early Lessons Learned—
the Hard Way

M.G.Sgt. Rene Regalot, USMC (Ret.), served as the intelligence chief (S-2) for Company A, 3d Reconnaissance Battalion, in the summer of 1965. Here, he recounts those events leading up to the contact made by an eighteen-man reconnaissance patrol led by 1st Lt. Frank S. Reasoner, the commanding officer of Company A. Mistakes made, at the cost of one Marine officer killed and three Marines wounded, would have a far-reaching impact on the reconnaissance community.

CLASSIFIED

DESIGNATION OF PATROL: SCAT A 12 July 1965

MAPS: 6658 IV

SIZE AND COMPOSITION: 2 OFFICERS, 15 ENLISTED, 1 CORPSMAN

MISSION: AREA RECONNAISSANCE RAOR-4

TIME OF DEPARTURE: 121530 H JULY 1965

TIME OF RETURN: 122130 H JULY 1965

ROUTE: SEE OVERLAYS

OBSERVATIONS:

TIME	COORDINATES	OBSERVATION
121730 July 65	922602	Received 20 rounds of sniper fire.

Returned fire and attempted pursuit with no success.
121815 July 65 927608 Flushed enemy position.

Defended by estimated enemy company. Received MG, A/W and small arms fire from three sides. Returned fire and knocked out one MG with four rounds M-79. Called for helo evac and fought way back to LZ. Picked up at LZ at approximately 2115.

OTHER INFORMATION: See enclosure one (1) statement of LCpl F. L. Murray, PFC. H. L. Pannell; PFC. K. R. Hahn; Cpl. B. C. Collins; PFC. T. Gatlin.

See Enclosure (2) sketch of zone of action and positions.

See Enclosure (3) chronological report of all messages received from Co. A.

Upon approaching the village of An My (3) the platoon was split into two teams with Lt. Henderson to approach the village and Lt. Reasoner to continue along the road. Upon reaching the village the first two houses approached were apparently deserted. Continued past a hedge row and discovered a family of eight hidden in a protective hole. At this time we determined that we had located something and then we started to receive AW [automatic weapons] fire from two sides. Lt. Henderson received word from Lt. Reasoner to withdraw toward the LZ south of us and at that time Lt. Reasoner and the remainder of the platoon started to receive MG and AW fire from three sides.

SSgt. Knee, the platoon sergeant, was with Lt. Henderson and WIA [wounded in action] early in the firing. LCpl. Shockley was with Lt. Reasoner and was the next Marine WIA. Lt Reasoner attempted to make his way to Shockley under heavy fire from the machine gun that had the area bracketed. It was at this time that Lt. Reasoner received gun shot wounds. The platoon fought its way back from its position carrying the WIA's with them and all that was left behind was one (1) M-14 with the bolt removed; one (1) PRC-10 radio set that had been shot in two and in an inoperable or [un]repairable condition and six (6) packs. At approximately 2115 the platoon was evacuated by helicopter under heavy fire from all sides.

RESULTS OF ENCOUNTER WITH THE ENEMY:
   Estimated strength of VC Company 75–125. From reports from members of platoon it is fixed that there were 18 VC KIA and a probable 4 more KIA. Three to five were from the results of the M-79 rounds and the remainder from rifle fire. An unknown number of VC WIA resulted from the throwing of grenades.

CONDITION OF PATROL, INCLUDING DISPOSITION OF DEAD OR WOUNDED:
One (1) KIA (Lt. Reasoner); three (3) WIA (LCpl Shockley; SSgt Knee; LCpl Hall) all to C&C. Remainder of patrol all good.

CONCLUSIONS AND RECOMMENDATIONS: Platoon apparently flushed out an enemy company that was possibly preparing for an attack on the HQ located at Dai Loc.
It is recommended that the T/E of the Reconnaissance Battalion be modified to include at least two M-79's per platoon.

W. T. HENDERSON
2nd Lt.   USMC

ADDITIONAL COMMENTS BY DEBRIEFER: It is possible that the VC attack was conducted by the company mentioned in I Corps ISUM #190 para.2.1. The VC contacted were noted to be wearing steel helmets and of particular note was the fact that all appeared to be wearing ponchos. In this particular patrol the scout dogs did not perform as well as expected as indicated from previous use.

J. R. LEMIEUX
GySgt.   USMC
BN S-2

<u>STATEMENT</u>

13 July 1965

On the 12th day of July 1st Platoon Co A were moving down the road proceeding toward checkpoint #2. At the point were LCpl Murray and Cpl. Collins. Behind the point was LCpl. Hall carrying the M-79. Following Hall were Lt. Reasoner, LCpl Shockley the radio man, & PFC. Hahn. Lt. Reasoner spotted a man with a poncho and rifle. The point was coming around the road and they spotted the man along with two other men wearing ponchos and helmets. They were under a tree and seemed to be an OP. Cpl Collins opened fire and at the same time a MG opened up from a hill. The point moved up the road and laid down frontal security. Lt. Reasoner followed by LCpl Hall, LCpl Shockley, and PFC. Hahn moved to the left of the road and set up left security. The point pulled back down the road to find out the situation. Lt. Reasoner called and asked how many men were over our way. We answered two men. Lt. Reasoner told us to come over to Hall and Hahn and give the wounded men cover fire. Cpl Collins gave Murray cover fire and he made it to LCpl Hall and Hahn. Murray put a bandage on Hall's arm and Cpl Collins moved over to where Murray, Hall, and Hahn were.

Cpl Collins and Hahn laid down a base of fire for Lt. Reasoner who was trying to reach LCpl Shockley. The field Lt. Reasoner was located in was barren and offered no cover at all. He moved toward Shockley and was hit by MG fire. Shockley called and told us the skipper was hit, hit real bad. I finished the bandage on Hall and sent him crawling toward the ditch. I followed him and PFC. Hahn followed me. Hall and I reached a grave, and we had some cover. Cpl Collins

moved out toward the skipper and Shockley. He told
Shockley to crawl back toward the ditch. Cpl Collins
took the skipper's AR-15 and left his M-14 with the
bolt taken out. I called to him and told him to get the
radio and we would give him covering fire. He made it
to the radio under heavy fire. At this time PFC.
Brewer called and told me they had a radio and were
up on the air. I told Cpl Collins to leave the radio and
make it back to my position. He was making it toward
me and met PFC. Hahn. Cpl Collins directed the fire of
the M-79 which Hahn was carrying. Collins and Hahn
knocked out the MG. Then Collins and Hahn made it
toward my position. At this time I sent LCpl Hall back
toward the ditch. Cpl Collins and Hahn joined me at
my position on the grave. It was getting dark, I called
to PFC. Gatlin and told him we needed help up front.
Gatlin and Pannell, under heavy fire, moved up to our
position. Gatlin and Murray and Pannell moved out
at a low crawl toward Lt. Reasoner's body. Collins and
Murray pulled the Lt.'s body at a low crawl for
about 30 yards. Pannell then joined them and we
carried the body back to the ditch. Pannell, Gatlin, and
Murray returned to Cpl Collins and helped him carry
Shockley back to the ditch under fire. Cpl Collins
picked up the Lt.'s body and moved out toward the LZ.
Pannell, Murray, and Gatlin picked up Shockley and
carried him toward the road. We were followed by
Hahn and Brewer the radioman. We moved out of the
ditch onto the road and we were hit again, we returned fire and kept going. We were hit three times
before we made it to the LZ.

The first copter came in and we loaded the dead and
wounded aboard, while the rest of the platoon was
giving us covering fire. The rest of the men were gathering up all of the loose gear. The second helicopter
came in and we loaded the rest of the wounded and all
the personnel with the exception of Lt Henderson and

Doc Lewis. We took off and a third bird came in and picked up the remaining two Marines.

The above is a true and correct statement to the best of my knowledge.

LCpl Freddie L. Murray

PFC. Horace L. Pannell

PFC. Kenneth R. Hahn

Cpl Bryant C. Collins

PFC. Thomas Gatlin

Interview with Master Gunnery Sergeant Rene Regalot, USMC (Ret.), 1997, San Diego, CA

I knew 1st Lt. Frank S. Reasoner very well and I thought of him as a first-rate Marine Corps officer. My assessment of what happened to him and his men, as a result of a series of mistakes made before and during the conduct of his reconnaissance patrol on 12 July 1965, serves as a small collection of "lessons learned" that not only influenced subsequent recon Keyhole and Stingray patrols, but may still serve to save the lives of a few good Marines who will, undoubtedly, someday be asked to conduct a reconnaissance or combat patrol, somewhere, someday, deep in hostile territory.

First is the undisputed fact that Lieutenant Reasoner made a serious mistake in deciding to move his reconnaissance patrol away from the village of Dai Loc 4 at approximately 1500 hours, in broad daylight, and then move his men down a primary road which led directly by the villages of An My 1, 2, and 3. This was not, in my opinion, the proper nor practiced method of conducting a large patrol in enemy territory.

It was quite obvious that the enemy was well aware, and prepared for the fact that Lieutenant Reasoner was proceeding in a particular direction with his reconnaissance patrol. This combination of the time of day, and more importantly the terrain, gave the enemy ample time to put together an effective and deadly hasty ambush.

When Lieutenant Reasoner made his initial observation of

the enemy, he thought the unit he had sighted only moments earlier was a reinforced "PF" (Popular Forces) squad. In fact it was a reinforced squad of Viet Cong soldiers who ambushed his recon team only two minutes later.

After Lieutenant Reasoner's recon team and the Viet Cong unit had passed one another, at a distance of no more than several hundred yards in open terrain, a VC sniper fired first. This signaled the initiation of the enemy ambush, and was joined by an enemy machine gun team opening up and wounding PFC Shockley, the team's primary radioman.

The team immediately took what little cover was available and began to return fire. Lieutenant Reasoner ran out to assist Shockley, and that was when the lieutenant was shot through the throat

Lieutenant Reasoner was awarded the Medal of Honor (posthumously) for his heroic actions that day. One of his corporals, B. C. Collins, left the safety of his position and ran out to assist Lieutenant Reasoner and carried him to a covered position. He then went back and retrieved the lieutenant's weapon. He was later awarded the Navy Cross.

At the time of this incident I was assigned as the company's intelligence chief. Because I was wearing a cast at the time and could not go to the bush, I was assigned to assist Gunnery Sergeant Lemieux in the company's S-2 (intelligence) section.

To help Lieutenant Reasoner prepare for his reconnaissance patrol, I had checked all of the current information on enemy activity available to me prior to the execution of his mission. I learned that the division G-2 did not have very much information on this particular area, but a local U.S. Army Special Forces group did have some current information. They said that two hard-core VC companies were known to be operating in the area of Lieutenant Reasoner's planned patrol. I briefed the lieutenant on all the information I had gathered together, and he was quite pleased with what I had provided.

When I asked him about his planned patrol route, he indicated to me that he was supposed to skirt the Charlie Area

Ridge (a piece of terrain well known to all of us). I made a note of this and told him that if he were going to pass by Charlie Area Ridge, he should have indicated this on the copy of the map overlay he was required to leave with us, which enabled us to trace the team's progress along its patrol route. The route he had traced did not show his proposed route on his overlay. This was his second mistake.

His submitted overlay showed that he planned to take his reconnaissance team by the villages of An My 1 and 2. He did not say anything else and I did not take the discussion any further. I was a staff sergeant and he was the company commander.

He took down the information I gave him and then asked me if, after my cast was removed, I would like to be assigned as his company gunnery sergeant. I was honored and replied, "Yes, sir. I would like that very much." I was in the zone for promotion to gunnery sergeant and I wanted the job.

Lieutenant Reasoner then mentioned to me that his team was going to be inserted near the Dai Loc Fort, an old colonial French structure, and then move up the road by foot and cross over a small bridge, continuing on toward An My 1 and 2.

I thought it rather odd that he planned to depart the area at 1500 in the afternoon and proceed during full daylight in the direction of where there were known to be two active VC companies. In the heat of mid-July in Vietnam, the only people foolish enough to be moving were American.

Lieutenant Reasoner didn't say anything about this and I didn't pursue it either. I did question why this recon company commander—and he had just recently been appointed commander of A Company—would be allowed to lead a reconnaissance patrol. That was the battalion commander's call but, in my estimation, the third mistake.

The fourth mistake was that Lieutenant Reasoner's reconnaissance patrol proceeded to move up the road, and I recall this because I was called upon to go and identify his body. We taught every Marine who came into the company that we never, ever, walk on a road. We didn't make the road, so why walk on it?

At approximately 1600 that afternoon Lieutenant Reasoner's recon team radioed in that they had just sighted a platoon-size unit of PFs wearing black pajamas and carrying automatic weapons. They passed one another at a pretty close distance and the lieutenant assumed they were "friendlies." Less than two minutes later the recon patrol was ambushed and the machine guns opened up on them.

I was not present at the debriefing of Lieutenant Reasoner's team because I was busy taking care of the lieutenant's personal effects. But this particular incident happened in just one hour of one afternoon. Alpha Company had been in country for quite a while, operating around the Da Nang area. Third Reconnaissance Battalion had been in country since early 1965, and B Company had been operating exclusively around the Phu Bai area more than fifty miles north of Da Nang.

As I recall it, Lieutenant Reasoner's team was ambushed just a little after 1600 that day. He was designated as the patrol leader, and for whatever reason he split his patrol into two groups, with a lieutenant named Henderson in charge of the second group. The actual patrol report states that Lieutenant Reasoner's team was attacked by a VC company estimated to be of a strength of 75 to 125 men. This supports the intelligence data I had received from the Special Forces group and had passed on to Lieutenant Reasoner before he departed the company area for An My 1 and 2.

As I have already stated, I knew Frank Reasoner very well. He had been out on numerous reconnaissance patrols before this particular mission and was no stranger to the bush. He was experienced and, in my opinion, a good patrol leader. We learned early on, when we first got in country, that it wasn't smart to move during the heat of the day, particularly where you could be seen by the enemy. This included walking on trails and/or roads.

What was the biggest mistake made during this recon patrol? All of the "little mistakes" added up to a recipe for disaster. To be inserted by CH-34s in the afternoon, dismount, and begin walking across open ground in front of the Dai Loc Fort appears now as foolish. The west side of the small bridge the team crossed over was considered to be friendly territory, but the area to the east was always considered Indian Country.

The Marines were also poorly equipped for the patrol. In my opinion they also lacked the firepower needed to break contact. The patrol report states, "Upon approach of the village An My 3, the platoon was split into two teams. This was another mistake. Lieutenant Henderson was to approach the village and Lieutenant Reasoner was to continue on along the road." They were transported to the southwest side of Dai Loc Fort, considered a friendly area, by truck. They moved toward the north once they crossed in front of the fort, toward An My 1 and 2 near the east side of the Annamite Mountain Range.

The VC knew it was getting late in the day and, in my opinion, knew that no one was coming out to help the team once they had them under fire. There was no plan for any re-action force to come to their aid, and that was another mistake we learned from.

The only reason the entire platoon was not completely an-nihilated, with them receiving enemy automatic weapons fire from three sides, was because of the Marine helicopter gun-ship support they received. The two helicopter pilots who went out to provide suppressive fire for Lieutenant Rea-soner's patrol, once contact had been made, received Silver Stars for their efforts that afternoon.

The U.S. Army Special Forces team which had been oper-ating in that area for nearly a year was known to use paid in-formants, and the information we received from them was, in my opinion, far better than anything the division could pro-vide us at the time. It was considered "fresh," and Lieutenant Reasoner, for whatever reason, chose to ignore it.

Two final mistakes were made during the conduct of that reconnaissance patrol. First, there was no preplanned sup-porting artillery fire, and second, there was no plan for any close air support should contact be made. A serious lack of preplanning that cost us lives, if you ask me.

Because of the ultimate results of this single patrol, it was immediately recommended that the T/E (table of equipment) for 3d Recon Battalion be modified to include at least two M-79 40mm grenade launchers for each recon platoon.

The ultimate question that will forever remain unanswered is: Why did Lieutenant Reasoner initially head north instead of moving south? His patrol overlay indicated that he was going to skirt Charlie Ridge. I told him, "This isn't the way you are supposed to be going, Lieutenant." But he looked right at me and said, "You know, I'm tired of Delta Company and Captain ["Patty"] Collins's getting all of the glory. We're going to put Alpha Company in the limelight." Those were his words exactly. If you check his patrol route and use his overlay, you can see how it all happened.

MEDAL OF HONOR CITATION

Reasoner, Frank S.

Rank and organization: First Lieutenant, U.S. Marine Corps, Company A, 3d Reconnaissance Battalion, 3d Marine Division. *Place and date:* near Da Nang, Republic of Vietnam, 12 July 1965. *Entered service at:* Kellogg, Idaho. *Born:* 16 September 1937, Spokane, Washington.

Citation: For conspicuous gallantry and intrepidity at the risk of his life above and beyond the call of duty. The reconnaissance patrol led by 1st Lieutenant Reasoner had deeply penetrated heavily controlled enemy territory when it came under extremely heavy fire from an estimated 50 to 100 Viet Cong insurgents. Accompanying the advance party and the point that consisted of five men, he immediately deployed his men for an assault after the Viet Cong had opened fire from numerous concealed positions. Boldly shouting encouragement, and virtually isolated from the main body, he organized a base of fire for an assault on the enemy positions. The slashing fury of the Viet Cong machine gun and automatic weapons made it impossible for the main body to move forward. Repeatedly exposing himself to the devastating attack he skillfully provided covering fire, killing at least two Viet Cong and effectively silencing an automatic weapons position in a valiant attempt to effect evacuation of a wounded man. As casualties began to mount, his radio operator was wounded and 1st Lieutenant Reasoner immediately moved to his side and tended his wounds. When the radio operator was hit a second time while attempting to reach a covered position, 1st Lieutenant Reasoner courageously running to his aid through grazing machine gun fire fell mortally wounded. His indomitable fighting spirit, valiant leadership, and unflinching devotion to duty provided the inspiration that was to enable the patrol to complete its mission without further casualties. In the face of almost certain death he gallantly gave his life in the service of his country. His actions upheld the highest traditions of the Marine Corps and the U.S. Naval Service.

8

Operation Hastings

July–August 1966

With the relocation of Marine reconnaissance teams from Task Unit Charlie into Quang Tri Province in the summer of 1966 came the realization that elements of the NVA (North Vietnamese Army) were operating south of the DMZ. The role of the reconnaissance Marines became ever more important. With the increase of enemy activity came new rules for the conduct of Stingray patrols, including the use of Marine artillery in direct support of the recon teams. Marine artillery began to serve as a defensive and offensive weapon for the teams and ultimately saved many lives in the process.

The responsibility for executing the reconnaissance mission, of course, lay with III MAF. Since the beginning of the month General Walt had completed contingency plans to reinforce the 1st ARVN (Army of the Republic of Vietnam) Division and continued to work with General Lam on the possibility of starting combined operations with the South Vietnamese in Quang Tri Province. Following extensive sightings of enemy forces in the Cam Lo sector and, on 18 June, a mortar attack on the ARVN Cam Lo outpost some eight miles west of Dong Ha on Route 9, the Marine command decided to begin its reconnaissance of the DMZ region.

At Phu Bai the 4th Marines had expanded their reconnaissance capability. Since March, Reconnaissance Group Bravo, 3d Reconnaissance Battalion, had been reinforced by a platoon from Company A and the 1st Force Reconnaissance Company. Maj. Dwain A. Colby, commanding officer of Force Reconnaissance Company, as the senior officer, assumed command of Recon Group Bravo. By the end of May the 4th Marines' reconnaissance zones had grown from three to six, extending from southern Thua Thien to southern Quang Tri. With the decision to begin an extended reconnaissance in the DMZ sector, Colonel Paul D. Sherman ordered the formation of Task Unit Charlie with Colby in command, consisting of two reconnaissance platoons, one from the Force Reconnaissance Company and the other from Company A; Company E, 2d Battalion, 1st Marines; and Battery H, 3d Battalion, 12th Marines, reinforced by two 155mm howitzers.

On 22 June, Task Unit Charlie moved from Phu Bai to Dong Ha and Cam Lo. The Marine artillery established firing positions at the latter base, while Company E, reinforced by an infantry platoon already at Dong Ha from the 3d Battalion, 4th Marines, provided security for both sites. Covered by artillery, the reconnaissance Marines were to "determine the size, designation, and equipment" of enemy units in the Cam Lo area.

III MAF, which still had its reservations about the existence of a large enemy force in the DMZ sector, was soon to have all of its doubts removed. On 28 June the NVA mortared the Cam Lo base, which resulted in two dead and five wounded, and, as Major Colby recollected, "a personal visit by Major General Kyle." More significantly, every reconnaissance insertion, according to Colby, ". . . encountered armed, uniformed groups, and no patrol was able to stay in the field for more than a few hours. Reports of this activity brought General Walt to the scene (probably to relieve the incompetent who couldn't keep his patrols out). But after talking to the reconnaissance teams, one of which was still in its jungle garb, having been extracted under fire minutes before Gen-

eral Walt's arrival, he apparently decided there was something to the rumor that the NVA was crossing the DMZ."

The reconnaissance phase of the operation in the North
was to last a couple more weeks. With the arrival of Lt. Col.
Robert T. Hanifan's 2d Battalion, 1st Marines, at Dong Ha, he
assumed operational control of the Dong Ha–Cam Lo sector.
Major Colby recalled that the resulting command relations
were delicate, in that Hanifan's mission was to support the reconnaissance effort without exercising control over it. The
reconnaissance commander credited both Hanifan and himself with "A great deal of tact and self-control . . . to make
this relationship function."

Despite infantry reinforcement and additional reconnaissance units as well as a change in designation from Task Unit
Charlie to Detachment A, Recon Group Bravo in early July,
little of substance had changed for Colby's reconnaissance
Marines. They continued to observe and encounter, in increasing numbers, uniformed regulars of the North Vietnamese Army. On 4 July a patrol led by 1st Lt. Theard J.
Terrebone Jr. moved into the area sixteen miles west of Dong
Ha, where a seven-hundred-foot hill known as the Rockpile,
a "sort of toothpick-type mountain stuck out in the middle of
an open area" with "sheer cliff straight up and down," dominated the landscape. During the twenty-four-hour period that
the patrol remained in the vicinity of the Rockpile, the Marines
observed several well-camouflaged enemy firing positions
including trench lines, mortar pits, and fighting holes. After
calling in an artillery fire mission on some nearby enemy
forces, the patrol returned to its base area. For the next ten
days the Marines continued their reconnaissance effort, but
of the eighteen patrols conducted during this period, fourteen
had to be withdrawn because of enemy contact. The reconnaissance Marines sighted more than three hundred North
Vietnamese troops.

During that period, South Vietnamese Army units operating in the same region obtained more evidence about the

movement of North Vietnamese regulars across the border. On 6 July, 1st ARVN Division troops captured an NVA soldier near the Rockpile. He identified his unit as part of the 5th Battalion, 812th Regiment of the 324B Division, and stated that the other regiments of the division, the 90th and the 803d, also had entered South Vietnam.

With the withdrawal of the [Marine] infantry battalions to the south, the role of the reconnaissance Marines became even more important. From the beginning of the operation (Hastings), Major Colby's men had conducted deep patrols and called supporting arms upon enemy forces. Colby had laid down four basic rules:

1. Stay together no matter what happens.
2. Upon reaching an observation post, call artillery fire upon a set of known coordinates so later fire missions can be called by shifting from a reference point.
3. Maintain constant radio communications with headquarters.
4. Never stay in one spot more than twelve hours.

On 28 July 1966 one of these patrols, led by Sgt. Orest Bishko (and accompanied by Capt. Francis J. West, a Marine reservist on a special assignment from Headquarters Marine Corps to develop small-unit combat narratives of Marines in Vietnam), reported approximately 150 to 250 North Vietnamese troops about three and one-half miles southwest of the Rockpile. The team adjusted artillery fire on the enemy force. As a result of this particular action the enemy lost fifty men.

According to West, after he returned to III MAF headquarters and described the patrol to General Walt and Colonel Chaisson, they both expressed the opinion that such missions deserved a special section in the reporting system and selected the name "Stingray" for that purpose. Major Colby claimed that the marriage of reconnaissance Marines and artillery was one of the major innovations of the Vietnam War, declaring, "Recon elements are a truly deadly force in hiding among enemy units with this capability in hand."

Other uses of artillery involved flushing the enemy from concealed positions, denying him use of escape routes, and deceiving him as to the direction of attack. Night employment included illumination of avenues of approach, harassing and interdiction fires, and navigational orientation for friendly elements. The Marines also used jungle applications dating back to the island campaigns of World War II. A lost patrol could reorient itself by requesting a "marking round" on a nearby grid line intersection. Another common jungle technique was to use artillery fire to guide units toward their objectives. Following the advancing fire by only a few hundred yards, the infantry worked their way forward while the artillery forward observer adjusted the firing to suit the situation.

The Stingray concept represented an innovation that blended the maximum use of supporting arms and the talents of III MAF's reconnaissance personnel. As III MAF initiated large-unit operations beyond assigned TAORs, and as TAORs increased in size to accommodate the operational tempo, reconnaissance teams operated at ever-increasing ranges from their battalion command posts. The lightly armed and equipped recon teams usually landed by helicopter at points near their operational areas and then moved stealthily to a designated observation post. Their primary mission was to gather intelligence in areas of suspected heavy enemy movement, but the Marines soon learned that the recon teams could call in artillery fire and air strikes and remain undetected. That led to the evolution of Stingray, which caused substantial enemy casualties at the risk of a very few Marines. Enemy troops away from main battle areas relaxed and, feeling relatively safe, moved with less caution and often concentrated in large numbers. Alert Stingray teams exacted a heavy toll on such unwary Communist units by hitting them with accurate artillery fire and precision air strikes.

For the Stingray teams, artillery served both as a defensive and an offensive weapon. If the enemy detected and pursued the team, artillery put a ring of fire around its position while helicopters moved in for the rescue. Though enemy units hotly contested many extractions, a surprisingly large number of Stingray teams escaped with only minor casualties while Communist losses multiplied greatly from the heavy concentration of fire. To overrun a Stingray position the Communists had to concentrate their forces; but as soon as helicopters extracted the team the abandoned site became a killing zone.

The Viet Cong

"Viet Cong," i.e., Vietnamese Communists, was the common name for the armed forces of the National Liberation Front (NLF). Founded on 20 December 1960, the NLF was ostensibly a broad coalition. Its president, Nguyen Huo Tho, was a noncommunist, and members of religious sects as well as national minorities such as the hill tribesmen were represented.

In fact, as the communist rulers of Vietnam have since admitted, the NLF was in effect a North Vietnamese front run by members of the Politburo in Hanoi, and its armed forces were directed by experienced North Vietnamese guerrilla commanders like Vo Nguyen Giap, who had directed the defeat of the French at Dien Bien Phu in 1954.

The core of the Viet Cong were the 10,000 or so former members of the Viet Minh who had remained in the South after the partition of the country in 1954. The North formed two transport commands in 1959, and those had infiltrated at least 28,000 trained personnel into the South by the end of 1964. Together with local recruitment, all those forces combined resulted in a guerrilla army of some 300,000 men under NVA orders in South Vietnam.

The Viet Cong were divided into two main sections: paramilitary units of villagers who might undertake sabotage by night, act as intelligence gatherers or porters, or, in the case of the young, become members of assassination or suicide squads; and full military units, the regional forces that provided backup and the main force. By 1965 this army was some 50,000 to 80,000 men strong and able to act in large self-contained formations.

A vexing question, one that assumed enormous propaganda importance, was the role of the North Vietnamese Army (NVA) in South Vietnam. It is now accepted that by March 1966, three complete NVA regiments (some 5,800 men) were operating with the Viet Cong, in addition to support units and political cadres. At the time, that could not be verified, and both sides made claims that bore little relation to the truth, purely to justify their actions.

— 9 —

Stingray in Operation Prairie

August–September 1966

War in the North

In stark contrast to the sporadic guerrilla operations in the southern war zones, American military strategy in the north was designed to trap large VC and NVA units that had been infiltrating across the demilitarized zone and through Laos into the coastal provinces of Quang Tri, Thua Thien, Quang Nam, Quang Tin, and Quang Ngai, which together made up I Corps Tactical Zone.

After the frustration of Operation Eagle (January–March 1966), when three Marine battalions failed to locate enemy forces in Binh Dinh Province, the action moved closer to the DMZ. During Operation New York (February–March), a Marine force swept through Phu Thu Peninsula, unearthing a VC battalion from a network of fortified bunkers.

Reports of NVA and VC units infiltrating into the northern provinces intensified, and the Marines made contact with enemy forces on a number of occasions when they were called in to help out beleaguered ARVN garrisons. From March to June, Marine operations were hampered by civil disorders in Hue and Da Nang, and NVA attacks led to the abandonment of several Special Forces camps along the western border with Laos and in the A Shau Valley.

The situation became critical when recon intelligence revealed that the NVA 324B Division had moved across the Ben Hai River into Quang Tri. Guarding that region now became the Marines' primary mission, with large conventional formations confronting one another across a fixed battle line—the DMZ.

Launched from Dong Ha, Operation Hastings (15 July–3 August) saw three battalions of the 4th Marines sweep through the Ngan Valley and inflict 882 casualties on the NVA division before contact faded out. The Marines remained in the area, and when the NVA renewed its attempt to take over Quang Tri Province the battle entered a new phase with the launching of Operation Prairie.

Operation Prairie

Enemy intentions in the DMZ area remained a matter of conjecture during the latter stages of Operation Hastings. On 22 July, Lt. Gen. Victor Krulak stated his opinion to General Westmoreland that the North Vietnamese were attempting to avoid direct contact with the Marines. Westmoreland replied that "just the reverse was the case and that the NVA forces were not seeking to get away."* The MACV commander believed that III MAF could expect to encounter large numbers of NVA and that elements of the 324B Division, although bloodied, were still south of the DMZ. Furthermore, he had received reports indicating that the North Vietnamese were moving two more divisions, the 304th and 341st, into the area immediately north of the DMZ. Marine commanders recognized a buildup of enemy forces in the DMZ but took exception to terms such as "massive buildup," "go for broke," "significant serious threats," and similar expressions contained in messages originating from Westmoreland's Saigon headquarters. Although MACV,

---

*U.S. Marine Operations in Vietnam, 1966. History and Museums Division, USMC.

FMFPac, and III MAF used identical intelligence data, they continued to interpret it differently.

After the closeout of Hastings on 3 August, the Marine command retained a small task force around Lt. Col. Arnold Bench's 2d Battalion, 4th Marines, at Dong Ha to monitor the potential threat in the north. Bench's command consisted of his four infantry companies supported by the 1st Force Reconnaissance Company and Battery G, 3d Battalion, 12th Marines, reinforced by two 155mm howitzers. Also attached to the 2d Battalion were a platoon each from the 3d Tank Battalion, the 3d Antitank Battalion, the 3d Engineer Battalion, and a logistics unit from Force Logistics Command. The battalion CP was established at the Dong Ha airstrip, but the attached artillery and tanks were at Cam Lo; two infantry companies, F and G, provided security for the artillery positions. Two helicopter detachments, one from MAG-16 and the other from the U.S. Army's 220th Aviation Company, were at Dong Ha to support the ground force.

The Marine plan for the operation, code-named Prairie, to determine the extent of NVA force in the DMZ sector, relied heavily upon reports of Major Colby's reconnaissance Marines. UH-1Es ("Huey" helicopters) from VMO-2 were to insert four or five Stingray teams along suspected enemy avenues of approach. If the reconnaissance teams made contact with NVA, they could call for artillery from Cam Lo, helicopter gunships, or Marine aircraft from Da Nang or Chu Lai. The infantry companies at Cam Lo and Dong Ha were poised to reinforce the reconnaissance patrols. Colonel Cereghino, the 4th Marines' commander, held two battalions on eight-hour alert at Phu Bai to move to Dong Ha in the event of a major infiltration from the DMZ.

The first significant encounter during Prairie involved a Stingray patrol. On 6 August, a UH-1E inserted a five-man team into a jungle-covered hill mass four thousand meters north of the Rockpile, approximately a thousand meters to the southeast of the Nui Cay Tre ridgeline. The team, code-named Groucho Marx, reported that it saw NVA troops moving along the trails and could smell smoke from enemy campsites. The patrol twice called for the artillery at Cam Lo to fire on the suspected locations. On the morning of the eighth the Marines saw ten to fifteen North Vietnamese troops moving in a skirmish line one hundred meters away, apparently looking for the American patrol. The team leader, S.Sgt. Billy M. Donaldson, radioed Major Colby and reported the situation. Colby sent a pair of gunships to cover the patrol and asked "if they thought we could get some prisoners out of there if I sent in a reaction force. They said affirmative and that there was a landing zone within 150 meters of them."

Shortly afterward, six HMM-265 CH-46 helicopters landed in the zone, debarking a forty-man Marine platoon from Company E led by 2d Lt. Andrew W. Sherman. By the time Sherman's platoon reached the reconnaissance team's perimeter, the enemy had disappeared. After a short, futile search for the North Vietnamese, Sherman asked for helicopters to lift the Marines out of the area.

In mid-afternoon, eight UH-34s from HMM-161 arrived overhead to extract the Marines. The first helicopter landed without incident, but when it took off, North Vietnamese troops opened fire from a ridgeline to the north. Five UH-34s landed, but were able to evacuate only twenty of the forty-five Marines because of the heavy fire. Lieutenant Sherman waved off the rest of the helicopters and set up a defensive perimeter.

At that point the enemy, in company strength, tried to assault the Marine position. The American defenders turned them back with hand grenades and small-arms fire, but Sherman was killed. His platoon sergeant, Sgt. Robert L. Pace, took command but was wounded during the next NVA assault, and command was passed to Staff Sergeant Donaldson.

Surrounded, the small force called for supporting arms. The 155s at Cam Lo responded immediately, and at 1830, F-4B Phantoms from MAG-11 arrived overhead and stopped one NVA assault. Sergeant Donaldson was severely wounded during the last attack.

At Dong Ha, the Company E commander, Capt. Howard V. Lee, asked Lieutenant Colonel Bench for permission to take a relief force into the battle area to evacuate the Marines. The battalion commander finally acceded to Lee's entreaties and the captain gathered seven volunteers besides himself. Three HMM-161 UH-34s flew the relief force to the battle site, but enemy fire forced the helicopters to land outside the Marine perimeter. Only three of the volunteers, including Lee, were able to reach the defenders. A VMO-2 UH-1E, piloted by Maj. Vincil W. Hazelbaker, evacuated the remaining Marines from the aborted relief expedition and flew them back to Dong Ha. Upon arriving in the shrinking Marine perimeter, Captain Lee immediately took command, reorganized the defenses, and supervised the distribution of ammunition that the helicopters had dropped inside the position.

The enemy continued to close in on the Marines and, at the same time, prevented any more helicopters from landing. NVA ground fire drove off two HMM-263 CH-46s carrying additional Company E troops and hit one UH-1E gunship, killing a crew member and wounding another. The Marine defenders repulsed repeated assaults on their position, but their situation deteriorated. At 2030, Lee radioed Bench that he had only sixteen men still able to fight. The company commander himself had been wounded twice, a slight nick on the ear when he first debarked from the helicopter and later severely, when an "NVA grenade . . . exploded no more than two feet" from him, "sending fragments into . . . [the] right eye and the right side of [his] body."

Lieutenant Colonel Bench provided what support he could. He ordered all available artillery, firing at maximum range, including a section of 81mm mortars from the Marine outpost on the Rockpile, to hit the enemy-held hill mass north of Lee's perimeter. The 105mm battery was out of range, and Bench ordered it and a section of M-48 tanks to displace so that at first light they would be able to support the surrounded Marines.

Although Marine high-performance close air support was called off because of darkness and a low ceiling, VMO-2 UH-1E gunships made numerous rocket and strafing runs on enemy positions. A Marine C-117 flare ship arrived to provide illumination, but each lull between flare drops allowed the enemy to move closer. Later that night two Air Force AC-47s arrived and strafed the hill slopes outside the Marine perimeter.

Several helicopters from MAG-16 made repeated resupply attempts. Major Hazelbaker, when he evacuated the stranded Marines outside the perimeter, was able to get close enough to the defenders' position for his crew to push out several boxes of 7.62mm linked ammunition. Enemy fire, however, aborted all other such attempts. Shortly after midnight Lee reported that his troops were almost out of ammunition. Hazelbaker volunteered to fly another resupply mission and successfully landed his aircraft inside the Marine defenses.

While the UH-1E was on the ground and the troops and crew were unloading ammunition, an enemy rocket "impacted on the rotor mast," crippling the helicopter. After helping two wounded crewmen out of the damaged craft, Major Hazelbaker and his copilot joined the fight on the ground.

The enemy attack that damaged the Huey was the last major effort against the Marine position. The helicopter crew distributed ammunition and incorporated the helicopter's M-60 machine guns in the defense. Major Hazelbaker and Captain Lee waited for the NVA to make the next move. According to a Navy corpsman in the perimeter: "The rest of the night was quiet. . . . You could hear them [the NVA] drag off the bodies. Some would come right up to the brush line and just start talking. Every time we shot at them another grenade would come in. They were trying to feel out our position."

In the early morning hours, Captain Lee, weak from loss of blood, relinquished command to Major Hazelbaker. At dawn the major directed a Marine napalm strike on the enemy positions; NVA fire completely stopped. Two hours later Company F and the battalion command group arrived at the Marine-held hill, followed shortly by the rest of Company E. The two units fanned out, but the enemy had left the immediate area.

The Groucho Marx fight was over and the last Marines

were lifted out that afternoon. The Marines had lost five killed and twenty-seven wounded. Four of the dead were from Company E, while one was a UH-34 gunner from HMM-161 killed by enemy ground fire. Of the wounded, fifteen were from Company E, one from 1st Force Reconnaissance Company, and the remainder from the MAG-16 helicopter crews, including three pilots.

The Marines counted thirty-seven enemy bodies on the slopes of the hill, but bloodstains and drag marks indicated that they had suffered much heavier casualties. The Marines recovered a document from one NVA body which indicated that the dead man had been a company commander. For the Groucho Marx action, Captain Lee received the Medal of Honor, while Major Hazelbaker was awarded the Navy Cross.

— 10 —

Just Another Day
in October: 1966

Success has a thousand fathers. And, apparently, so did
Stingray operations. But Lt. Col. Clovis C. "Buck" Coffman's contribution on the subject—written in longhand
on a yellow legal pad while the author was in hospital—is
by one of the concept's true founders. Buck Coffman had
occasion to be there not only at the beginning, but also
during Stingray's later, theoretical, development at Quantico, with Lt. Col. Alex Lee (whose own contribution on
the subject is included later in this volume).

BUSTED

1 September 1998
Greetings, Doc,

Your recent missive requesting my labor has arrived. I will
strive to provide some small input that I hope will prove to be
of value. But you should have some understanding of my material and that of Lt. Col. Alex Lee (see Chapter 22, "My
Thoughts about Stingray Operations in Vietnam").

First: You must realize that Lee's view of Stingray and
mine differ in point of view. To him—back in the States when
it all started—Stingray was a semiabstraction; to me, operating in RVN, it was entirely different.

Second: Lee has never had to function in a combat (or

peacetime) environment as an elegant Marine enlisted man in more than one small conflict as I did. I speak of my service in Korea, Malaya, Suez, the Dominican Republic, and Vietnam. Having been an enlisted man yourself, you can understand my point of view.

Third: My reconnaissance experience in the Republic of Vietnam alone totals 54 months; Alex had 10 months. So the base of experience is a *skosh* wider on my part if you consider 1965 to 1970 as my recon time frame, with 14 months as a Marine officer and 40 months as a Marine enlisted man.

Fourth: I found things all the way around to be very different when working with Alex than with anyone else; he knew me quite well and he trusted me completely, and so did Lt. Gen. Herman Nickerson. The result was nothing short of terrific! I got to *operate* with little direct interference from the boots-and-buckles wallahs at III MAF headquarters.

Fifth: In large part my comments concerning the history of the Stingray concept will be anecdotal. I will start in 1965, when I was serving with 1st Reconnaissance Battalion in Chu Lai.

In March 1965, 1st Force Reconnaissance Company was dumped into the lap of an understrength 1st Recon Battalion, due, in part, to the fact that the 1st Marine Division (1st MarDiv) commanding general was new and understood very little about reconnaissance work of any type—Lou Walt had been promoted to commanding general, III MAF (new name), because the 3d MarDiv was already there in country.

First Force Recon Company was almost instantly raped and scattered throughout 1st Recon Battalion ("for the greater good"); its officers, SNCOs, and E-5/E-4s were likewise sprinkled around 1st Recon Battalion. Our company commander, Maj. Chuck Riney, became the battalion S-3, and the previous S-3 (a useless show-pony, boots-and-buckles type who *never* left the battalion command post), became the battalion executive officer.

The battalion commander was a feisty lieutenant colonel named Sullivan. The A Company CO was, in my opinion, another travesty: a teetotaler named Hockaday Walker who was the heir to the Johnny Walker Distillery. B Company went to Capt. A. K. "King" Dixon II, a former All-American football star at Alabama. C Company (my company) was led by one Timothy J. Geraghty, who as a colonel in 1984, was the sacrificial lamb in Lebanon. D Company was lead by Capt. "Billy the Kid" Bonney.

A Company had two officers and four SNCOs; B Company had one officer and five SNCOs; C Company had one officer and four SNCOs. (1st Platoon, C Company, S.Sgt. Jimmie Howard; 2d Platoon, G.Sgt. Buck Coffman; 3d Platoon, C Company, G.Sgt. "Guts" Gutierrez). The C Company first sergeant was Neal Avery.

We were armed with a mixture of M3A1, .45-caliber grease guns, M-14s in several configurations (pistol grips from off stocks, front forearm grips made out of hand-cut wood, etc.), 12-gauge pump shotguns, several configurations of the M-1 carbine, and so on. The only universally carried weapon was the K-bar fighting knife.

From 1965 to early 1966, our supply system was virtually nonexistent. We had no real messing facilities; we lived in open, canvas tents on the beach; socks and soap did not exist unless they arrived in packages from home; our 782 gear, jungle uniforms, and boots were either traded from Special Forces soldiers or stolen by the truckload from the Chu Lai air terminal, or during sneak trips to Da Nang and Okinawa. We were truly the homeless bastards of WestPac.

As Alex Lee so accurately put it, we had an internecine battle going on at the same time that field commanders used us as praetorian guards at the battalion command post, as lifeguards at the beach, and on all sorts of nonreconnaissance jobs. We were in an eternal squabble between the "raiders," who thought we could attack tanks with K-bars, and the "rabbits," who wanted us to hide, see, and report but not mix it up.

The sizes of patrols varied from a full company that was outposted and patrolling from a base camp to four-man light ambushes that were used at close-in trail crossings. We had three basic types of patrols at first. Bushmaster ambush or raid patrols designed to kill all hands, cut throats, take ears, and leave behind the ace of spades as part of the terror tactics. Next were keyhole missions, during which we were to look and report but do nothing else. And last the OP—observation post—mission where we worked from a hilltop as spotters and radio relays. This last type of mission was strictly static.

Two almost simultaneous events caused a dramatic change in our little recon world. Before I get to these events, some additional background information on communications is necessary.

The "standard" patrol radios used from 1965 to early 1967 were the AN/PRC-25 (an AM/FM radio that could transmit to ships or aircraft) and the AN/PRC-10, neither of which was particularly well suited to reconnaissance patrolling because of their weight (which was increased by the requirement that at least three extra batteries be carried), lack of range due (their line-of-sight range required us to employ radio-relay sites), and built-in antenna problems (the whip antenna was too long for bush country, but it had far more range than the tape type of antenna; the tape antenna traveled well but lacked effective range. To obtain greater range, the radio relays had to erect a long-pole AN/292 antenna, which was cumbersome, heavy, and hard to conceal).

When operating close enough to the South China Sea to call fire from a ship (usually a destroyer with 5"/38 or 5"/54 deck guns), we had to use the AN/PRC-47 HF (high frequency) radio, which was also extremely heavy and cumbersome, or place a receiver on the naval vessel that could enable our communicators to talk to the AN/PRC-25.

To further compound this already difficult situation, our communicators were constantly changing their encoding systems, a habit they continued throughout the entire Vietnam conflict. We had changing authenticators, KAC sheets, whizwheels, keypunches, and so on. Try changing an encrypted message into something understandable in the rain at night while laying a few meters off a trail well-traveled by enemy formations!

Some senior communicators sold the wonderful idea of

everyone changing unit call signs on the first day of each month, along with giving code names to almost everything.

A CO's three platoons were Average Age, Applegate, and Animal Cracker. You see? The name had to be a compound word or two words beginning with the company's letter—Beehive, Blasting Cap, or Butterworth; Carnival Time, Cakewalk (my second platoon, C Company), and Cornwalis; Doghouse, Drama Day, and Deep Diver. A jeep was a jitney, a 6×6 truck was a rumble, a helicopter (UH-34) was a hummingbird, and these code names were used for one month only. If we were going to be out in the bush for a period of two months, we had to carry two lists.

Call signs went to Charlie Ace, Charlie Deuce (me), and Charlie Trey. They were soon changed to names of cars and trucks. First Platoon, C Company, was Cadillac Coupe; 2d Platoon (our platoon) was Corvette Stingray; and 3d Platoon was Chrysler Country. As Marines will often do, they shortened the names to more easily spoken and remembered ones; Cadillac Coupe became Caddy, Corvette Stingray became just Stingray, and Chrysler Country became Crissy.

The first of the catalyzing events I mentioned earlier took place when Team Carnival Time, S.Sgt. Jimmie Howard's first platoon, C Company, became famous before Operation Colorado. His *fifteen-man* recon team—"too big to hide, too small to fight"—was inserted preoperation as a radio-relay team near Tam Ky. There is no way to hide fifteen Marines, an A/292 antenna, and an AN/PRC-47 radio on top of a hill in 12–15 inch grass. The results of this incident are history: 5 Marines dead, 10 wounded, 143 main force VC counted dead. This action resulted in the awarding of one Medal of Honor, four Navy Crosses, and ten Silver or Bronze Stars.

The rifle company that was already heliborne and on its way to Operation Colorado was hastily diverted to Howard's hill and saved the day. It was nothing in the world but luck! It was a truly valiant fight where a mix of real bravery, determined leadership, and old-fashioned Marine "hanging tough" prevented a tragic total wipe out. But it was not proper employment of reconnaissance elements, and we all knew that.

The second event occurred just three or four days later, when second platoon (Team Cakewalk), C Company, was tasked with a very similar mission south of An Hoa: to "observe/communicate for a battalion from the 7th Marines" sent to protect the South Vietnamese rice harvest in Quang Ngai Province.

Odin smiled upon Cakewalk. I had two men on R&R, two at SCUBA School, three at Jump School, one on emergency leave, two at NCO school, one assigned as a lifeguard, and two in the hospital. My team fielded seven Marines and one Navy corpsman.

After inserting on a grassy ridge top overlooking a horseshoe-shaped valley no more than a mile from the shoreline, we immediately observed hundreds of uniformed enemy troops in the valley below us and three columns of inbound enemy moving to our west.

Three things made it a perfect situation for the team. One, as a gunnery sergeant I had been trained as a forward observer for artillery and as a naval gunfire spotter. So I called for fire from the 7th Marine's 105 direct-support battery, which I could actually see to my east. Then Odin really must have laughed, because the USS *Mullinnix* (DD 944), newly reporting on the gun line, cut in on my radio net to offer assistance. She had a 5"/54 rapid-fire mount forward and a twin-mount 5"/38 aft with more than 5,000 rounds of ammunition. I was delighted! Especially as many more enemy troops were pouring into the valley. By now we had several thousand men in the open and more on the way.

I called the infantry battalion CP (command post) and informed them they were outnumbered by at least eight or ten to one, and their CO came back with "Good, Cakewalk."

I had not seen an enemy in that kind of number since Korea, but I told the CO to save his 105 ammunition because I was going to use the ship's firepower first.

The *Mullinnix* came into alignment no more than 1,000 meters from the beach and dropped anchor. I gave them a center of mass, and all three of her guns commenced to rearrange the valley terrain and lots of people. In the midst of this, the UHF ground-to-air radio, which I had scrounged at Chu Lai, came to life:

"Cakewalk, this is Pea Patch Leader, overhead with six A-4s with snake-eye and napalm. How about a piece of this?"

"Welcome aboard, Pea Patch. I'll turn off the ship, and you can help yourself."

In less than ten minutes the A-4s had completely expended their ordnance, and I turned the *Mullinnix* loose again. We fired the ship empty. The entire 21st NVA Regiment and 501B NVA Battalion had ceased to exist.

The difference between Howard's action and mine are abundantly clear. We never had to fire a shot.

Although unauthorized by the comm-o (communications officer), I had split my platoon into two teams of eight men, any six of whom would usually go out at one time. Splitting the platoon accomplished two things simultaneously: it doubled our assets and gave us teams of a size that could easily be handled. I knew that too many were too much, and Captain Geraghty and First Sergeant Avery agreed with me. Now we had Corvette and Stingray in the same platoon. Company B did the same thing.

I leaned on my buddy with the Air Wing at Chu Lai and "acquired" six more UHF air-ground radios. Then I caught a hop to Da Nang and picked up about 100 sets of jungle cammies (tiger stripes), 100 pairs of jungle boots, and 30 or 40 cases of long-range patrol rations (LRRPs)—all of which were the first we had ever had—courtesy of Flamingo Special Forces HQ Detachment, thus proving a good Marine gunny can do almost anything—I was and I did.

On 11 October 1966, I got into a major brawl that was to change my life. That day was my pay entry base date. I had joined the Marine Corps on 11 October 1949, seventeen years earlier. I had been through thirty-five months in Korea and at Yokosuka Naval Hospital (due to having been hit four times), fifteen months in Malaya chasing Ts with the 7th Gurka Rifles, and jumped into the Dominican Republic just before coming to Vietnam, where I had already been wounded for the fifth time on an earlier patrol.

Team Stingray was sent down to an area south of Chu Lai, a place known as Ba To that was a Special Forces camp, to help locate the originating point of daily enemy mortar attacks. For some reason SF could not get the job done, and we were given the mission.

Ba To was in the middle of nowhere. Having had to deal with Special Forces folks on previous occasions, I had concluded that they were a lazy lot. The young army captain in charge of the A-team (A-107) wasn't particularly interested in much except going back to the States.

The camp's defense consisted of three old and dirty 4.2" (called four-deuce) mortars, two 60mm mortars, and six M-60 machine guns. Some of the local CIDG troops carried a few BARs (.30-caliber automatic rifles) left over from World War II, but the majority of them were armed with M-1 carbines (i.e., semiautomatics).

The mission started off badly. We landed in an army Caribou on a short, muddy, dirt airstrip, and the aircraft got stuck in the mud.

The army SFC who was their communications tech handed me a message that said that within a couple of days 1st Battalion, 1st Marine Regiment, was going to be conducting one of the endless search-and-destroy sweeps only 5 kilometers north of Ba To and we were given a secondary mission of screening their left flank. The message included their tactical radio frequencies.

While I was reading this little piece of news a shot was fired outside. One of my Marines had been gut-shot by one of the locals—an accidental discharge. About two hours later, while waiting for our UH-34s to take us into the LZ I had selected, my primary radio operator, Corporal Dove, began vomiting and turned as white as a cotton ball. The medic found that he was running a temperature of 104 degrees. I had come in with ten men, was already down to eight, and hadn't seen one minute of action.

As the helos dropped altitude to let us off, we took a couple of long-range small-arms rounds, and as they left us, I thought, Well, so much for a clandestine insertion.

We had landed in high, thick saw grass, and I told "Mouse" Wren, my point man, to head downhill moving westward. We could not see a full arm's length ahead of us, and it was tough going. Just as Mouse got to the edge of the forest of grass, he leaped forward cursing. I was directly behind him, followed by Corporal Tommy Brown, my radio operator.

The Mouse had literally collided with the last man in an enemy six-man heavy-mortar crew that was skirting the heavy grass. He slammed his K-bar into the enemy soldier's belly as my radioman and I both opened fire on the remaining five NVA soldiers. The two grease-guns made it quick work; all were very dead, and I was somewhat surprised to note they were all uniformed NVA regulars.

"Jesus, Gunny, look over there!" Mouse said.

About 200 yards to our south, what looked like two separate enemy rifle companies were hastily deploying with a 50-yard gap between them. After tearing off two NVA shirt-pocket flaps (their letter-box numbers would be useful in identifying the unit), I told everyone to back into the grass. We went about 50 yards deeper so we could move between the two units when they came to the edge of the grass.

"Gunny, Ba To just came up on the net and said that the lead company from the 1st Marines has already landed," my secondary radio operator whispered. Shit, I thought, Two days early and these NVA bastards are moving to flank them from this side. . . . They knew before we did.

"Okay, listen up. I want to form a single line of movement. We are going to try to get between these two units. Open fire when I tell you. We can hit both sides while they are fumbling in the grass."

We did as I planned, and the result was more than we could have hoped for. We managed to get through, leaving the two NVA companies unwittingly firing on each other while we took off for the top of the closest hill. Halfway up we ran into a squad-size rear element of NVA soldiers and traded fire at about 8 yards. We killed seven, and the rest ran for the bush. I had one Marine killed and two wounded. Taking the dead Marine and helping the wounded, we made it to the top of the hill. A couple of rocket-propelled grenades exploded in our wake, but no one was harmed. Looking down the eastern side of the hill, we saw another company of enemy soldiers moving toward a lower ridgeline that formed the left flank of the area where the Marine infantry was landing.

We tried using our radios to warn the incoming Marine units but got nothing. We radioed Ba To, and they came in very weak. We told them our situation. At about the same time an air-spotter flew overhead. I was able to contact the pilot on my stolen air-ground radio, and he replied that Marine air support was on the way. I nearly cried with relief. That was my old unit during the Inchon Landing in 1950. Meanwhile, Stingray was surrounded by some very angry people.

I moved the team a short distance down the eastern slope where we could still see the top, and the first probe of enemy soldiers skylined only moments later. We blew the hell out of them and moved back up onto the hilltop. The NVA left nine of their dead behind, and it became an intense firefight for several minutes. I had another Marine killed and four more wounded including myself.

Suddenly, one NVA soldier stood up and waved a white rag on a stick. "You surrender, Marine, we treat you good!" he shouted. I shot him through the head, and we heard aircraft approaching. We ran air, both A-4 jets and C-model helo-gunships, until the lift birds finally came in and took us out.

I had two Marines killed and the other six wounded, and God only knows how many NVA died or were hit between our firing, their shooting at each other, and the air strikes.

After the medical people patched us up, we were debriefed by the new commanding general of the 1st Marine Division and his staff. The general was none other than Herman Nickerson Jr., who was soon to become known as the Marine Corps' godfather of long-range reconnaissance.

Lessons learned and relearned included, again, the fact that the weakest link was our communications equipment. Also, glaringly exposed, was the fact that being small in numbers and possessing very limited team firepower necessitated that we have dedicated outside fire support to enable our teams to survive. Additionally, the senior officers, however involved, *must be taught the proper use of reconnaissance assets.*

The only good to come out of the small firefight was that my old battalion, 1/1, did not get smashed on an exposed flank by the NVA.

On our return to our forlorn Recon command post in old Chu Lai, we found 1st Reconnaissance Battalion in the throes of moving north to Da Nang. I was summarily whisked off to Cam Ranh Bay, far to the south. I sat on a plane with all sorts of VIPs; the only other enlisted Marine I saw was the sergeant major of the 1st Marine Division.

Asking him what the hell was going on was a mistake because he chewed me out about having unshined boots, a wrinkled uniform, and no helmet. Then some protocol puke snatched my bush cover from my head and replaced it with a spotless helmet. I was herded in front of a reviewing stand with three other guys, two army and one air force, and in less than a minute, I was looking into the face of President Lyndon B. Johnson. A citation was read, and he pinned a Navy Cross on my starch-free bush jacket.

After an incredible lunch with the president, I went back to Da Nang, where I was hustled up to General Nickerson's office and meritoriously promoted to first sergeant, "pending battlefield commissioning," as was stated in the message from Lt. Gen. Lewis Walt, Commanding General, III MAF.

I was made the 1st Reconnaissance Battalion operations chief, took my Mouse with me as a driver, and was given the seat supposed to be used by a captain, Assistant Operations and Training Officer, which we didn't have.

My new boss was Capt. (Major elect) Charles M. Welzant, a capable officer with his finger firmly planted on his number in the lineal (promotion) list. Anxious to make some sort of mark, he was busily scribbling together a project book for a patrol SOP (although he had never been on a single patrol). He asked me what my team's patrol name was, and I told him Stingray. He smiled and said, "I'll call this Project Stingray."

I took out only special patrols after that, bird-dogging new officers (Andy Finlayson of Team Killer Kane fame being one), checking out special areas of interest for General Nickerson, teaching classes in the RIP (Reconnaissance Indoctrination Program), going in after downed pilots. But the best part, in my opinion, was teaching young officers and NCOs how to direct artillery, naval gunfire, and air strikes—the meat of the Stingray concept. I wrote it all up, and then the good Major Welzant put his name on it as part of "his" Project Stingray book.

On 15 March 1967, I got busted to a second lieutenant (at least that's what it felt like). Marine Corps Base, Quantico, Virginia, was not my idea of an ideal place to put a thirty-five-year-old professional warrior, but I got to meet and work with Alex "The Hun" Lee, the man who, through trials and tribulations not to be recounted here, became my blood brother. Of the projects we worked on—and they were numerous—Stingray was by far our favorite, and we put heart and soul into it. Then one day we were directed to report to HQMC at now–Lieutenant General Nickerson's office. General Nick greeted us warmly and got right down to business.

"Bucky, Alex, this morning the commandant asked me to go back to Vietnam to be the commanding general of III MAF, and I, of course, accepted. I want you two to come and build me a Force Recon Company. You, Alex, as the CO and you, Buck, as the operations officer. Will you do it? I want Stingray to work, and you two are the best in the business. It will be difficult in the extreme, with many heathens obstructing all you try to do, but you two can do it."

You already know most of the rest, Doc, it's all written down in Alex Lee's book *Force Recon Command*.

Semper Fi,
Buck Coffman

=== 11 ===

The Story Is in the Letters

In 1995, Mr. David Jensen came to San Diego and told me about the events surrounding the death of his brother, Alan. David had kept every piece of correspondence related to the event, the patrol reports, maps, photographs, and letters that described what happened to his brother, the assistant patrol leader of a sixteen-man recon patrol in October 1967. The patrol report, and the personal letters of condolence from fellow Marines to Sergeant Jensen's parents and to David, are noteworthy, as they detail the heroic actions and the ultimate sacrifices made by Marines from 1st Force Recon Company (Team Petrify), and the helicopter pilots assigned to support Stingray operations in 1967. The extremes that Marines will go to "to recover their dead" are no less remarkable.

The Death of Sgt. Alan T. Jensen, USMC

(17 October 1967)

The patrol report, two pages of the COC (Combat Operations Center) logbook entries, and personal letters of condolences from fellow Marines to Sergeant Jensen's parents and brother, describe the heroic actions and ultimate sacrifices of Marines from 1st Force Recon Company (Team Petrify) and helicopter pilots in support of Stingray operations in Vietnam in 1967. The extremes that Marines will go to "to recover their dead" are no less incredible.

OPERATION ORDER: 563-67   1st RECONNAISSANCE
BN
PATROL: F-2-1 PETRIFY   DA NANG, RVN
DEBRIEFER: Capt. R. C. KICKLIGHTER   DTG 191-
500H Oct. 67
MAPS: VIETNAM 1:50,000 AMS L7014;
SHEET 6541 I, 6541 II, 6641 III,
6641 IV.

PATROL REPORT

1. SIZE, COMPOSITION, AND EQUIPMENT:
   A. COMPOSITION: 1 OFF. 16 ENL.
   B. SPECIAL ATTACHMENTS: NONE
   C. COMM. AND OBSERVATION EQUIPMENT: 2PRC
      25S; IM-49 SCOPE, 1 7X50'S (BINOCULARS)
   D. SPECIAL EQUIPMENT: CLIMBING SPIKES
2. MISSION: CONDUCT RECONNAISSANCE AND SUR-
VEILLANCE WITHIN YOUR ASSIGNED NFZ/FFZ TO
DETECT POSSIBLE VC TROOP MOVEMENT OR ARMS
INFILTRATION IN THE UPPER SONG BU LU RIVER
VALLEY IN THE LOC THUY SECTOR OF THE NORTH-
WESTERN PORTION OF THE PHU LOC DISTRICT,
THU THIEN PROVINCE. SPECIAL EMPHASIS TO BE
PLACED ON HIGHWAY #1 AND ROUTES OF ACCESS
THERETO. BE PREPARED TO CALL AND ADJUST
ARTY, NGF, AND AIR ON TARGETS OF OPPORTUNITY.
3. TIME OF DEPARTURE AND RETURN:
150745H/191445H
4. ROUTE: SEE ATTACHED OVERLAY
5. SYNOPSIS: PATROL COVERED A PERIOD OF 113

HRS. WITH A CONTACT OF AN UNDETERMINED NUMBER OF ENEMY. THE PATROL COMMENCING ABOUT 1600 ON THE SECOND DAY HAD ALMOST CONTINUOUS CONTACT WITH THE ENEMY. THE PATROL SUSTAINED 2 FRIENDLY KIA'S AND 3 SERIOUSLY WOUNDED WIA'S. A BALD EAGLE (REACTION FORCE) WAS LAUNCHED FROM 2/7 TO REINFORCE TEAM THE FOURTH DAY. THE REACTIONARY FORCE ALSO HAD MUCH CONTACT BEFORE THE PATROL WAS EXTRACTED. THE INITIAL REACTIONARY FORCE WAS LINKED UP WITH ANOTHER REACTIONARY FORCE IN ORDER TO BE EXTRACTED.

6. OBSERVATION OF ENEMY AND TERRAIN:

A. ENEMY: ALL THE ENEMY THAT WAS SPOTTED WERE DRESSED IN KHAKIS OR IN A MIXED UNIFORM WITH AUTOMATIC WEAPONS. WEB GEAR WAS NOT DETECTED. IT WAS QUITE EVIDENT THAT THESE WERE WELL TRAINED PROFESSIONAL SOLDIERS AND NOT VC. THEY WERE ALL LARGER IN SIZE THAN THE AVERAGE VC.

B. TERRAIN: THICK SECONDARY GROWTH CONSISTING MOSTLY OF BAMBOO AND VINES. NO CANOPY. MOVEMENT WAS DIFFICULT.

7. OTHER INFORMATION: INSERT LZ ZC177988 UH-34 BIRD ZONE. EXTRACT ZONE ZC175005, MULTIPLE BIRD ZONE VERY GOOD. AT COORDINATES ZC173977, IS A POSSIBLE ONE UH-34 BIRD ZONE, BUT 4-5 TREES WOULD HAVE TO BE BLOWN. AN OP SITE WAS ESTABLISHED AT ZC174987, BUT IT WAS NOT VERY GOOD. TRAILS WERE PREVALENT OVER THE ENTIRE AREA. THEY ALL SEEMED TO BE WELL USED. ALSO CLEARED OUT LANES WERE EVIDENT ALL OVER THE AREA LOOKED LIKE THEY WERE CLEARED FIELDS OF FIRE. COMM WAS BAD DUE TO ENEMY INTERFERENCE.

8. RESULTS OF ENCOUNTERS WITH THE ENEMY: PATROL WAS BELIEVED TO HAVE MADE CONTACT WITH A LARGE ENEMY FORCE. THE PATROL

LEADER DETERMINED DURING THEIR LENGTHY EN-
COUNTER WITH THE ENEMY THAT THE PATROL IN-
FLICTED 20 KIA'S CONFIRMED ON THE ENEMY. HE
HAS NO WAY OF DETERMINING HOW MANY
PROBABLE. KIA'S RES.

9. CONDITION OF PATROL: THERE WERE 2 FRIENDLY
KIA'S AND 3 WIA SERIOUS, HOWEVER EVERY MAN
IN THE PATROL RECEIVED SHRAPNEL.

10. CONCLUSIONS AND RECOMMENDATIONS: NONE

11. EFFECTIVENESS OF SUPPORTING ARMS: FAIR;
GUNS DID NOT SEEM TO BE REGISTERED. WEATHER
HAMPERED SATISFACTORY USE OF AIR SUPPORT.

12. COMMENTS BY DEBRIEFER: NONE

13. PATROL MEMBERS:

LONG, P. E.	2005909	JENSEN, A. T.	1949496 (KIA)
WILKINS, C. D.	2347185	LANSBURG, H. E	2171599
CRUZ, D. S.	2249686	WILLINGHAM, T. A.	2212213
GAINEY, L. R.	2315707	MOFFETT, G. A.	1012893
KLEVEN, G. J.	2278448 (WIA)	DEGRAY, J. F.	2320041 (KIA)
HENSLEY, T. A.	2295677 (WIA)	CHILSON, D. G.	2245039
ADAMS, H. S.	2229701 (WIA)	ROSHONG, P. B.	7964400
KELLY, J.	0102043	WOO, D. M.	2057528

PATROL ROUTE OVERLAY   ZD 19
                        ZC 16   OUT

                                        00
                                   99
                                   IN

COC Logbook Entries

CONFIDENTIAL

TO ATTN: MED-EVAC OF SERIOUS WIA'S. 1615H
CH-46A (BONNY SUE) COMPLETED MED-EVAC ON 2

WIA'S. 171450H 2D REACTION FORCE F/2/7 LANDED BY LVT VIC AT865861. 171513H CH-46A (BONNY HERO) COMPLETED MED-EVAC OF LAST SERIOUS WIA. 171520H REACTION FORCE I/3/7 LINKED UP WITH TEXAS PETE. 5 VC BODIES AND MANY BLOOD TRAILS FOUND IN VIC OF PTL'S LOCATION. 1/3/7 & TEXAS PETE, CARRYING KIA'S, PROCEEDING TO F/2/7 POS UNTIL MORNING WHEN EXTRACTION WILL BE ACCOMPLISHED BY LVT & TRK. REMAINING WIA'S TO BE MED-EVACED AT FIRST LIGHT.

3. PETRIFY F-2/1MD-1037

a. 171658H: PTL RECEIVED HVY SA & AW FIRE & GRN FRM EST VC SQUAD FROM 360 DEGREES AROUND PTL'S POS VIC ZC178987, RES IN 2 USMC KIA & 11 USMC WIA (2 MED-EVAC) & 9 MINOR. PTL RETURNED SA & M79 FIRE & GRN RES IN 1 VC KIA CONF & 1 VC KIA PROB. 171725H UH-1E'S (DEADLOCK 3-0 & 3-2) ARRIVED ON STA & DELIVERED SUPPRESSIVE FIRE. 171775OH AO (DREAM HOUR 48) ON STA AS TAC(A) & TO ASSIST AS RADIO RELAY. 171750H UH-1E'S (DEADLOCK 4-0 & 4-2) ARRIVED ON STA & DELIVERED SUPPRESSIVE FIRE. 171800H CH-46A (BONNY HERO) ARRIVED ON STA & ATTEMPTED TO MED-EVAC SERIOUS WIA'S. ON ATTEMPT HEL'S RECED HVY VOL SA & AW FIRE, FORCING ABORTION OF MSN & RES IN 1 USMC CREW CHIEF WIA (MED-EVAC). 171900H RECED REPORT THAT REACTION FORCE G/2/7 INSERTED BY TRKS VIC ZC 165994 & COMMENCED WALKING TO PTL'S POS. 171920H UH-1E'S (DEADLOCK 7-0 & 7-2) ARRIVED ON STA. FRM THIS TIME PTL HAS NOT RECED ANY FIRE. 172035H SPOOKY 1-1 ARRIVED ON STA FOR SUPPORT & FLARES. PTL STANDING BY FOR LINKUP WITH G/3/7.

(d) 181900H 2 LIGHTS MVG "S" TO "N" VIC AT

898396 FM CALLED. OUTSTANDING COVERAGE. 1
LIGHT WENT OFF. 1 LIGHT STAYED ON.
(e) 181930H 4 LIGHTS MVG "W" TO "E" IN VALLEY
VIC 909390 OUTSTANDING COVERAGE. LIGHTS
WENT OFF.

2. PETRIFY F-2 1MD-1037
(a) 180725H CH-46A (BONNIE SUE 1-0) ON WAY TO
PTL TO ATTEMPT MED-EVAC OF SERIOUS WIA'S.
RECED SA FIRE FROM RIDGE LINE "SE" OF PTL. POS,
RESULTING IN BROKEN FUEL LINE. BONNIE SUE 1-0
HAD TO SET DOWN ON ROAD VC ZD168012. PTL IN
DEFENSIVE POS VIC ZC178078 AWAITING MED-
EVAC AND LINK UP WITH G/2/7. 180740H PTL HAS
VC MVG TOWARDS THEIR POS. (DEADLOCK 3-0 &
3-2) ON STA; DELIVERED SUPPRESSIVE FIRE. (DEAD-
LOCK 4-0 & 4-2) ON STA; 180850H FIXED WING
(SWISS 0-60 & OXWOOD 0-1) ON STA. 180915H
DEADLOCK 4-0 & 4-2 DELIVERED SUPPRESSIVE
FIRE TO THE "E" OF PTL POS. AO (BENCH-MARK 1-2)
MARKED HIGH GROUND ABOVE PTL POS. WITH
YELLOW SMOKE. FOR LINK UP WITH G/2/7. PTL
HEARD 4 GRENADES GO OFF IN VIC ZC178973,
WHEN SMOKE WAS DROPPED. 181185H PTL &
G/2/7 LINKED UP VIC ZC 175985. BONNIE SUE 1-0
DOWN IN VIC ZD 168012 RECED MORTAR FIRE.
FIXED WING ON STA. 181455H PTL & G/2/7 STILL
RECEIVING SA FIRE. PTL & G/2/7 MVG DOWNHILL
TO LINK UP WITH I/3/7 * 2/7 CMD GRP. AT LZ VIC
ZC167988. PTL & G/2/7 STILL RECEIVING SA FIRE.
(END OF PAGE)

Dear Mr. Jensen,
　　29 Oct 1967
　　I am sorry I have taken so long in writing you, but I was
just released from the hospital ship *Sanctuary* today.
　　I am writing you in connection with your brother's death. I
do not have the words to tell you how sorry I am that all the

events that took place occurred. He was the first man who was a casualty in my platoon in the four months I have been here, and the fact that he was my best man compounded the incident that much more.

My platoon was scheduled for a routine patrol in a relatively pacified area. During my briefing, a call for volunteers was put out for another patrol to go into an area where one of our teams had taken heavy casualties. Your brother volunteered to go along with one of my other men and was the assistant patrol leader for the 16 man patrol. I have spoken to the patrol leader and several other troops who were there and this is the account I got:

The patrol was hit as they set in for the night during the second day. Sgt. Jensen took a group of seven men down the trail as retaliation and successfully dispersed the enemy. The next day, the Viet Cong picked up their trail again (they were deep in VC territory) and a fire fight broke out. Sgt Jensen was hit by the first grenade in the head and body. However with his fighting spirit, he disregarded the wounds and he headed for cover, disregarding his own safety, to deliver a heavy volume of fire on the VC. In the ensuing fire fight he maneuvered the point (which he was in charge of) and the patrol killed 19 Viet Cong confirmed, and many other probable. During this fight he was shot through the heart. Later, as the patrol was taking his body to an evacuation point, they were ambushed. The patrol suffered many casualties (2 KIA and 11 WIA out of 16) and they were unable to carry the KIA's. The infantry sent a reaction force and two other men lost their lives trying to recover the bodies. (They got the other Marine's body, but could not locate one of the other infantry man's body or Sgt Jensen's.) They decided that the price for recovering the body was too high to pay. Had my patrol and I been there, we would have disagreed with that decision, but we weren't. Two days ago, the infantry recovered the body and it was positively identified as your brother's.

We here have no knowledge of where he is to be buried. If it is in Arlington, please write my father, Capt. J. K. Tanssig,

Jr., USN, Wardon, Annapolis, MD, as he may be able to be of some help.

Sgt Jensen was one of the most professional Marines I have yet run across. There are a Bronze Star and Silver Star pending, which should be approved and awarded for his fine achievements.

Again, I deeply share your loss.

Sincerely,

Joseph K. Tanssig, III

1st Force Reconnaissance Company
1st Marine Division (Rein), FMF
FPO San Francisco, Calif 96602

2 Nov. 1967

Mr. David Jensen
5931 South 116th Street
Hales Corners, Wisc 53130

Dear Mr. Jensen:

Received your letter of 25 October, 1967, inquiring about your brother, Sergeant A. T. Jensen's death.

I would like to answer your questions myself because I thought of your brother as more of a friend than just that of another one of my men. I have gone on several patrols with Alan, and he did nothing but an outstanding job at all times.

Alan was the assistant patrol leader of a 16-man long range reconnaissance patrol north of Da Nang, deep within Viet Cong controlled territory. On the patrol's second day out they were attacked by a numerically superior communist force, which at first wounded Alan with a grenade and then minutes later mortally wounded him with a gun shot wound in the chest. One other man was killed instantly and all but two of the remaining patrol members were wounded. Everything that was possible was done to extract the team that day, but the enemy force was too great and three helicopters were shot down, killing one of the crew members. When extraction by helicopter failed, a Marine rifle company was sent up the densely vegetated hill to help the team out. It took the company all that night and half of the next morning before they made contact with our reconnaissance team. The team held on all this time with occasional enemy contact. Once the linkup was effected, heavy enemy fire came into their positions. As they were pulling off the hill they ran into heavily fortified enemy positions. The fire was so intense that it was impossible to recover Alan, and one other Marine from the rifle company without sustaining more casualties. You can be assured that all was done to recover Alan at this time. The next day a regimental size team was put into the area to recover Alan's body. The body was recovered and brought to Da Nang where several close friends and myself identified Alan.

This company and the U.S. Marine Corps suffered a great loss by losing Alan. You can be very proud of the work your brother did.

If you have any questions, please do not hesitate to write.

B. L. RUPP
Captain, U.S. Marine Corps
Executive Officer

Dear Mr. and Mrs. Jensen,
22 Nov 67
I have read the letter that you sent to the First Sergeant, and saw the package that you sent and it was given to the new men of the fourth platoon (which was Al's platoon) and they enjoyed it very much.

My name is Sgt. Thomas E. Machulda, and the fellows all refer to me as "Pappy." I came into the Marines in 1949, got out in 1956, and came back in again in April of this year. My wife, Mary, lives in Garden Grove, California, along with our daughter, 9 years old. We have two boys 15 and 16 living in Kansas, and a married daughter 19 who lives in Kansas also. She has a little boy 6 months old, so that makes me a Grandfather! The time sure flies by doesn't it?

I knew your son Al very well, we weren't what you may

call real close, as in this business you never get real close, as you don't know what will happen. But we were pretty tight and we talked together quite a lot and sort of shared our life's secrets if you know what I mean.

Mary and I lost our son on June 7th of this year, at Quang Tri, just about fifty miles north of here. He was hit by a mortar round and was killed instantly. He was just 21 on the 18th of May. I was at Camp Pendleton and would have left to come over here on the 10th of June. I hadn't told him I was coming as I wanted to drop in on him and surprise him. But I guess that wasn't the way things were meant to be. Al and I always felt the same way, that whatever will happen will happen, and we never worried about going out and not coming back. The mission that Al went out on, he volunteered for, it was a special mission into an area where a team had been shot up before, and we had to go back in there and see what was there. I was about half a mile away operating a radio relay for the team back to headquarters when they got hit.

In the initial attack Al was wounded in the arm, and then a few moments later was shot, this killed him instantly, so he did not lay there and suffer. They were hit about four o'clock in the afternoon and did not get out until the next day. It took that long for a rescue force to climb the mountain to reach them and bring them out.

I have several pictures of Al, all of them, however, I've sent home, but I'm sure my wife would be happy to have copies made of them and send them to you if you would like. I know my wife was very happy to get any pictures of our son.

It made me feel very good to hear that you had buried Al at Arlington. I know it would be his wish to be placed with other professional soldiers and Marines. I know he is very proud to be there. Al was a proud Marine just like all of us who are in for "twenty." Al was happy here, I know he wouldn't want to have been anywhere else, even if he could have foreseen the outcome. Sometimes we can't understand why things happen the way they do, but I know that our son Gale, and your son Al, went out of this world for a reason, "So that the rest of us could have a reason." They gave everything they could, the rest of us will have to see that it wasn't in vain.

Well, I would appreciate it very much hearing from you folks, of course anything I have said here is unofficial and just between friends. If ever the opportunity arises, I would very much like to meet you folks, not to relive any unpleasant memories, but to shake the hands of you two, for I know you can always be proud of your son, Al. I know that the grief is very hard, but now you have a reason to walk a little taller.
Yours truly,
Sgt. Thomas E. Machulda, 1114301, USMC

Dear Jensens,
26 Nov 67
Please allow me to introduce myself. I am Sgt. Harry Grace. I was in the same platoon as Al. A letter was received from you stating that you would like to hear from some of the people who served with your son. So, I'll do my best to scratch out some kind of letter.

I have been in Nam for 18 months. I am now on a six month extension. Al and I worked together for a little over two months. I made Sgt. in September and at that time was taken out of the bush and put in comm. relay. I am a radio man. I must say that in the short time Al and I were together, I really learned to admire him.

Many of the persons of whom Al sent home pictures are not here now. Quite a few of them have already rotated home. I should be leaving Nam in January. I was hoping to make Christmas this year but it appears I will have one more in Vietnam.

I have a few extra pictures of Al that I took while on patrol. If you would like to have these just drop a line and I will send them.

Got to run for now. Hope you didn't mind my writing to you. If you have any extra time, drop a line. I would enjoy hearing from you.
Yours truly,
Harry W. Grace

Dear Mr. and Mrs. Jensen,
22 Dec. 67

Hello, I'm Sgt Livingston. I write to express my sympathy. You are going to have to forgive me for being late with this letter. I'm afraid I'm not much at this, but then I guess none of us are. I was Al's Team Leader. I'm sorry that I was in the Philippines when it happened.

Al and I were a lot alike in quite a few ways. We were both Sgts. and got out of the Corps. Mainly for the same reasons, and I guess we came back for the same reasons. We both looked at the Corps as professionals. We all worked well together. The eight of us as a team set a pretty impressive record. We had been in some pretty hot spots this summer and on two occasions, if it wasn't for Al we wouldn't be here at all. Since October, we, the rest of us, have been split up. I think you know that Sgt. Huff drowned the following week in the same area. Simmons (Slim) is back at Camp Pendleton, Cal. Sgt. Grace is in the comm section now training radio men. Cpl Owens is now a Sgt. I was given the job of building a new team from the team that Al was with when he got hit. It's the second platoon. Sgt Owens is helping me, but he leaves in ten days for the States. This is his 20th month so he has earned it. Skip Landsburg and Doc Jackson are still in the 4th platoon. Skip goes the same time Owen does.

Well, I better go. I'm going out in the morning on patrol. Once again, I want to tell you how proud I was to serve with Al and how proud we are of him. He's the finest Marine I've ever known.

Here's hoping you have a Merry Christmas and a Happy New Year.

Semper Fidelis,
Sgt. L. H. Livingston

STATEMENT OF CORPORAL HAROLD E. LANSBURG, USMC

On 16 October 1967, while on patrol in the Republic of Vietnam, with 1st Force Reconnaissance Company, the security element, which consisted of a two man team, was taken under fire with M-79 rounds and automatic weapons fire. Sergeant JENSEN, who was with the main group, charged through the underbrush hollering and screaming in order to take the Viet Cong's attention from the rest of the men. Then after the enemy fire had ceased, he proceeded down the trail to confiscate the enemy's weapons. He also checked the area thoroughly. Then, and only then, did he return to the main group. Due to all the fire put out by him, heavy casualties were inflicted on the enemy, and probably aided in saving the lives of his comrades. His extreme valor proved to be inspiring to the men at this crucial time. His actions were a credit to himself and the United States Marine Corps.

Harold E. Lansburg,
CPL. USMC

1st Force Reconnaissance Company
1st Marine Division (Rein), FMF
FPO San Francisco, Calif 96602

DSN/efh

1650

14 Nov 1967

From:	Commanding Officer
To:	Secretary of the Navy
Via:	Commanding Officer, 1st Reconnaissance Battalion
	Commanding General, 1st Marine Division, (Rein), FMF
	Commanding General, Fleet Marine Force, Pacific
	Commandant of the Marine Corps (Code DL)
	Chief of Naval Operations
Subj:	Bronze Star Medal, recommendation for
Ref:	(a) FMFPersO P1650.1A
	(b) DivO 1650.4S
Encl:	(1) Proposed Citation

(2) Statement of Master Sergeant George A. MOF-
FETT, USMC
(3) Statement of Corporal Harold E. LANSBURG,
USMC

1. In accordance with the provisions of references (a) and
(b), it is recommended that Sergeant Alan T. Jensen, 1949496/
0311/0651 U. S. Marine Corps, attached to and serving with
the 1st Force Reconnaissance Company, FMF, be awarded the
Bronze Star Medal for his heroic achievement, posthumously.
2. While serving as the assistant patrol leader of a 16-man patrol with 1st Force Reconnaissance Company, 1st Marine Division, (Rein), FMF, Sergeant Jensen participated in a long
range reconnaissance patrol in enemy held territory during
the period of 16 to 17 October, 1967. On 16 October, 1967,
the patrol's position was probed by an estimated squad of
North Vietnamese army soldiers. Another member of the patrol spotted them and opened fire, killing one and driving the
rest away. Sergeant Jensen led an aggressive assault on the
retreating enemy in an attempt to capture weapons or documents. The patrol then began receiving heavy M-79 fire.
Sergeant Jensen, often exposing himself to the fire, helped
the patrol leader break contact and move to a harbor site. On
17 October, 1967, while the patrol was establishing a new
harbor site, they were attacked by a large, well-disciplined
unit of North Vietnamese Army soldiers. Sergeant Jensen immediately moved to the positions receiving the heaviest attack, where he proceeded to direct the fire of the men and to
offer them encouragement. Although painfully wounded by
an enemy grenade, Sergeant Jensen continued his aggressive
performance, encouraging patrol members and directing fire
until he was fatally wounded by a small arms round through
his heart. By his selfless devotion to duty, despite painful
wounds, and in the face of withering small arms fire and
grenades, Sergeant Jensen upheld the highest traditions of
the United States Marine Corps.
3. The facts as stated in the proposed citation are completely

substantiatcd by thc statcmcnts of cyc-witnesses which are contained in the enclosures.

4. This award is for direct participation in combat operations and the combat Distinguishing Device is recommended.

5. Sergeant Jensen had not been recommended for any awards, nor had he received any foreign awards.

6. Sergeant Jensen died as a result of this action.

7. The following additional recommendations are being submitted in connection with this action.

AWARD	NAME	RANK	SERVICE	LTR
BRONZE STAR	GAINEY, L.R.	Cpl.	USMC	My ltr 1650DSN

1650 dtd 14Nov67

BRONZE STAR	LONG, P. E.	SSgt.	USMC	My ltr DFN ever

1650 dtd 14Nov67

8. This document is being submitted late due to the fact both the people who gave statements for this recommended medal were either hospitalized or committed operationally.

D. J. KEATING, JR.

1st FORCE RECONNAISSANCE COMPANY
1st MARINE DIVISION (Rein), FMF
FPO SAN FRANCISCO, CALIF 96602

30 August 1968
Mr. and Mrs. Theodore Jensen
5931 South 116th Street
Hales Corners, Wisc 53130

Dear Mr. and Mrs. Jensen,

The Marines of 1st Force Reconnaissance Company received your generous and thoughtful packages once again. The sausages found their way into our new enlisted club as well as numerous other "goody lockers." Please accept my most sincere thanks on behalf of all of us.

My name is probably new to you. I commanded C Company, 1st Recon Bn when your son was in 1st Force, and relieved Major Walker here in Phu Bai, this past May. Gunnery Sergeant Trevathan and Staff Sergeant Cole are still here, on their second extensions. 1st Sergeant Holemon is our new Top.

Many of your son's friends are still in the Company and the newcomers hear his name repeated often, most particularly when we make parachute jumps in the "Jensen Drop Zone" here in Phu Bai. Sorrow still abides in the ranks over our fallen Marines, yet consolation is found by continuing to fight in the cause for which they gave their lives.

Major Dan Keating, your son's former Commanding Officer, and my best friend, was killed in action this past May. He died on patrol in much the same situation that befell your son, Alan. He and his family are now remembered in our prayers along with Sergeant Jensen and you, his parents.

We're all (believe it or not) looking forward to the start of the Monsoon season. It'll be a relief over the heat and dust which the summer brings to Phu Bai, RVN.

Once again, please accept all our thanks for your continued generosity and thoughtfulness.

Semper Fidelis,

J. V. Sullivan
Major, U. S. Marine Corps
Commanding

══ 12 ══

Mike McKenna, Radio Operator, 3d Force Recon Company: 1967*

Dr. Mike McKenna, now an anesthesiologist in San Diego, describes his experiences as an eighteen-year-old Marine radio operator assigned to 3d Force Reconnaissance Company, in 1967. Along the DMZ and operating in the "back yard," near Con Thien, Stingray teams used Marine artillery with telling effect.

My Biography

I enlisted in the United States Marine Corps after spending one pitiful semester at Syracuse University. At seventeen I was not ready for college. The war was rapidly escalating and I had become prime draft material. Vietnam was in my future and I decided that if I was going to go to war, I wanted to go with the professionals. My wish was granted, and I spent two of my three years in the Corps with force or battalion recon.

Thoroughly motivated, I returned to Syracuse and went on to medical school and a specialty in anesthesiology. While anesthesia is said to be a "high stress" specialty, it doesn't even come close to a day in combat in the Corps.

*An interview with Dr. Mike McKenna, San Diego, California, 1998, formerly a radioman with 3d Force Recon Company.

My First Stingray Mission

I was the veteran of a hundred reconnaissance patrols and a
score of firefights with the North Vietnamese Army. All in my
head. I had played the tape of what I would see and do in
combat over and over in my eighteen-year-old mind. I was
playing the same game that Henry Fleming had played in *The
Red Badge of Courage* before he had "gone to see the elephant" at Chancellorsville in 1863. Henry Fleming and I
were both very young and very naive.

This was Phu Bai (pronounced "foo-bye") in 1967, not the
rolling hills of Virginia in 1863, but Henry and I had the same
questions and fears. What was combat like and how would
we act?

Our eight-man recon team of the 3d Force Reconnaissance
Company was making its first patrol. The team consisted of
two decorated veterans of previous recon tours, a point man
who had been in country for six months, and five virgins.

We five neophytes thought ourselves fully trained recon
Marines. We were ready to slip silently through the hills of
Vietnam and bring death to the North Vietnamese Army. We
knew the NVA were out there. Our mission was to locate
them and report all we could about their size, equipment, and
direction of movement. Our small recon team was not to engage the enemy at close quarters, but to kill them surrepti-
tiously, even scientifically, with artillery and airpower. Our
goal was to remain undetected for four to seven days, deep in
hostile territory.

If detected, the team would fight, attempt to break contact, then evade an inevitably larger enemy force until it
could be extracted by helicopter. Each recon team had
to carry with it enough firepower to survive that kind
of critical time, plus enough water and food to be self-
sufficient for a week or longer. Each team member had to
carry up to eighty pounds of gear on his back. It is difficult
to be swift and stealthy with so much equipment, but anything less meant risking annihilation.

Corporals Moragne and Case, and lance corporals Gottschalk, Christie, and I were first-timers; Staff Sergeant "Val" Valpando, our team leader, was a career Marine with a number of distinguished recon tours in Vietnam under his belt. Val was the quintessential Marine noncommissioned officer: he ordered and we obeyed; we instinctively trusted this man with our lives.

Doc Bridges was our Navy corpsman. Technically a noncombatant, Doc had probably participated in as much combat as Staff Sergeant Valpando, and like Val, had been awarded a Bronze Star for his recon exploits.

Lance Corporal Thompson, our experienced point man, was halfway through his thirteen-month tour of duty. I can only wonder at his thoughts as we boarded the helicopter at the Phu Bai airstrip. Thompson, like Val and Doc, knew that in the field a single blunder by a new man could kill the team very quickly; there was no margin for error in the bush. This was not Camp Pendleton or the jungle school in Panama. Mistakes and inexperience could be and would be fatal.

The helicopter ride was noisy but cool. There was no attempt at conversation; the Plexiglas windows of the CH-46 had long ago been removed, and the openings served as firing ports when necessary. The helicopter was a functional, nofrills tube designed specifically to move Marines quickly in and out of trouble. There was some armor plating for the pilots and the engines, but none for the passengers. The CH-46 was a nimble and powerful transport, but it was not designed to be a gunship.

With map in hand, Staff Sergeant Val had been seated between the two pilots, guiding them to the insertion point. When we were about six hundred feet above the deck we quickly moved back to our crouched position near the open ramp at the rear of the helicopter. Val ordered "lock and load," and we held onto the nylon-web seats on the sides of the CH-46. The helicopter stopped its tight downward spiral suddenly and flared to a solid landing in a meadow of deep elephant grass. The team bolted down the ramp and quickly spread out into a tight defensive circle. Suddenly the bird's rotor-wash and the scream of the turbine engines were gone.

"Insertion" was an apt term; the helicopter had been on the ground less than ten seconds, and all that remained of it was the thick smell of jet fuel.

The elephant grass depressed by the CH-46 sprang back to its six-foot height and I realized I could only see the team member on each flank. We were surrounded by low, nondescript rolling hills. The terrain looked very different from what I had imagined when using the map and looking down from high above in the CH-46.

Case signaled to me to call in. I keyed the handset and called in with the cryptic message that meant we were safely inserted. No response. I called again. Still no response. The radio had worked when we tested it at the airstrip. It was on the correct frequency and the battery was new. Now what? Eight of us were on the ground, the helicopter was long gone, and we had no communications with Phu Bai. Gottschalk, the primary radio operator at Val's elbow, was already replacing his short "tape" antenna with a twelve-foot folding whip, hoping for better reception. Of course, to me it just looked like a flagpole pinpointing our position. Still no communication. The longer antenna came down and we slowly moved out toward higher ground.

The heat was stunning. Sweat was dripping camouflage grease paint into my eyes faster than I could clear them. Our green utility uniforms were black with sweat. There was no breeze, yet I could smell something foreign but oddly familiar in the air. Phu Bai had smelled of dirt, diesel fuel, and Americans. This smell in the bush was very different. It was not the sweet musty smell of the Panamanian jungle nor the dried-out sage smell of the Camp Pendleton hills.

Case turned back to me, slowly pointed to his nose, and mimed eating with a fork. We had landed in the midst of someone's chow hall. My alertness, already off the scale, ratcheted up to animal-like heights. Our team continued to move to higher ground. My head swiveled constantly, watching our flanks and the Marines to my front and rear in the file. The radio handset attached to my lapel murmured something, and I realized we had moved out of the radio's dead spot. I didn't respond. Gottschalk was the primary radio operator, always at Val's side, and I would use my radio only if something happened to Gottschalk or if Staff Sergeant Valpando directed me to do so.

Suddenly we heard voices, men's voices, jabbering away. We froze. My thoughts were simple: Here it comes . . . time seemed to slow. My head had only one paramount and very chilling thought—be ready to pull the trigger when it starts. The voices faded. We remained in place for another five minutes as our heads swiveled. I realized I was breathing deeply again and the sweat was still dripping heavily into my eyes. I started to think again in a rush of questions. Were they farmers? Woodcutters? Probably not. Any noncombatant would have moved out of the area after seeing a Marine helicopter land then quickly depart. The locals had been watching recon teams insert longer than I had been in the Marine Corps. They knew that a recon insertion made the neighborhood dangerous for all parties involved. They knew the drill.

I was perplexed. The NVA/VC had obviously seen us land in their midst, but they didn't seem that impressed with our arrival. Were they complete idiots with no noise discipline, or, more ominous, were they watching us, waiting for us to make a mistake? I didn't expect the enemy to rush into a headlong retreat in the face of only seven Marines and one corpsman, but neither did I expect them to be so nonchalant.

The team moved out. Moragne, on point, came upon a well-worn trail. Staff Sergeant Val's earlier experience with trails in and around the Da Nang area had convinced him that they were not to be used by us. We could move faster and quieter on a good trail, but trails reeked of the probability of ambush.

Val snaked the team parallel to the trail until he was convinced that a crossing would be safe. We then quickly crossed over it in single file and set up an ambush overlooking the enemy's principal route of travel. Case and I were sent further into the bush behind the team to provide security to the rear and flanks. It was nerve-racking. There was no sound or movement for twenty minutes. Case and I could see each other and the backs of some of the ambushers, but we could not see the trail or, more important, the killing zone. The first shots would startle us as much as the enemy in the trap. I was parched but didn't dare risk making any movement to get one of my canteens.

A high thin cloud cover had moved in and the heat eased up. It was still a sauna, but not as vicious. How would I ever acclimate to this heat?

To me the mission was frustratingly incomplete. We had landed and detected enemy activity, but had no hard data on him. We had heard him and even smelled his food and his cooking fires, but had yet to see him. After we waited for some time, our ambush position was quietly abandoned and we slowly moved on to higher ground. There were no more voices or smells—just an aura of anticipation and suspense. A violent meeting was inevitable, but on whose terms?

Our point man came to a small stream. We paused while Moragne checked the area and then we slipped through the water as silently as possible. It was about a foot deep and sluggish. Everything out there seemed slow and listless.

Another ambush was set up, looking down on the streambed. Again, Case and I acted as security to the rear of the team. The two of us looked across a small meadow pockmarked with shallow artillery or bomb craters. About eighty feet from us the clearing was bordered by an eroded earthen dike about five feet high. The more I looked at the dike, the more ominous it became. What was on the other side? Was that a trail coming over it or simply an old artillery scar? I glanced over at Case to see if he shared my concern. He was quietly checking out a snub-nose .38 revolver. We were cautioned not to carry any personal sidearms and I was fascinated by his blatant disregard for company policy. I was still naive.

Doc Bridges silently came up from the ambush site, gave Case a withering look, and told us to stay put. The team was still behind him and we were to fall in as it passed us.

Moragne and Thompson skirted the clearing and quickly slipped over the dike.

There was a startling blast of gunfire. Here it was at last. No shouts or screams, just a torrent of automatic-weapons fire as Moragne and Thompson scrambled wildly back over the dike. Thompson fired long bursts from his M-60 machine gun as Val sent Doc Bridges up to see what Moragne had run into. Doc bolted across the clearing, fired a full magazine from his M-1 carbine into the melee, and then scrambled back to report to Val. Moragne had collided with two NVA soldiers walking down the trail and had killed both of them with his M-14 rifle. But there was plenty of movement and shouting in the bush on both sides of the dead bodies.

Doc reported that to Val in a cheerful manner, totally devoid of drama or excitement. Doc, I realized later, was not trying to be cool under fire, he simply *was* cool. Nothing to get too worked up about, simply another day of people running around trying to kill each other.

Val told me to fire into the brush directly across from the clearing as he scurried up to confer with Moragne and Thompson. Gottschalk was calling in the report of our contact while I did my best to obliterate the opposing tree line with my M-16.

Doc asked me, "Just what in the hell are you doing?"

"Covering Val," I explained. He gave me a tight grin and advised me to save a few rounds "for later on." I was learning. Within minutes Val had Marine artillery rounds crunching into the tree line in front of Moragne. Case was lobbing M-79 grenades over Moragne's head into the area around the two NVA bodies. The noise of the machine gun, grenades, and impacting artillery fire was exhilarating. We were like coiled springs releasing the tension of the morning's cat-and-mouse game with the enemy. The whispering was over, the game had begun, and it was oddly exciting.

The artillery fire paused and an 0-1 spotter aircraft was orbiting above our position. The pilot apparently had seen some movement to our rear and was firing an M-16 out his open side window. Great, I thought, they are to our front and rear and they're not running away.

Two Marine Huey gunships arrived and began chewing up the area with rockets and machine gun fire. The helicopters were making firing runs toward our position, holding fire only when sixty to eighty feet from our loose defensive perimeter. The incoming rounds were spattering into the dense bush around us long before the noise of the guns reached our ears. I had never been shot at before and the sequence of sounds seemed peculiar. It was unnerving and I hugged the ground even tighter during the passes made by the gunships. The pilots were good shots. All they could see of our position from an altitude of fifteen hundred feet was a three-by-six-foot colored marker panel I had positioned in the middle of our clearing.

Val had ordered me to unfold the "air panel" earlier in the engagement. I had promptly dashed out to the center of the clearing, firing my M-16 from the hip. I threw the panel out as flat as possible, fired another burst, then scrambled back to cover. I was quite pleased with my John Wayne style of "fire and maneuver" until I saw Doc and Val smiling at me. Those two would be very hard to impress in combat. They were professionals and I was just an overly eager amateur in his first big game. I could only hope to reach their cool, detached level of competence in this deadly business, and I was worried more about screwing up than getting hit.

I was too green to worry much about the intentions of the enemy maneuvering around us. I knew that Staff Sergeant Valpando would get us out and away from this contact. He was a Marine SNCO, I was his charge, and would unhesitatingly follow him through the gates of hell itself.

The Huey gunships ceased their fire and the area grew strangely quiet. I glanced up. Two F-4 Phantoms were orbiting above us at thirty-five hundred feet. The F-4s had apparently impressed the NVA in the past, for all movement and shooting had stopped. Staff Sergeant Val was like a demented maestro, orchestrating firepower on the radio, summoning artillery, gunships, and a flight of F-4s. What next? A flight of B-52s?

Val told me to retrieve the air panel, which I did with a minimum of theatrics. We were being extracted. The patrol had been compromised. There were plenty of NVA in our area, but our efforts to break contact and continue our mission would inevitably lead to another encounter with the NVA, probably under less favorable conditions and most likely at night.

The Phantoms climbed several thousand feet but continued to orbit our position as the helicopter gunships returned to strafe the area in preparation for our extraction helicopter, another CH-46. The tempo picked up as Christie threw a yellow smoke grenade into the center of the clearing. While the rising smoke gave the pilots our location and the wind direction, it also announced to the NVA that helicopters would be arriving, the probable direction of their approach, and that we might be leaving the area.

We had made our decision: extraction. What would the NVA do? They could leave several riflemen behind to harass the helicopters while the remaining main body quickly cleared the area. The NVA knew that as soon as our team was lifted out the area would be pummeled by gunships and the Phantoms. Did the NVA have heavy machine guns positioned to knock down the CH-46 as it made its approach? Would they turn our LZ into a pyre of burning helicopters and a swirling melee of ground combatants? Did they plan, as their General Giap expounded, to "grab us by the belt" and slug it out so close that our airpower would be useless to defend us? That scenario could also be very costly to them. They knew that a trapped recon team was not as easily rolled over as an isolated and exhausted infantry squad. A recon team is top-heavy with seasoned NCOs, is much more heavily armed, and all members of the team can call in artillery and airpower. More important, a recon team is accustomed to being outnumbered in precarious situations. Its members are not superhuman, they just train for the worst to happen and do not panic when it does. A good recon team will fight savagely until it is annihilated. Few prisoners were taken by either side in those vicious firefights.

The CH-46 landed in a swirl of blowing dirt and yellow smoke. Val sounded the command *"Go!"* and we bolted from cover and ran to the ramp. The screaming jet engines obliterated all noise of gunfire except for that from the two door gunners, who were using heavy .50-caliber Brownings. We rapidly positioned ourselves at each of the portholes and fired outboard as the helicopter lifted us from the LZ. My first Stingray patrol was completed. My first combat experience, and no Marine casualties. We sat in the nylon-web seats of the CH-46 and simply stared at each other as we flew back to Phu Bai. I had a hundred thoughts and as many unanswered questions. It had not been at all what I had expected. Were we lucky? Would things get worse? Would I manage to survive an entire year of it?

We had been lucky, and, yes, it would get worse—much worse. The company soon moved north to Dong Ha and we began running patrols inside the DMZ (demilitarized zone). Con Thien, Khe Sanh, Tet, and the meatgrinder infantry sweeps along the DMZ all loomed in our future.

Doc Bridges, Christie, and Thompson would all be dead within the year. Staff Sergeant Valpando would later die in a parachuting accident in Southern California. In my youthful bravado I had used a subminiature camera to take photographs of this first contact. I never had the opportunity, or the nerve, to show the slides to Val. He would probably have just smiled and told me never to do it again.

Con Thien—1967

Victor was the name of our radio relay site, located at Con Thien, and that was my first assignment after leaving the bush as a recon team radio operator. I left the bush relatively early in my tour. Heat stroke and M-16s had damaged my hearing to such a degree that I was a liability to the team. What do you do with a half-deaf radio operator? Send him to a relay site that is not too intense. Let him learn the ropes and then rotate him through more challenging and remote radio relay sites. It was similar to training an air traffic controller. Start him out in Des Moines, not at Chicago's O'Hare. Con Thien, in June of 1967, was Des Moines.

Con Thien had been in the news. In the spring an NVA ground assault had been repulsed by 1/4 (1st Battalion, 4th Marine Regiment). The bodies of the NVA were buried in a mass grave located just outside our perimeter. Sporadic NVA artillery, mortar, and recoilless fire still hit the base at Con Thien, but not as if the enemy were conducting a siege. Con Thien was lively but not deadly. It seemed a good place for me to learn how to work on a radio relay site.

Corporal Peacock and I had ridden in a truck from the Marine base at Dong Ha through Cam Lo and then north up to Con Thien. The infamous "McNamara Line" had been physically cleared from the South China Sea to its western anchor of Con Thien, but the road north from Cam Lo to Con Thien was still bordered by thick vegetation that could literally be touched from the bed of an open truck. An ambush would have been quite simple and most devastating, but our trip was uneventful. Perhaps Con Thien had cooled down.

I was told that the name Con Thien translates to "The Hill of Angels," and the French missionaries who had come earlier to Vietnam had no doubt named it during happier times. As we approached it from the south the hills more resembled Golgotha, the Place of Skulls, the location of the crucifixion. It consisted of two barren hard-baked mounds of earth connected by a grassy saddle. The flat summit of each hill was the size of a basketball court. Other than low grass, there was no vegetation on the slopes. It was a grim place that certainly did not bring the thought of angels to my mind. A narrow single-lane road led to each summit. A detour off the road meant finding uncharted land mines left by the ARVN (Army of the Republic of Vietnam), French, Viet Minh, or even the Japanese. Con Thien was the high ground in a strategic area, and all previous military men in the area had gravitated toward it.

The view from the summit was spectacular. To the north I could look out over the DMZ and into North Vietnam. To the east, the cleared "trace" of the McNamara Line. To the south, virtually every emplacement of the Third Marine Division. Con Thien also proved the old military maxim: if you can see them, they can see you. The exact coordinates of the compact little base could be recited by any NVA gunner. NVA 152mm and 130mm cannons, with crews of nine men and a range of twenty-seven thousand meters, were emplaced in North Vietnam and knew how to hit Con Thien without much trial or error.

Corporal Peacock and I moved into the aid station bunker on the eastern hill and started our radio watch. Our only excitement was the occasional arrival of ARVN soldiers wounded by incoming mortar fire. The ARVN were invariably wounded in the legs. A Navy corpsman explained to us that the ARVN would extend their legs out of their trenches during enemy mortar attacks in the hope of getting a "million dollar" wound. It was risky business but seemed to work. Their legs would get peppered and, if they survived, they would soon be shipped out to a (hopefully) safer place.

Those troops and their U.S. Army Special Forces counterparts were leaving Con Thien to the control of the Ninth Marines. The American Special Forces had occupied a large bunker on our hill, rumored to contain a theater-size popcorn machine. We didn't socialize with the Special Forces, but we could smell the aroma of popcorn at night. The Vietnamese troops spent their days at Con Thien roasting potbellied pigs and trying to sell me their weapons. They told me that Con Thien was a "very bad place," and when I asked why, they would only smile and start to giggle. These soldiers may not have been the best fighting force in Vietnam, but they did know what was coming.

The Special Forces contingent finally moved out and Corporal Peacock and I quickly took over their underground "Connex" shipping containers for our new radio relay site. The boxes were made of steel and about the size required to ship a VW beetle. They were dry and covered with two feet of dirt and layers of sandbags. The boxes had served as the Vietnamese armory, and during a previous unescorted tour of their facility I had managed to stuff a Browning automatic rifle, virgin in its cardboard box, up the ventilation shaft. The ARVN didn't miss it when they left, so I had a new BAR, complete with several cans of .30-caliber ammunition.

They had also left behind a .50-caliber machine gun in a covered gun emplacement directly atop our Connex box bunker. The 1/9 Marines didn't act like it belonged to them and I didn't ask any questions about its ownership. I kept the .50-cal. machine gun cleaned and lubricated with WD-40 and schemed on how I could take it back to Dong Ha for our company.

For a while Con Thien remained quiet. The hills baked during the day but Peacock and I stayed cool inside our boxes. We slept atop the bunker at night and listened as sticks of B-52 Arc Light bombs fell across the DMZ from thirty thousand feet above. The bombers were noiseless, but the bombs left a ghostly sucking sound as they fell from the sky. A string of orange flashes would light up the DMZ, our hill would shake, and then the growling impact wave from the five-hundred-pound bombs would sweep across our position.

Recon Stingray teams were being inserted in the area around Con Thien at an accelerated rate as more and more NVA units were observed on the move. Marine artillery fire would be called in, the NVA would take heavy losses and then melt into the abandoned villages and dried-up rice paddies. They were staging, for something. Con Thien? Dong Ha? Gio Linh? No one knew.

I was impatient to fire my new BAR. The Ninth Marines advised me that if I walked north, down from our hill, and then turned west I could test-fire the antique but effective weapon from the days of World War II. Another Marine and I grabbed our M-16s and the BAR, walked down the hill, and out to a cleared strip of land. I noted the thin perimeter as we walked by the last strand of concertina wire and past bored grunts in two-man fighting holes. The grunts waved us through and assured us that there were no land mines in our path. We fired the BAR, learned how to adjust its rate of fire, and took some "hot dog" slides of the event before returning to the safety of our bunker.

Looking back from the north our twin hills position looked formidable, but we knew that was just an illusion. There were no minefields, the defensive perimeter was thinly manned, the grunts were not under heavy cover, and the fortress of Con Thien was not bristling with heavy weapons. There were some tanks, a battery of 4.2-inch mortars, and a couple of thin-skinned Ontos.* But Con Thien was not meant to be a copy of the Maginot Line. It was just a piece of high ground that served as a base for Marine infantry units that constantly swept the area. The real defenses of Con Thien were the grunts sweeping the land in front of the base, and because of them the NVA would have to go through 1/9 to take possession of Con Thien.

Two days later Alpha and Bravo Companies of 1/9 left Con Thien on their regular sweep. They had advanced about three klicks (kilometers) north toward the DMZ when they were ambushed and virtually annihilated by several regiments of the North Vietnamese 324B Infantry Division. The solid and continuous roar of automatic weapons could be heard on our hill. The chilling sound went on and on, unlike anything I had ever heard, or want to hear again.

The Stingray teams out in the bush also heard the noise and wanted to know what was going on. At that point no one knew enough to tell them. The teams were watching as the NVA brazenly trotted toward the noise of the 1/9 battle; the Stingray teams wanted to call in artillery fire, but all the artillery batteries were tied up answering calls from spotter planes sent in to assist the ambushed Marines.

The bombardment of Con Thien began in earnest. Earlier incoming fire had apparently been nothing more than registration rounds. Salvos of 152mm and 130mm rounds started walking over the area. Our base was compact and it didn't take very long to sweep. When fired, the Soviet guns made a distinct boom, then a pause of a few seconds was followed by the scream of the incoming shell as it impacted with a dull

---

*"Ontos" means "thing" in Greek. It was a lightly armored speedy tracked vehicle that carried six 106mm recoilless rifles as its armament.

crunch. The sound was distinctly different from that made by an incoming rocket or mortar round. The artillery rounds were more crisply sinister; they were going deep into the earth, looking for bunkers. The enemy artillery wasn't wasted on mere ground-level blasts that smashed helicopters, mortars, or even ammunition dumps. They were going for Marines dug in deep. Thin-skinned surface targets were left to enemy mortars, rockets, and recoilless rifle fire. By that point there was no good reason to be above ground other than to take a quick look to see if the place was crawling with NVA. A lot of rifle fire would be the signal to move topside in a hurry. The generator was hit and most field telephones had their lines shredded. Our bunker on the hill stayed underground and remained isolated.

The incoming fire paused but the distant booms grew more numerous. I looked to the northwest and could clearly see the white muzzle flashes of enemy guns. The shells were whispering directly over Con Thien as they headed for Dong Ha and its airstrip. The long-range artillery raked Dong Ha for half an hour before it shifted back onto Con Thien. The NVA knew that a reaction force to help 1/9 would be assembling at the Dong Ha airstrip, and their attack was obviously well organized.

The shelling resumed and I retreated deeper into the corner of my Connex box. There simply was no safe place to go as the hill shook. It was a bright afternoon, but I remember it as night.

My radio proved to be no source of encouragement. Several Stingray teams had been inserted with the reaction force from 3/4 (3d Battalion, 4th Marine Regiment). The NVA had hit 3/4, located at Dong Ha, and they targeted them again as they landed in the open LZ south of the battle. I tuned my third radio to the 1/9 frequency and listened to reports of NVA wearing Marine gear and carrying M-16s and M-60 machine guns. Our Stingray teams had been mistaken for NVA under much less chaotic conditions, and we were worried about friendly fire from above and ground level fire from confused and paranoid grunts.

I drank cold C ration coffee and talked to familiar voices out on the DMZ as the night staggered on. Corporal Peacock had gone to Dong Ha that calm morning and planned to return with any mail that afternoon. I didn't plan on ever seeing Peacock again. I was experiencing a feeling of exhausted detachment, probably similar to the thoughts of soldiers under intense artillery fire at Verdun or the Battle of the Somme. There is simply nothing one can do other than sit and endure it. A 152mm artillery round was more than capable of penetrating six feet of reinforced concrete. The dirt above my little Connex box wouldn't even slow it down.

The radio reports from Stingray teams kept me busy enough that I couldn't dwell on my situation. The NVA chose not to withdraw, but continued to slug it out with the grunts. B-52s saturated the area with bombs. Marine, Navy, and Air Force strikes were continuous. Army 175mm guns located at Camp Carroll were firing deep into North Vietnam to help counter the Soviet cannon fire. A Marine C-130 flare-ship kept the area bathed in a putrid light throughout the night. It was World War II–style total warfare and the NVA were not running from it.

In the morning the command group of 1/9 arrived and moved to occupy the bunker that had formerly belonged to the Special Forces unit at Con Thien. It was considered the sturdiest bunker on the hill, but a 152mm round blew it to bits the second afternoon after their arrival. I felt the impact but had no urge to get up and bear witness to what had happened. In a few moments my hatch was opened and a grunt asked if I had communications with Dong Ha. I told him that I did. Another Marine crawled in and told me to get a 1/9 representative on the radio. The Marine's utilities were black with soot, his mouth and nose were crusted with blood, and he stank of burned hair and flesh. He calmly advised Dong Ha that the command group of 1/9 was dead, he could not locate his CO, and that he was assuming command. He handed me the handset and stepped back out of the cover. Dong Ha was both furious and baffled. Who was he, and why was he talking so openly on the radio? I explained that the caller was WIA and in shock. An unknown heavy-duty voice came over my radio and told me to find out the situation. I scrambled up to ground level to get the necessary answers. The command bunker was just a smoking hole swarming with a rescue party, all under fire.

The .50-caliber machine gun emplacement on top of my bunker had disappeared. The heavy machine gun and its bunker had simply vanished, swept away by something I didn't really want to think about. I returned to my radio and informed Dong Ha that the unknown wounded officer was probably correct.

Con Thien had suddenly become newsworthy. TV film crews scrambled up the hill, filmed a short clip of the smoke out on the DMZ, and then raced back to safety. Close enough. I doubt that any of them wanted to get any closer, even if allowed.

A large black lady in army fatigues knocked on my bunker and asked if there were any "Negro Marines" she could interview for *Jet* magazine. By that time, I hadn't slept in more than seventy-two hours and I thought I was beginning to hallucinate. I told her that Corporal Peacock would probably love to talk to her, but recent events had kept him stranded at Dong Ha. She heard "Peacock," thought I was nuts, and quickly departed. I don't blame her. I looked, smelled, and sounded very strange at the time. She wore no helmet nor flak jacket. Who the hell had directed her up to our hill? Was anyone alive down below or were they trying to kill the woman?

That same afternoon a pretty young Frenchwoman provided the perfect ending for my Con Thien experience. She sauntered up the hill, took photographs of some grunts, stripped off her blouse, and proceeded to give herself a topless sponge bath. The grunts were furious. They didn't feel that she was teasing them—they just thought it was a very unladylike thing to do. Their indignation was more sad than funny.

Corporal Peacock returned and we decided to move down the hill to an even more humble bunker position than we previously had; anyplace else was safer than that small summit. It was a wise move. Several days later I walked up to take a few slides of our former relay site and discovered that our Connex box on the Hill of Angels had been shredded by a large mortar round.

That's the way I recall my time in Vietnam.

13

U.S. Strategy
for Vietnam in 1967

During 1967 the American forces pursued two strategic aims in Vietnam. On the one hand they were determined to disrupt the buildup of NVA/VC main force strengths in the South by creating a protective shield of "free world" forces astride likely infiltration routes and destroying enemy formations that tried to break through. On the other, they recognized the need to clear existing communist bases in the South as a preliminary to more effective pacification.

The two aims were meant to be complementary: as U.S. main force units followed a policy designed to "find, fix, and destroy" their NVA/VC equivalents in the jungles and mountains of the border provinces, they would isolate in-country bases, denying the enemy the means to replenish material captured or destroyed in clearing operations. Once that happened the South Vietnamese could begin to provide security in the villages, persuading the ordinary people to support the Saigon government.

Unfortunately it did not work out like that, chiefly because the various strands could not be tied together. As 1967 progressed, Gen. William C. Westmoreland devoted more and more attention to militarily dramatic operations designed to destroy NVA/VC units in a deliberate war of attrition. The protective shield was gradually extended until its aim was not to cut off infiltration but to impose unacceptable losses on the forces of the North. Westmoreland summed it up: "We'll just go on bleeding them until Hanoi wakes up to the fact that they have bled their country to the point of national disaster for generations. Then they will have to reassess their position."* But as the North proved both willing and able to absorb the losses imposed, the obsession with "big battles" backfired. Too many U.S. units were concentrated on the shield, searching out the enemy main force units to such an extent that the village war, where the insurgency was taking place, was ignored.

Communist Strategy, 1967

Throughout 1967, as the full weight of U.S. commitment was brought to bear, communist units in South Vietnam were forced to adopt a more reactive role. Infiltration and subversion still took place, especially in areas less strongly defended by the ARVN, but in the key areas of confrontation—the northern provinces, the Central Highlands, and the approaches to Saigon—NVA and VC formations followed a policy of absorbing U.S. attacks, inflicting casualties as part of a strategy of attrition, and pulling back as soon as the pressure became too great.

This inevitably led to losses. In the area around Saigon, for example, the VC 9th Division, backed by elements of the NVA, was badly mauled during Operation Junction City. Although the Communists had mounted effective ambushes at Prek Klook and Ap Bau Bang in March, U.S. firepower had inflicted heavy casualties. As a result the VC pulled back to sanctuaries inside Cambodia.

The picture was much the same in the Central Highlands. The NVA 1st and 10th Divisions made life difficult for U.S. Army forces as the latter pushed into the western enclaves during Operations Sam Houston and Francis Marion. But by December the NVA 32d and 66th Regiments had virtually ceased to exist. Even in the northern provinces, where infiltration was the major aim, the establishment of Marine de-

---

*Stanley I. Cutler, ed., *The Encyclopedia of the Vietnam War,* Stanley I. Cutler (New York: Macmillan, 1996).

fenses south of the DMZ effectively blocked communist movement. Farther south the NVA 2d and 3d Divisions found the going tough.

But that did not mean that the Communists were anywhere close to defeat. On the contrary, their willingness to fight, accept casualties, and revert to guerrilla operations showed that they were continuing to oppose the American forces. Furthermore, by the end of the year General Giap had recognized that he would have to match his enemy in terms of commitment, and was already building up his forces for the Tet Offensive.

14

"Marines Should Know about This Thing Called Stingray"

By 1968, after nearly three years of combat in Vietnam, Marines who had seen action with either of the two reconnaissance battalions, or with the two force recon companies, wanted to share their observations with others. A "primary source" paper not only recorded those observations but allowed juniors, peers, and seniors to read about them, too. The following two chapter articles—the first on the importance of division recon capabilities, and the second on the Stingray concept—appeared in the pages of *Marine Corps Gazette* and *Proceedings of the United States Naval Institute*, respectively.

A Direction for Division Recon
by Maj. R. S. Kaye, USMC

The division recon battalion finally has emerged as an indispensable asset to Marine Corps tactical operations. It happened in Vietnam.

For years, thousands of Marines trained and conditioned themselves in the rigors and skills so frequently associated with "recon," SCUBA, escape and evasion, rubber boat drills, and rappelling. For years many commanders argued the relative merits of employing recon units. Some ignored the subject altogether. In most cases the procedure was simply to attach recon platoons or companies to infantry units and hope for the best. The results were frequently marginal, unproductive, and inconclusive. Little attention was paid to how, where, or why they would be employed. As a result they were frequently relegated to screening, CP, and perimeter security missions.

Two schools of thought dominated the subject of reconnaissance and its employment. The attachment or detachment method was popular. Another school pondered the general support concept. Proponents of this approach would put the battalion under the direct operational control and direction of the division commander. The flexibility this approach suggests found few takers outside the reconnaissance battalion. It was not until Vietnam that any serious thought was given to recon, its employment capabilities, potential, and limitations.

To understand this dilemma let's take a brief look at the battalion's history. The reconnaissance battalion was formed in 1957 to complement the dispersion concept. Facing a nuclear threat capability, planners envisioned a widely separated complex of tactical areas of responsibility (TAORs). Unfortunately, peace is a poor relation, and in the case of recon it fostered little opportunity to advance an active role. Although recon participated in many large and small operations, few were impressed with what the battalion could or couldn't do. Hampered by a lack of available helicopters, restrictions imposed by limited training areas, and general apathy on the part of commanders outside the battalion, Reconners were often left to their own devices. Training skills peculiar to recon continued. Clearly lacking was a *direction*.

Col. J. B. Carpenter Jr., a former CO of 3d Reconnaissance Battalion, commented in the March '63 issue of the *Gazette* ". . . there hasn't been, and probably never will be, a situation demanding use of the battalion in accordance with its formal mission." Events of recent years have overtaken this view, but I think it tends to highlight the obvious frustration of one who was required to command a reconnaissance battalion during its formative years.

If controversy be the mother of change, I think we can

credit it with prompting a significant modification to the T/O of the battalion. Changing little in relative strength, the battalion expanded from three to four companies in direct support and, at the same time, afforded the division commander a general support or special mission capability. A test of this newfound flexibility was not long in coming.

In Vietnam, recon Marines have been roaming the hills and valleys, the border country and the beaches, in search of the enemy. What they've accomplished tends to mitigate any opinions one may have had regarding recon and its employment. Why? In an effort to answer this question I have selected eight factors which relate directly to the battalion's present success and its future course in the years to come.

* The TAOR concept has been validated.

Tailored to a counterinsurgency environment, the principle of establishing tactical areas of responsibility has enabled Marine forces to stake their claim to huge areas of the Vietnam countryside. Limited manpower precludes a permanent occupation of the ground. Through the employment of a comprehensive system of observation, detection, and reporting, an acceptable level of control can be exercised. Reconnaissance, both ground and air, provides the division commander with needed information. Exploitation of the information provides the control.

* "Charlie" isn't there!

To succeed with the manpower resources we have available to us, we must know where "Charlie" *isn't*. Our ability to eliminate an area as a potential trouble spot is crucial to the planning and execution of effective operations. Knowing where he isn't allows us to concentrate our efforts and attention on those areas where his presence is either suspected or known. Why should the division commander commit his forces to an operation when the efforts of a team of recon Marines can eliminate the area through quiet hours of watching and listening?

* Operation Stingray is a success.

The joint venture of artillery and reconnaissance units in exploiting our artillery capability has been a resounding success. Tying recon directly to its supporting artillery, Stingray has maximized the effects of accurate and devastating fires at a time and place when it's least expected by the NVA or the Viet Cong. Stingray has successfully foiled many enemy operations by frustrating attempts to mass his forces. Beyond this, it must be disconcerting to a conscientious aggressor to have his hootch, training areas, or CP blown away by artillery which he believes to be twenty miles away. Exploitation of this concept has accounted for many thousands of enemy KIA and WIA. At the same time it has drastically reduced the loss of friendly forces.

* Survival presents no problem.

It has been shown, through years of experience in Vietnam, that small, well-equipped, and well-trained recon units can survive for extended periods of time in an unfriendly physical and enemy environment. Consistently, eight- and ten-man patrols have ventured into hostile country, stayed for five or six days, accomplished their mission, and returned. Mobility minimizes exposure of the unit and the helicopter to enemy fire during the critical insertion/extraction phase and maximizes the total coverage that we are permitted to give an area.

* Choppers make the difference.

A rationale for the success of the recon Stingray effort in Vietnam must include the helicopter. Speed, mobility, range, and the comforting thought that the chopper and the Marines who fly it can get you in and out of an LZ, combine to make it an indispensable tool. On countless occasions, helo pilots and their crews dared the fire of an enemy force in order to extract recon patrols from LZs deep in contested territory. The clear and simple fact is that we could not conduct a comprehensive recon effort without the helicopter. The nature of the terrain and the critical element of time preclude any other approach.

* Communication presents no problem.

The success of a recon mission, like most other operations, depends largely on communications. The object is intelligence. Continuous and reliable communications ensure that the information gathered reaches the user in sufficient time to permit exploitation. In the case of Stingray, it is a crucial element in a system of effective fire support. An example may help illustrate the point.

To support the 1st Reconnaissance Battalion in Chu Lai, RVN, a series of [radio] relay stations was established. The system consisted of three primary and three secondary stations. This permitted in-depth coverage of the entire TAOR and extended the reliable operating range of our radios out to a distance of thirty miles. Tied into this system were three batteries of general support artillery. Stationed at each battery FDC (Fire Direction Center) was a two-man team of recon communicators whose sole mission was to relay fire support requests from recon teams in the field. To round out the system, three recon communicators were stationed at the division Fire Support Coordination Center. Special operations call for special measures. When existing means failed to satisfy the requirements for long-range communications (thirty to fifty miles), airborne radio-relay was employed. Sandwiched in between all this were the Aerial Observers and the helos, who also provided radio relay services. Innovation, imagination, and superior equipment have contributed a free rein in exploiting our reconnaissance capabilities.

* **Sorry, no sanctuary, "Charlie."**

The no-sanctuary approach to tactics, employed throughout I Corps, has been instrumental in keeping the enemy off balance. For years, the sanctuary of the backcountry has meant survival and recovery to the Viet Cong. A place to train, rest, and recuperate has been denied the enemy. Aggressive search and clear missions, coupled with a comprehensive reconnaissance effort, make "Charlie" unhappy.

* **Economy of force—a by-product.**

A natural by-product of a successful reconnaissance effort is economy of force. Ability to close with and destroy the enemy is keyed to balanced combat power. Knowing the location, strength, and intentions of the opposition gives us this capability. Reconnaissance is an essential element in providing us with the tools to find the enemy and successfully defeat him. Beyond the obvious benefits of economy, the characteristics of the present approach to recon employment in Vietnam must be evaluated in terms of the future. We face the prospect of continued commitment to conflicts in a counterinsurgency environment. The success realized thus far is incontrovertible. The task now is to crystallize and mold this success into a plan for the future. The guerrilla chose the tactics. Unconventional, hit-and-run, choice of ground tactics have been his bag. We know now that we can beat him at his own game.

Our direction is obvious. We must refine the capability which we now possess. Sophistication in our means of insertion, reporting, surveillance, and detection are areas which need our attention. The new and exciting world of sensors may provide some of the answers. Serious thought should be given to enlarging the size of the battalion to meet the increased demand for reconnaissance. General support is the current and correct approach. A centralized reconnaissance effort will place the emphasis where it belongs. Find the enemy first: then destroy him.

15

Stingray '70

by
Francis J. West Jr.

In ancient battles the principle of mass led to organizational cohesion and tactical strength. The Roman soldier marching in the phalanx knew that his flanks and rear were protected by the shoulder-to-shoulder formation. As long as a unit remained tightly knit, it was least vulnerable and its chances of victory over less tactically cohesive enemies were highest. Modern weapons have upset this balance. The principle of mass now leads to organizational confusion and tactical vulnerability. Each man in a firefight is safest when he seeks individual cover and concealment. Men on the march are vulnerable precisely because they feel secure. In the scattering effect of the initial battle, control over units decreases in proportion to the size and intensity of the engagement.

The honored battle principle of mass should not be applicable axiomatically to Vietnam, or to any future conflict involving American forces. In the nineteenth century and the first half of the twentieth, masses of men were needed to supply with their rifles the volume of firepower necessary to establish fire superiority, inflict substantial enemy casualties, and ensure victory on the battlefield. The place of manpower in the causality of these events is now severely questionable.

If the objective is simply to wear down the enemy main forces, then in examining the course of engagements, one should distinguish between what may be called "involved presence" and "proximate presence." When, for instance, a battalion mounts a search-and-destroy operation, it is not the battalion commander's intention that all one thousand of his men engage the enemy simultaneously. Indeed, it is his fervent hope that this does not occur; for if it does he is most probably in the midst of an enemy ambush and has lost control of his troops. A commander posts point and flank elements to avoid the simultaneous and sizable engagement of his troops. When contact is made, he wishes to let the situation develop slowly, so that he can identify enemy intentions and strengths and then commit his forces carefully and under control.

Of course, the confusion of real battle generally twists the concepts of control and measured response. But, both in theory and in practice, a unit of a hundred men or more almost never intends to or actually does commit all its riflemen to the battle in one fell swoop. There is a distinct time lag in the development of engagements, either offensive or defensive, which allows an observer to characterize chronologically and spatially the participants in terms of either involved presence or proximate presence.

To traditional military strategists, this distinction was of little importance for operational planning since the forces necessary for victory had to be massed within striking distance. In the past, troop mobility was so slow that the only way to ensure the proximate presence of soldiers for reasons of firepower and replacements was to travel in large units. Although the commander may have intended that only a minority of his troops would become involved initially, he had to have a large backup force physically close at hand in order to command and control them. The proximate presence deployment had to be measured in terms of meters; reinforcements many miles distant were of no use at all, for they could not converge on the battlefield rapidly enough to be of any use.

This principle of proximate mass still holds true for the North Vietnamese. For the Americans time has largely replaced space as the crucial factor determining the position of those forces needed as the proximate presence. The gradual development of a firefight from the time of initial contact to the time when the situation is that of involved presence is generally sufficient to allow relief, first by fire support and second by reinforcements.

The means of mobility, communications, and firepower at the disposal of American forces represent major technological breakthroughs in the tools of warfare. Although these breakthroughs mainly have been adapted to the task of making traditional tactics and maneuvers more easily executed, they have also raised the possibility of some revisions in organizational structure and unit missions, as the evidence mounts that for certain tasks several small units are more effective than one large unit.

One set of such small units is the strike teams. Strike team is a generic term used to describe a variety of friendly units in Vietnam whose common characteristics are smallness in size, missions in enemy areas, concealment in movement, surprise in attack, and suddenness in withdrawal. Strike teams include among other elements the two U.S. Marine Corps reconnaissance battalions in I Corps, the hundreds of U.S. Army Long-range Reconnaissance Patrols (LRRP) in I, II, and III Corps, the Australian Special Air Service (SAS) in III Corps, several Special Forces detachments working in the Central Highlands with the Vietnamese irregular defense groups, the Vietnamese provincial reconnaissance units, and the U.S. Navy Sea-Air-Land commando (SEAL) platoons in III and IV Corps.

Strike teams have been growing in terms of total numbers and acquired skills since the spring of 1965. They represent a classic case of strategy slowly evolving from tried tactics. When Marine reconnaissance platoons, for instance, first were sent out into the hills of I Corps, their mission was to find and report the location of enemy units; the infantry battalions would then do the fighting. This tactic did not work well. Recon found enemy soldiers but not units; the enemy preferred to travel dispersed during the daytime, that period when recon could observe their presence. The common sighting of two, three, five, and seven enemy infantry did not warrant the commitment of a battalion. For the sake of morale of his recon units, Lt. Gen. Lewis W. Walt, then commanding general of III Marine Amphibious Force, allowed the recon teams to begin shooting the enemy from ambush, using air and artillery whenever possible so as not to expose their own positions. Thus were born the strike teams in I Corps.

At the same time and under similar bureaucratic conditions, the Navy SEALs were starting to stalk the guerrillas along the waterways of III and IV Corps. Again, it was a case of not knowing quite what to expect. As one SEAL put it, "When we first started going out small at night, guys from regular units told us the Viet Cong would just eat us up. I can remember sitting in muck up to my neck being eaten alive by mosquitoes but afraid to move because I had been told the Viet Cong were everywhere."

Exactly what these small teams, be they Army, Navy, or Marines, were to do, or how they were to do it, could not be mapped out ahead of time by senior staffs. There was no body of experience directly applicable. With doctrine lagging, strike teams blazed their own tactical way. While their main assignments have been to find and to wear down the enemy, their specific missions, deployments, and growth rates have depended more upon operational factors than predetermined objectives.

The first and most obvious factor was the *enemy*. The initial forays of the strike teams often caught the enemy at great disadvantage. In the summer of 1966, for instance, my assignment as a tactical analyst for the Marine Corps took me to the DMZ, where the first large operation against the North Vietnamese 324B Division was being mounted. Rather than join one of the five infantry battalions engaging the enemy, I joined a force reconnaissance team. The five of us were given a simple mission: get into the bush, find the enemy, and destroy him if you can.

At dawn on a windy morning a helicopter dropped us five miles east of Khe Sanh and we quickly moved off into the jungle. For two days we moved through the thick undergrowth, staying well hidden, occasionally hearing the enemy chopping wood or shouting back and forth, once at mid-evening seeing lanterns bobbing down a valley floor. By the third morning we knew where their battalion bivouac area was and called in artillery fire. To escape, the North Vietnamese had to cross a wide stream; first a few crossed, then dozens, then scores. That was where the artillery caught and annihilated them. Chased by a North Vietnamese Army platoon, we left the scene at top speed and before we could be overtaken or hemmed in, jet fighters were scrambled and they erased the pursuit force. Following the debrief, General Walt and his G-3, Col. John C. Chaisson Jr., decided that such missions merited a special section in the reporting system and chose for the strike teams the operational code name of "Stingray." The operation itself remained classified until 1968.

The strike teams wedded individual training and initiative with advanced technology; five men with one radio had the firepower of a regiment at their disposal. The same idea was occurring to others, including Brig. Gen. Willard Pearson, U.S. Army, who often so deployed major elements from his brigade of the 101st Airborne Division.

But the NVA was learning, too. One simple counter was dispersal, since hitting a moving point target is difficult given the indirect-fire weapons, problems of circular error probability (CEP), map coordinate estimates, and short response times.

To cover some large movements the NVA took to sending out its own counterstrike teams, which roamed like destroyers around a convoy. These flankers could sweep aside small units; it cost the enemy, however, his previous advantage of invisible movement, for its pattern indicated his shifts. And in some other areas the enemy was so thick and entrenched that he could mass firepower against helicopters called in for extractions. Strike teams were loath to enter locales where infrared detection readouts indicated large enemy forces, because they learned from experience that the enemy had come to expect strike teams and planned accordingly. In the A Shau Valley and along the DMZ, for instance, the enemy by 1967 had adapted to our strike teams and sent small outguard patrols roving the sides of the hills looking for Marines. The Marines did not fear the initial contact, however, since the opposing force was generally of their own size and they could usually settle these engagements satisfactorily with their M-16s. It was the subsequent piling-on tactics that they hated. For once the firefight began, other enemy units moved in. If the team was lucky it broke contact and escaped from the area. If not, it had to defend itself until reinforced or extracted by helicopter.

Other strike teams faced other enemies. Lt. Gen. William A. Peers, commanding I Army Field Force in II Corps, found an added bonus in using LRRPs [long-range reconnaissance patrols]. Not only were they seekers and harassers of encroaching NVA units, they were pinging away at two Viet Cong local-force battalions which had proved too elusive for entrapment by large U.S. units. In the Mekong Delta, SEAL platoons sometimes were even more selective, targeting individual members of the Viet Cong political apparatus. In short, strike teams cut across the spectrum of enemy forces.

The second factor which affected the operations of strike teams was *terrain*, defined demographically. Between 60 and 70 percent of Vietnam is unpopulated wilderness. In the sharp hills of I Corps, Marine recon teams frequently used hidden observation posts from which to call air and artillery fire upon unsuspecting enemy groups. Even when the enemy presence was thick and encounters were at short range, the small-arms effectiveness of strike teams matched their ability in using supporting arms, as the dozens of patrols and hasty ambushes in the scrub growth of the DMZ north of Dong Ha attested.

The kill ratio was the most ballyhooed statistic quoted in regard to reconnaissance. This ratio was partially a function of terrain but mostly a function of tactics, especially of the principles of concealment and surprise. In the denser jungles of II Corps and the flatter forests of III Corps, the Army's LRRPs and Australian SAS relied more on trail ambushes using small arms and claymore mines. In many sections,

long-range visibility was not possible. Then it became an Indian war. There, too, the strike teams kept the balance of casualty exchange far in their favor since surprise was on their
side in the majority of encounters. In all three corps, Stingray
operations were generally conducted in areas with little or no
villager population, and the teams relied upon the bush to
hide from the enemy.

The [Mekong] Delta was a different case altogether, however, since there the population density was high and the
amount of vegetation concealment low. So the SEALs substi-
tuted the night for the jungle and the boat for the helicopter.
By using the waterways they had a substantial selection of
entry points and could conduct comparatively discreet insertions. By using the darkness they could proceed to their ambush sites undetected, even when they moved near or within a
hamlet.

There are essential differences between the strike patrols
and the ordinary small-unit patrols conducted by U.S. forces
in the populated areas. In fact, the roles of the opposing
forces are exactly reversed. In the populated areas, friendly
forces must patrol constantly to prevent enemy infiltration,
and they must carry on the administrative routines of supply,
communications, and travel. Thus, their daily exposure factor
is high and the chance of meeting the enemy low. The strike
teams, however, are guerrillas in the enemy area. Whether
the enemy is carrying on a daily routine or simply resting, he
feels safe and secure in his own area. He then becomes the
hunted for these silent teams.

Mobility constituted the third operational factor for the
strike teams. Mobility took two levels—first, to avoid patterns detectable by the enemy there had to be an element of
nonconsistency in the insertion and area coverage frequency
of strike teams.

Since the ability of the enemy to mass clandestinely or
swiftly could not often be predicted with sufficient geograph-
ical specificity, the strike teams added a second level of mobility. This counter was footpower, a willingness to get up and

get away after making a hit or when the enemy seemed alerted and strong.

Whereas a large unit often endeavors to inflict as many casualties as possible regardless of the cost to itself, a strike team endeavors to inflict as many casualties as it can on the enemy at no cost to itself. Like the Viet Cong, strike teams will try to refuse contact when they don't like the situation. The size and high conditioning level of the teams make pursuit of them fruitless and dangerous. Seven men can squirm through brush that will stop a company; in other situations they back off into the night. For the enemy to plunge unplanned into pursuit has invited them into hasty ambushes, confronted them with tear gas, and made them vulnerable to claymore mines with delay fuses.

Reaction forces were the fourth operational factor. Passive defense by evacuation did not always work. When a strike team had to go to ground, it needed help, and it was crucial that whatever assistance was required to save a team was forthcoming. By their actions, senior commanders in all services have keenly manifested this attitude. The most spectacular example of this awareness occurred one night in June 1966, when an eighteen-man Marine reconnaissance patrol (S.Sgt. Jimmie Howard's patrol) was surrounded on a hilltop by an NVA regiment and attacked repeatedly. During that long night, reaction forces included a U.S. Army Special Forces team and their South Vietnamese gunners pounding the hillside with artillery; continuous sorties by U.S. Air Force and Marine fixed-wing aircraft expending over twenty-five hundred items of ordnance; a Navy destroyer standing by offshore to deliver fire support from five-inch guns; and a Marine infantry battalion called into the attack at first light. When the siege was broken at noon, the strike team had taken six fatalities, and earned one Medal of Honor, two Navy Crosses, fifteen Silver Stars, and eighteen Purple Hearts. The leader of the strike team told the first Marine from the reaction force to reach his position, "Buddy, I never expected to see the sun rise. When it did, I knew you'd be coming."

A strike team is not independent; its members must feel that they belong to a powerful system that cares. A team member must have a high degree of confidence in himself, in the other team members, and in the system that backs him and puts him out there in the first place.

Reaction forces tie in directly with the fifth factor which affects the operation of the strike teams: the *training* and *attitude* of the strike teams. Until recently, the question had remained unanswered whether large bodies of troops could ever be trained and supported to fight a war using the strike team concept, combining superior individual jungle skills with sophisticated equipment. The techniques, the mission, and the training threatened to remain relegated to the very few, stamped "nontransferable." Thus, awe, pride, and resentment inhibited emulation. The belief was widespread that strike team training and tactics could not be successfully applied to regular infantry battalions.

While commanding the U.S. Army 4th Infantry Division in II Corps in 1967, however, General Peers proved differently. He adopted the small teams on a division-wide scale, and his division included a substantial percentage of two-year draftees. It was important that they believe they could do the job, and that they were not really all alone. The division went on to establish an extraordinary record.

And by 1967, the Marines who came to reconnaissance were not handpicked; they were simply assigned as they would have been to any other infantry unit.

Not all men adapted, but over 90 percent of them did. There was no difference between the young recruit placed into an infantry battalion and the one sent to a reconnaissance battalion. They were sorted out according to the numbers needed. Reconnaissance Marines had no difficulty with the recruits. They kept them, when they could, for the first few weeks in garrison at Dong Ha or Da Nang, to train them, particularly in reading maps and calling in fire. Even then they didn't have the time to do this in all cases. So many young privates learned the way soldiers do in every war—by keeping

His face covered in camouflage paint, Marine PFC Robert L. Scheidel looks out on the landing zone for his Stingray team from inside a Boeing Vertol CH-46 Sea Knight helicopter. Note the smoke cannisters strapped to his chest. (Abel Collection)

3D RECONNAISSANCE BATTALION
11 JULY 1968-12 DECEMBER 1968

	Jul	Aug	Sep	Oct	Nov	Dec	Total
No. of Patrols	133	147	143	165	158	105*	851
Average Duration	2.13	2.05	2.00	3.18	2.60	2.89	2.77
Average Size	6.00	6.61	6.72	7.22	7.10	6.50	6.72
No. of Sightings	45	54	78	71	55	20	323
No. of Enemy Sighted	288	778	508	289	314	114	2291
No. of Contacts	20	52	52	34	31	22	211
No. of Fire Missions	16	28	39	64	64	22	233
No. of Rounds Fired	416	1203	911	1749	1363	849	5891
No. of Air Strikes	5	14	5	24	3	5	56
Enemy KIA (C)	00	00	102	25	23	13	248
Enemy Captured	0	0	0	1	0	0	1
Weapons Captured	2	5	8	0	7	1	23
Friendly KIA	4	1	5	1	3	1	15
Friendly WIA	26	5	20	4	6	8	69

* Includes 31 teams deployed in the field as of 12 December 1968

Chart provided by LtCol Donald R. Berg USMC (Ret).

Chart provided by Lt. Col. Donald R. Berg, USMC (Ret.)

A patrol from Company B, 3d Reconnaissance Battalion, moves along a trail south of the Demilitarized Zone in search of evidence of North Vietnamese infiltration into Quang Tri Province. (Department of Defense Photo [USMC] A192449)

Concealing himself in a grove of bamboo, a reconnaissance Marine surveys the terrain and directs artillery and air strikes on enemy troops and base camps. (Department of Defense Photo [USMC] A192444)

NVA weapons cache discovered by Stingray, 1967.

Dressed for "every occasion," Force Recon Marines from 1st Force show the diversity of uniforms and equipment, 1968.

Team Record, 1st Force Recon Company, November 1968. The poster of Uncle Ho was found in a large satchel near the body of a dead NVA officer. Team Record was credited with knocking out two anti-aircraft guns and killing thirteen NVA soldiers on that mission.

Radio operator L.Cpl. Mike McKenna at Con Thien, 1967.

Marines from 3d Force Recon Company at Phu Bai, 1969.

Marines from 3d Platoon, 3d Force Recon, preparing to leave Phu Bai for a Stingray mission, January 1970.

The author, HM3 Bruce H. Norton, with 3d Force Recon at Phu Bai, 1969.

Recon Marines from 1st Recon Battalion practice ladder extraction beneath a CH-46 helicopter just outside Da Nang, 1968.

Recon Marines from 1st Force on the beach at Chu Lai, 1965. Note the M3-A1 grease gun and WWII-style camouflage utilities.

Capt. "Reb" Bearce, MSMC, prior to a para-scuba jump, 1965. Capt. Bearce is credited with starting the Vietnam War.

Lt. Gen. Herman Nickerson Jr. in an official U.S. Marine Corps photo, 1970. Reconnaissance Marines nicknamed him the Godfather of Long-Range Patrolling.

1st Lt. Clovis C. "Bucky" Coffman Jr., operations officer, 3d Force Reconnaissance Company. (Courtesy Colonel Coffman)

Major Lee (left) and Lieutenant Coffman (center) enjoy a moment of relaxation with their mentor, General Nickerson, at Phu Bai, 1970. (Courtesy Bruce Norton)

L.Cpl. Charles T. Sexton, who was awarded the Navy Cross, poses in front of 3d Force Recon's ammo bunker at Phu Bai, February 1970.

Lt. Col. Alex Lee in an official U.S. Marine Corps photo, 1974.

Marines from 1st Force Recon Company, Camp Pendleton, California, wearing current capability equipment, 1969. Left to right: scuba rebreather, halo-ops, direct action, ground reconnaissance gear.

their mouths shut and following the lead of experienced team members.

To all new men the same line was preached: "You'll stay alive in recon, even if the work is harder than in the infantry units." It was a good selling point. General Peers emphasized this point to each of his LRRP graduating classes. While many men were scared in the bush, they knew they were safer there.

This factor of lower friendly casualties is a most important reason for evaluating the strike team performance and potential. The strike team work is more nerve-racking but less deadly than infantry work. The reconnaissance troops know this; and it makes a significant morale difference, especially since a reconnaissance Marine knows his survival depends largely on himself. He often has a distinct say in what his team does or does not do.

These operational factors set the parameters within which the strike teams could work, and delimited the objectives which the teams could accomplish. It became obvious that the strike teams had severe limitations. In fact, the concept was inapplicable to the fundamental missions of conventional warfare: strike teams could not hold terrain and they could not destroy the enemy forces. They traded terrain for survival, being most vulnerable when the enemy knew where they were, being safest when the enemy assumed the land belonged to him. While they occasionally disrupted an enemy unit to a major degree, as in the DMZ incident related above, most usually hoped to just sting and run.

These distinct limitations of the strike teams are implicit to their Fabian style. Cast in the mode of guerrillas in enemy areas, however, the strike teams have displayed three relative advantages over larger units. First, as one might suspect, their rate of contact is significantly higher. Engagements and attrition of the enemy, when measured on a per-man basis, have shown that the strike teams of all three services are more productive by these criteria than larger conventional units.

Second, contrary to popular belief, decentralization can decrease vulnerability. For three years, regular U.S. infantry battalions have suffered significantly higher casualties in proportion to those suffered by the strike teams of any of the three services. In fact, strike teams are often reluctant to move in groups of over a dozen men, believing that the larger size means noise, exposure, discovery, fire, casualties, and frustrated evacuations. When a battalion (or larger) operation is mounted, most often the telltale signs are there for the enemy to read: preinvasion air and artillery strikes on the objective, large convoys of men and supplies, unusual air activity, etc. Once on the ground near the objective, concealment is still the role of the enemy and exposure that of the allied forces. Tactically, this deprives the battalion of the element of surprise and leaves the opening round up to the enemy.

A large unit (a hundred men or more) on the move can forsake concealment for cover, which hopefully is provided in deterrent form by the suppressive capability of its firepower. The strike teams make it their business to disappear as fast as possible once they are in Viet Cong areas. They must cling to concealment, be it the jungle or the night; survival motivates them.

The size of the strike team represents nothing more than the economic principle of optimum productivity. Given as their mission the attrition of the enemy, and allowed to use (in strict moderation) the tools of technology, additional patrol members beyond the five to ten needed for watchstanding, defense, and first-burst ambushes have below-average productivity.

Third, in keeping with their reconnaissance aspects, the terrain coverage of strike teams is considerable. Deployed shrewdly and debriefed properly, the information collected by the strike teams can be collated and, together with other intelligence reports, be used to establish patterns of enemy activity and movement.

Over the past three years the actual performance of the strike teams has indicated the operation factors and their limitations. This history also points out two complementary missions to which the strike teams could be set so as to maximize their relative advantage, if a substantial number of strike teams were to be organized and incorporated into a strategic framework for Vietnam. These missions are harassment and surveillance.

The means to harassment is attrition. Although some important enemy cadres may occasionally be eliminated, attrition by strike teams does not imply the gradual destruction of the enemy. (Destruction is the rate of attrition minus the rate of regeneration.) Attrition would be undertaken not for the sake of kill ratios or other statistics, but for its psychological effects upon the enemy. The intent would be to lower the morale of the enemy in his own backyard. During the past year, especially, prisoner interrogations have revealed that many enemy units are aware they have been stalked by small teams with sudden ambushes and massive fire support, and that this awareness has unsettled them.

Harassment also restricts the enemy's movement, as some areas of enemy passage are no longer cost-free. The precedent is the Viet Cong's brilliant use of mines in certain GVN (government of Vietnam) areas. When American units start losing men week after week, without any pattern, without warning, without any solid contact, morale goes down and down. There is a distinct qualitative difference in how casualties are sustained, which affects how a unit fights and feels. It becomes difficult to persuade the troops that there is reason sufficient to justify the steady patrolling of certain areas. Once mine-shy, units will avoid the bad places or enter them only with great reluctance. Harassment of the enemy could effect a similar channelization.

The morale of a unit is affected worse by constant small attrition than by a few major engagements. Those who survive major engagements once or perhaps twice a year have the intervening several months to reorganize, recruit, retrain, and rest. This is not so when the pressure is constant and the casualties consistent, for then each man wonders each day if it is his turn. Confidence in the leaders wanes and critical questions about the wisdom of their tactics and strategy arise.

Enemy countertactics to the strike teams should be considered a gain if they raise his exposure factor or if they tie up resources otherwise of offensive use to him.

This recognized but unpredictable sort of harassment also affects the attitudes of the villagers and the morale of the GVN officials. Although the contact rate and attrition figures may be low, if the strike teams generate operations consistently, the word spreads through the rural communities: the GVN or the Americans are moving in small units against the Viet Cong. The SEALs, for instance, have been known to sneak into a hamlet in the dead of night, burst into a house, and shake their man awake. This arrest technique has had a psychological impact throughout the Delta far exceeding its actual accomplishments. The word had gone out from province to province: There are Americans with green and black faces who come from the water in the middle of the night to seize the VC. It is very unsettling to a VC to think he cannot come home at night to visit his wife. The reputation of the SEALs has far exceeded their physical capabilities. (There just are not that many of them, and the Delta holds over five million people.) The odds are very low that they would actually break down many doors in any given year. Yet the fact that they have done it successfully has set the Viet Cong on edge in many provinces.

The utility of strike teams is thus partially measurable by the extent to which gossip and repetition foster their reputation for invisible ubiquity. The intent would be to deter from active support to the enemy those fence-sitters who now cooperate because the penalty for refusal is higher than for compliance. If rice movement at night, for instance, were to run the unknown risk of ambush, many nondedicated activists in Viet Cong areas would try to desist.

The second major mission of strike teams is surveillance. Around several of the major cities, screens of strike teams are deployed with the object of picking up any signs of the enemy massing within attack distance of the urban centers. In large measure, strike teams can remove the burden of searching from conventional units conducting search-and-destroy operations. When lucrative enemy targets are found, battalion exploitation forces could be thrown in on spoiling operations. This use of strike teams could relieve many battalions that are tied up and yet not actively engaged. To this end strike teams are an economy of force measure which permits a higher proportion of American forces to be reallocated in keeping with more important tasks, such as developing a rural area security system which the GVN can gradually take over.

At first it was by trial and error that the strike teams learned. Later, however, institutionalized memories within units emerged as the men, naturally close, swapped sea stories, extracted lessons, wrote them down, and passed them along verbally and by example to newcomers. Desire for knowledge also led to interservice training. Australian SAS members have accompanied SEALs to learn their techniques, and Marine recon people have accompanied the SAS, and the Army LRRPs have accompanied Marine recon teams.

These innovations and accrued knowledge have proceeded so far in the absence of strategic doctrine—and in cases like the SEALs, perhaps because of it. When tactics prove themselves, however, it is time to extract the concepts and construct the doctrine to test for future applicability and influence on force structures.

To a future ground warfare conflict between modernized nations, the strike teams could by their small size bring the initial advantage of front-line target dispersal and by their radios bring the impact of massed firepower on troops in conventional formations. When the Viet Cong slam rockets into an American division headquarters, that is in keeping with the strike team concept.

And relating to future conflicts of a lower scale on the spectrum of warfare, institutionalization of strike teams would bring to the policymaker added selectivity in military instruments. The British actions in Sarawak and northern Malaysia over the past four years exemplify the use of unobtrusive small units. Strike teams apply force in a restrained manner. Discrimination in the selection of point targets is not an effect attributable to any comparatively enlightened morality on the part of the strike teams: it comes as a function of specificity. Infrared might read out a village, whereas five men staking out a trail select a man. And, of course, the structuring of forces to include flexibility in the use of strike teams relates to the development of a military option, not to a prior argument for its future use.

The present use of strike teams, however, is another matter. Many commanders still believe the role of small units in enemy areas is pure reconnaissance.

The history and military tradition of western nations have emphasized the dominant role of large units and mighty battles in determining the outcome of wars. Despite whatever lip service might have been paid to the tactical tenets of guerrilla warfare, the temptation remained to do most what one knew best, had studied the longest, and was best equipped for, mentally and materially: large-unit war. Many battalion commanders put an arbitrary time frame on the war: the number of months they had command. The central issue often became combat for the sake of combat, recognition, and reward. In a way the Army of Vietnam (ARVN) and Viet Cong commanders were more rational in choosing to refuse combat unless trapped or clearly holding an advantage. Now it is very true that the battalions have to perform a variety of missions and cannot always afford to be as discriminating as reconnaissance, but that does not lessen the validity of comparisons where the missions are the same, or the validity of questioning the concepts which underlie the missions.

The fascination with the individual battalion engagement is understandable on the part of the battalion commander and the press. For the commander, battle brings pride to his unit and to himself. For the press, a battalion action is large enough to guarantee footage back home and small enough to allow a summing-up editorial. At another level, however, engagements must be rated and alternatives weighed in keeping with known constraints and feasible goals.

The dilemma of deciding the worth and the opportunity cost of strike teams has a direct parallel in a naval operations research problem of World War II, wherein a study to destroy enemy shipping took as its criterion of performance the ratio of enemy ships sunk to U.S. man-years of effort. This criterion was discarded as misleading since sinking was only one of several means of preventing shipping and since man-years was only one of several means of measuring costs.

Similarly, the fascination with individual engagements in Vietnam has led to insistence upon a numerical parity or superiority that is not relevant for engagements against an unfixed enemy who will move. Attempts to minimize risks in each individual case can thereby lead to more casualties for lesser gain in the aggregate. Any given strike team runs the risk of being completely wiped out—an eventuality no battalion need worry about. Yet the average infantryman's chances of survival are twice as great in a strike team as in a battalion, while that same strike team member will inflict *six times* as many casualties upon the enemy.

A correct understanding of the problem and of the constraints should, although does not necessarily, precede the means taken to ensure a solution. A transition from the historical naval example to a fantasy might help explain the point. Suppose that in 1966 an American general had information that fifteen thousand troops from the NVA 324B Division were massing in the DMZ to swoop down upon Quang Tri City and "liberate" it. Suppose the general decided to let them come down into the flatlands, and proposed further that the 1st Air Cavalry Division be poised to cut the NVA division off from the mountains to the west while a Marine division made an amphibious landing from the east. Suppose the plan was approved enthusiastically by MACV and forwarded to Washington, the argument being that the proposed destruction of an elite enemy division would probably curtail any such future NVA invasion plans. Appalled, Washington rejects the plan and questions the sanity of the proposing general—on the grounds that Tarawa proved almost insupportable even in the crusade atmosphere of World War II, and that in Vietnam several hundred and perhaps thousands of

American deaths within a framework of one or two days cannot be sustained politically.

This fantasy should point out the futility of constraints and the wisdom of commanders who can properly identify the problem and structure the operations of their forces accordingly. It is not the author's intent to freeze force structure capabilities by suggesting that the Stingray style is axiomatically applicable in Vietnam or anywhere else. It is to suggest that strike teams ought to be an option added to the more established deployments and tactics. Whether the troops are then so used depends upon the commander's reading of the problem and the constraints within which he must move forward toward a solution. To add flavor to the platitudinous air of the last statement, the author would say that, from his observation, troop use in Vietnam far too frequently followed the risk minimization of indeterminate single-battalion sweeps when the more recent combination of strike teams and multibattalion cordons were markedly preferable within the context of the problem. Small-unit actions were looked on as an adjunct or an aid to a large-unit strategy, not as an alternative. But the tactics of the engagements, the technological potential for manpower substitution, and the political nature of the conflict indicated the wisdom of wider adoption of the Stingray method.

Moreover, there may be an additional role for strike teams to play—if and when a mutual U.S./North Vietnamese Army troop withdrawal is agreed upon in Paris. Strike teams then may be called upon to monitor the exfiltration routes. While infrared, side-looking radar and other technological devices can perhaps bring in the bulk of the evidence about such movements, the human element of strike team surveillance is both an added check and, to the press, also a more credible witness. This could be crucial in a situation wherein the strongest sanction for the North Vietnamese to comply with a mutual withdrawal pact might be the expectancies of world opinion, as mirrored and stirred by the press.

In Vietnam the crucial question now is not whether to use strike teams, but rather how many to use and for what ends.

Set to the objectives of harassment and surveillance, as outlined above, the strike teams have exhibited two strong relative advantages over larger, more conventional units: they can perform those tasks using fewer men, and with a lower casualty rate. Any such sub-optimized set of strike team objectives could have meaning only if it were placed within an overall Vietnam strategy in keeping with friendly performances, enemy capabilities, and political realities. Since this strategy does not seem to exist, lacking therefore also are rational criteria by which the strike teams could be judged and accorded strategic status and force deployment in keeping with their tactical worth.

Since I do not accept the strategy of attrition as a valid and attainable war objective, it must be made very clear that I believe the merit of strike teams does not lie simply in their ability to accomplish attrition more economically. I see strike teams as just one part of an overall strategy, part of a time-buying process while the South Vietnamese forces are being reshaped and a strong area security system is being established within the populated area.

In a war where there is a definite need to hold territory or to seize area objectives, a considerable number of troops is needed. But where the objective is to punish and prevent access to an enemy, the number of troops employed in the task could in large measure depend upon the tactics chosen. The Stingray concept, with its offensive power, psychological impact, and defensive elusiveness, has called into question, for certain objectives, traditional tactics and the classic ratios of friendly to enemy forces.

Military planners now must devise a Vietnam strategy that will ensure both a U.S. troop reduction and a decrease in fatalities. Since the enemy has demonstrated that he can drive up the level of U.S. fatalities, it is fallacious to assume that casualties will be automatically reduced proportionate to troop withdrawals. Therefore, to continue the current programs unchanged—attrition of the enemy, improvement of ARVN, and protection of the cities—by the same input mix of activities, i.e., battalion sweeps and platoon patrols, while hoping for casualty reduction is to assume benevolence or exhaustion on the part of the enemy.

Not all U.S. programs and activities, however, are equally susceptible to enemy pressure. More than most other activities, Stingray operations control the level of friendly casualties. Strike teams operate from large, secure ground and sea bases; they select the times, the means, and places of entry; and they, not the enemy, choose whether to engage. The Stingray mode has been used in all four Corps areas for over three years in the face of various enemy force levels. Friendly casualties have remained remarkably low despite determined and diverse enemy countertactics.

Control of casualties, of course, is a constraint in terms of cost-benefit analysis. It is rather like trying to work within a fixed budget for optimum effect, a contradiction of the traditional war strategy which fixed objectives rather than costs.

On the effect-side of the balance sheet, Stingray operations should be conducted so as to affect both the enemy and the armed forces of the GVN. The effects related to the enemy are surveillance and psychological as well as physical harassment. The effect upon the GVN may well be even more critical. The dilemma facing top U.S. decision-makers is how to de-Americanize the war while strengthening the morale of the GVN to meet the strong challenge of its adversaries. The SEALs have proven that Stingray, as seen from the enemy's point of view, can be dramatic as well as physically telling. The judicious employment of Stingray in 1970 toward ARVN could be similar in psychological scope but opposite in effect. The purpose would be to let ARVN troops see with their own eyes that U.S. troops were still willing to go anywhere at any time, even in small units. The basic rule of thumb would be: invisibility while on operations; visibility before and after operations. The intent would be to foster among both the enemy and the South Vietnamese Army a reputation for Stingray ubiquity and utility.

Thus far, missions and resources have been allocated to the strike teams in an *ad hoc*, tactical, decentralized fashion. Their growth has been impeded by tradition, organizational incentives, and above all a satisfied feeling that no radical changes in force structure or missions were needed in Vietnam. In a period of increasing constraints and uncertainty, however, careful planning and centralized control become imperative if chaos is to be avoided. Given planning and analysis, 1970 should see Stingray teams augmented in size and activity in order that they may play a major strategic role in keeping with their comparative advantages of low friendly casualties, ally morale-boosting, and enemy harassment and surveillance.

16

Employing the Recon Patrol: 1968

By Maj. Gen. R. G. Davis and Lt. J. L. Jones Jr.

"The conflict of stealth vs. force has been resolved in the application of reconnaissance procedures in 3d Marine Division's area of operations."

—Maj. Gen. R. G. Davis

From Quang Tri City north to the demilitarized zone; from the South China Sea west to the Laotian border beyond Khe Sanh—this is the thirteen-hundred-square-mile area of operations of the 3d Marine Division.

The terrain varies greatly. The coastal flatlands are interlaced with rich delta farm country and flat sand waste. Extending westward to Camp Carroll is the piedmont with its low rolling hills and scrub growth. In the west are mountains.

This area is secured by mobile forces ranging rapidly into areas where intelligence indicates the presence of enemy forces. But at any one time, less than 40 percent of the total area is covered by these operations. The remainder must be covered by reconnaissance, and the principal instrument is the Marine reconnaissance patrol.

During 1968 about sixteen hundred such patrols operated in the 3d Marine Division area, roughly 120 to 130 patrols per month. One out of every three patrols expects to make contact, and two out of three expect to find evidence of recent enemy activity. Rarely does a patrol go out on an uneventful mission.

Patrol contacts have occurred throughout the entire area from Quang Tri City into the DMZ, and in the mountains near the Laotian border. On a typical day approximately thirty patrols are used, including twenty in the field. The remainder are preparing for insertion or are in the process of extraction and debriefing. Of the twenty in the field, four usually are in contact with the enemy, and three of these will result in emergency exploitation by the insertion of additional forces or will require emergency extraction.

Exploitation operations are undertaken when it is apparent that the patrol is in contact with a sizable force, usually a hundred or more enemy troops. Emergency extraction is normal in remote areas beyond the range of friendly fire.

There are two general concepts to patrol operations. Within range of friendly artillery—the artillery fan normally covers 70 percent of the entire area—a patrol concept called Stingray is employed. In the outer reaches, beyond friendly range, a different concept called Keyhole is used.

These two types of reconnaissance patrols accommodate the variety of missions given to the total effort in the 3d Marine Division. Regardless of the breakdown into Stingray and Keyhole categories, the 3d Marine Division's reconnaissance effort is considered one cohesive effort.

Though they differ in several ways, the *essential* difference is that the mission of the Stingray patrol is to strike at the enemy, while the mission of the Keyhole is to observe him.

Stingray Patrols

The basic concept of this form of patrolling is carried over from the earlier days of reconnaissance. Though today's tactics may differ somewhat, the mission remains essentially the same: to find, fix, and engage the enemy with all available supporting and small arms.

The size of a Stingray patrol depends on expected enemy contact. This patrol consist of a team leader, assistant team leader, one or two medical corpsmen (depending on the size of the patrol), any special personnel necessary to accomplish the mission (e.g. demolition experts), and patrol members themselves.

The Stingray patrol is heavily armed, and organic arms are supplemented with weapons capable of sustaining heavy enemy contact. Members also carry quantities of grenades, claymore mines, and so on.

This patrol operates under the cover of the artillery fan. Artillery is continuously on call and gives the patrol constant protection even in adverse situations when air or reinforcements are not available, particularly in poor visibility.

Keyhole Patrols

The Keyhole concept is based on secrecy and stealth; its function is pure reconnaissance. This type of patrol is engaged by the enemy more often than its Stingray counterpart, because the Keyhole patrol operates in more remote areas. It is much smaller, and armed only with essential weapons and ammunition.

Of late, the division's effort to totally annihilate enemy activity has resulted in extensive use of the Stingray patrol, coupled with rapid reinforcement and exploitation. The success of any form of reconnaissance remains contingent upon the division's ability to respond immediately to particularly urgent requirements. Thus, the use of reconnaissance in the 3d Marine Division is a product of the needs of unit commanders. The challenge is the same as that which faces the commander with all of his assets: how best to employ them and support them.

Planning

The principal ingredient in successful reconnaissance is continuous, careful, detailed planning—with the overall intelligence collection effort a key factor in determining where and when reconnaissance patrols are best employed.

In an area as active as that of the 3d Marine Division, it is necessary to employ the full capability of the division reconnaissance battalion plus the force reconnaissance company to exploit available intelligence. The division G-2 coordinates the overall effort and plans the allocation of teams to areas controlled by major units, with detailed planning normally done at the subordinate task force or regimental level.

Full coverage of the division area is planned well in advance to insure frequent detailed explorations of all areas. However, immediate reaction to intelligence from other sources is also essential. This necessity for immediate reaction requires carefully designed SOPs and around-the-clock planning and execution.

Reconnaissance missions in the 3d Marine Division are developed from requests submitted by subordinate units to the division G-2. Based on the division appraisal of the overall enemy situation and immediate tactical requirements, these requests are appropriately included in the reconnaissance plan.

Once a request is approved for a patrol mission, a reconnaissance unit is notified and directed to prepare the patrol in detail: briefing, instruction and preparation, insertion, contact, reporting, protection, exploitation, extraction, and debriefing.

In undertaking a mission, all support elements must respond effectively and in a timely manner to ensure early and complete coordination. The support package for a reconnaissance team is a successful combination of both air and artillery. It includes delivery aircraft (usually CH-34 or CH-46), armed rotary aircraft (UH-1E), aerial observation aircraft (OV-10), fixed-wing cover aircraft (F-4, A-4, etc.), a responsive reaction force, and finally *direct support* of all available artillery when the teams are operating within range.

Before the team's insertion, the team leader and insertion pilot conduct an overflight of the assigned reconnaissance zone. This enables the team leader to study the terrain and permits the pilot and team leader to agree on a suitable LZ, one which can be approached by the insertion aircraft and which is tactically desirable for the team. A primary and alternate zone are selected during the overflight to add flexibility to the insertion plan. It cannot be overemphasized that the pilot who makes the reconnaissance flight must be the same pilot who flies the delivery helicopter.

The delivery aircraft with an accompanying search and rescue ship will be escorted by two UH-1E gunships. These four rotary aircraft, with the team, constitute the reconnaissance package.

In both planning and execution, no detail is too small to be overlooked. Since the focal point of the entire operation is the reconnaissance team itself, the team must undergo careful preparation before the mission.

Once the reconnaissance unit receives the division requirements for a specific mission, it issues a warning order and tasks one of its elements, normally a company, with the mission. The company then designates the appropriate team. The warning order is a preliminary effort to provide as much initial information as possible to assist the reconnaissance team in its overall preparation. From this order the reconnaissance team leader can determine where his team is going, how it will get there, and the method of insertion and extraction. Meanwhile, the reconnaissance battalion staff prepares a more detailed operations order for both the company and the team.

Preparation

Once the operation order has been issued, the team leader and his assistant are briefed by the battalion S-2 and S-3. Then the patrol leader formulates his order and issues it to his team, following up with several rehearsals and inspections. Meanwhile, the aircraft wing has been alerted on requirements of the mission and the pilots concerned come to the reconnaissance battalion COC to be briefed. A copy of the warning order is sent to artillery units concerned with the area where the reconnaissance team will be inserted.

The most important aspect of the team's preparation is the

briefing. This briefing follows no set pattern and is based partly on experience and precedents. One basis is to consider actual reconnaissance debriefing reports such as this example:

1. Recon team: Snaky 2–3, 3d Force Recon Company.
2. Time inserted/extracted 301400H/311800H (28 Hours)
3. Route: From YD 843576 to YD 863594 to YD 886613 to YD 895624
4. Terrain: Steep hills with triple canopy. Rate of movement 75m per hour.
5. HLZ: YD 843576. Site can accommodate one CH-46. Site is on top of a hill. Best approach: East to West. High canopy to the south of zone. YD 86559 will accommodate 8 CH-46s. Site is a ridge line, 360 degree approach with no obstacles.
6. Enemy: None
7. Comments: None

A detailed debriefing report is maintained on every reconnaissance team launched. These reports are filed and available for reference. When a patrol leader is assigned a mission in a specific area, he receives in his brief the latest enemy intelligence available and the most current friendly situation (including a weather forecast), all of the debriefs by prior patrols into that area, the latest aerial observation reports, and information available from the civilian population and POW interrogation. Thus he has at his disposal a vast amount of information. A careful study of this information gives the patrol leader a sound basis for his order, which should basically follow the standard five paragraphs used in operations: situation, mission, execution, administration and logistics, command and communications/electronics. Within this order the standard infantry outline is followed, with various adjustments to the needs of reconnaissance.

The patrol leader's order, when issued orally, is usually a forty-five- to sixty-minute undertaking. The patrol leader must cover every conceivable difficulty that the patrol may encounter. He is responsible for insuring that there is no doubt about the course of action the patrol will take when faced with a critical situation.

To minimize potential problems, the patrol leader conducts a series of rehearsals, repeated until he is satisfied that every man knows exactly what is expected.

The rehearsals cover such items as movement order, medical evacuation procedures, immediate action drills, and the plan for insertion and extraction.

The team leader also makes a detailed inspection before the mission to ensure that every man has the assigned equipment. The variety and quantity of equipment varies with the requirements of each mission.

When preparations are complete, the team assembles at the loading zone. Meanwhile, the pilots for the mission have been briefed and have coordinated with the patrol leader as to exactly how the insertion will be made. A recon officer briefs the pilots and team leaders and covers a variety of information, including a team's call sign, aircraft call signs, various FM and UHF frequencies to be employed, the size of the team, LZ coordinates and elevation, various thrust points, and the specific techniques of insertion, extraction, and reinforcement.

Insertion

The time between the request for an insertion and the actual execution varies from thirty-six to forty-eight hours for a routine mission. However, the reconnaissance battalion can respond much more quickly to a priority mission.

The insertion is a critical moment for the entire mission, for often the LZ is not entirely clear of enemy and the team is met by ground fire and forced to abort the mission. For example, five minutes after insertion of one Keyhole patrol, the team heard voices and equipment rattling within thirty meters to their east, south, and west. In addition the team had radio communication only with the insertion helicopters. Because of the situation the patrol was extracted within twenty minutes of its insertion, and the helicopter took fire as they went in to extract the team. This is also a good example of NVA counter-reconnaissance techniques—they sometimes recognize a reconnaissance insert but will not fire on the insert itself, reserving heavy fire for the departing helicopters and then closing in on the reconnaissance team.

After a successful insertion and after establishing communication with the team, the gunship pilot confirms to them their exact location using thrust points. Upon receiving an "all secure" from the team and after the team has established radio communications with its base, all aircraft leave the area.

The initial moments on the ground after the aircraft leave are critical, for a reconnaissance team usually will be engaged within the first hour if the insertion has been detected. The first priority is to set up a hasty 360-degree defense to determine whether the enemy is in the area. As a case in point:

1. Recon Team: Red Dancer 1–5, 3d Force Recon Co.
2. @50830H the team was inserted at YD 816528. After deplaning the insertion helo, the team observed 25 enemy soldiers approximately 30 meters to the west. The enemy wore mixed green and brown utilities, cartridge belts, and bush covers, and carried SKSs and AK-47s. The team initiated small arms fire resulting in two NVA KIA confirmed. Gunships made four rocket and strafing runs on the enemy with excellent coverage of the target. The team was extracted 250915H at YD 816528.

Either the transport helicopter pilot or the team leader may abort the mission at any time before insertion. The LZ may be changed during the overflight if both the pilot and the team leader agree on another site.

Reinforcement and Extraction

If at any time the reconnaissance team's presence is detected by the enemy, a decision must be made whether to extract or reinforce it. If a team is compromised, immediate plans are drawn and transports and gunships are "fragged" for extraction. At the same time an alert is issued for possible reinforcement.

En route to the area the aircraft establish radio communications with the team. When they arrive in the area, visual contact is established. The gunships make gun runs on the suspected enemy positions during the pickup.

The extraction of a recon team is at best risky, because the team and the extracting helicopter are both very vulnerable to enemy attack when the team abandons its position on the ground to board the aircraft. During this critical maneuver the enemy usually makes his main thrust at both the team and the helicopters. This effort can vary from an all-out assault to intensive small-arms fire supported by accurate mortar fire. The gunship escorts, which are strafing suspected positions, must ensure that the transport helicopters and the reconnaissance team are always within sight and support range at the moment of extraction. Once the reconnaissance team is aboard, the transport helicopter departs and climbs out at the discretion of the pilot.

Concurrently with the planning and preparation for extraction, a unit is readied to reinforce the team. Normally the team will be reinforced and the force built for combat if more than a small patrol or screening enemy forces are present and if the patrol is within effective range of friendly artillery. As soon as enemy presence is discovered the reaction force is alerted, and plans for its insertion are completed along with plans for emergency extraction. As more information becomes available, the decision is made as to which course will be followed. In any event, supporting air strikes and artillery fire are employed while a decision is being reached.

The reaction force is inserted into an LZ secured by the reconnaissance team if practicable; otherwise a new LZ must be prepared quickly. In many situations elements of the reaction force can be inserted into several LZs to provide maximum shock and increase opportunities for destruction of the enemy force.

After successful extraction from the objective area, the reconnaissance team is returned to the battalion for immediate debriefing by a reconnaissance S-2 officer; other interested units often are represented also. The debrief consists of a verbal question and answer period followed by a written summary of the patrol's activities and findings. The patrol debriefing report follows a standard pattern and is best illustrated by an actual report:

RECON DEBRIEFING REPORT

1. Recon Team: Alpha Bravo 3–1 3d Force Recon Co. Opo313F68 (120 hours)
2. Date inserted/extracted: 10000/150000H
3. Route YD 231414 to YD 250121 to YD 194401 to YD 292341 to YD 221210
4. Terrain: Low rolling hills with 1 to 3-foot elephant grass. Poor cover and concealment. Rate of movement at the patrol leader's discretion. Any hill in the area is a good OP site. There are numerous well-used trails in the area which can be seen from the air. Trail at YD220190 is 5 feet wide and runs from north to south. This trail cannot be seen from the air.
5. HLZ's: YD 1400
6. Enemy: 120915H YD 210920 team observed 6 enemy at YD200915 moving north. Enemy wore white or khaki uniforms, bush covers, no packs, cartridge belts, and unknown type weapons. The enemy spread out like a recon team. 131200H the team observed an unknown size enemy force at YD 231610. Enemy wore green utilities, bush covers, web gear, and were armed with AK-47's. The helo took hits and landed at A-4. The team set out claymores and observed 4–7 enemy moving south in two columns about 90 meters north of the team. Team set up a 360-degree security inside a building. AO came on station and observed enemy strung out for 400 meters moving in groups of 5–9 men. Team initiated small arms contact and the

enemy returned fire with small arms, automatic weapons, and grenades. Fixed wing began making runs on the enemy with excellent coverage. Gunships came on station and fired on the enemy. 140911H YD244450 the team observed three enemy 30 meters northwest of the team moving south. Enemy wore green utilities, bush covers, web gear, packs, and AK-47 rifles. The enemy was heavily loaded. The team requested gunships and directed them on the enemy. The enemy returned fire. When the gunships finished only one AK-47 was still firing. The team then called for 50 rounds of artillery with excellent target coverage. 141150H reaction force from A-2 arrived to reinforce the team. The team directed tanks as they swept north for 900 meters. While they were moving north, the team, tanks, and reaction force were exchanging fire with the enemy. Results of contact were 4 friendly WIA's, and 14 NVA KIA (C). The team returned to A-2 with the friendlies. 141400H the team moved 80 meters east and observed an estimated company. The enemy was moving south through elephant grass approx. 150 meters north of the team. The team could only observe the heads of the enemy and they wore green bush covers. The team called a fire mission of approx. 50 rounds with excellent coverage. Gunships came on station and fired on the enemy. While the gunships were firing the team moved SE to Vic YD 247051. Team in a security halt, received one incoming enemy grenade resulting in one USMC WIA not serious. The team returned fire and the enemy continued to throw grenades and fire AW. The enemy pulled back and fired an RPG round and continued with sporadic SA fire. The team continued with 360-degree return fire. AO, gunships, and fixed wing came on station and fired on the enemy. 141700 the team was extracted and received no fire upon the extraction. Results of the team's contacts with the enemy were (1) USMC WIA minor and 17 NVA KIA (C).

7. Miscellaneous: All enemy soldiers observed by the team had new gear, fresh haircuts and new uniforms. The enemy was well disciplined and well trained. In contact the enemy used grenades and RPG's primarily and SA fire was well disciplined and accurate. The team discovered a corral 200 meters NE of YD 194015. There was a 30-meter-square fence of bamboo. When discovered by the team there were no cattle in the corral. Team believes that the corral is used for pack animals. It can be seen from the air and the area was hit by an airstrip.

Reconnaissance patrols have made a significant contribution in the overwhelming defeat of large North Vietnamese Army forces in the 3d Marine Division area in recent months. Regardless of this success, efforts are under way to refine and improve their operations primarily in terms of responsiveness. One major improvement need which is beyond present capability is in helicopter lift. The Bell UH-1H is a far superior helicopter for reconnaissance insertion and extraction. It has more power, requires smaller landing zones, provides easy loading and off-loading, and carries two side gunners.

In any review of overall helicopter requirements the support of an active, aggressive reconnaissance patrol effort should be seriously considered. The payoff can be high.

(Major General Davis commanded the 3d Marine Division for a year in Vietnam. Before that he was Deputy Commander, Provisional Corps. His assignment after CG, 3d MarDiv, was Deputy for Education, MCDEC, Quantico, Va., which carried the collateral authority of Editor-in-Chief, Marine Corps Gazette.*)*

— 17 —

The Defining Year, 1968: Marine Reconnaissance Operations

With nearly three years of experience under its collective belt, Marine reconnaissance operations were conducted by the 1st and 3d Reconnaissance Battalions, and the 1st and 3d Force Reconnaissance Companies. The Stingray operations were well defined and supported, greatly extending the effectiveness of Marine firepower by hitting the enemy in his own backyard.

The experiences of Recon Team Cayenne describe a "typical mature Stingray mission," if any mission can be described by that phrase.

The enemy activity report submitted by 3d Recon Battalion, detailing events from July to December 1968, attests to the effectiveness of the Stingray concept.

The more mobile Marine operations would also have an impact on the employment of Marine reconnaissance units. In 1968, the Marine reconnaissance assets consisted of the 1st and 3d Reconnaissance Battalions, and the 1st and 3d Force Reconnaissance Companies. The two reconnaissance battalions remained under the control of their respective parent divisions, the 1st with the 1st Marine Division and the 3d with the 3d Division. Each of the force reconnaissance companies was attached to one of the reconnaissance battalions, the 1st to the 1st Reconnaissance Battalion and the 3d to the 3d Recon Battalion. After mid-1966, the two divisions employed their reconnaissance battalions in much the same way, basically as extensions of their supporting arms in Stingray patrols, thus bringing Marine firepower to bear deep in enemy territory. In Stingray operations, a small reconnaissance unit (usually a squad, although platoon-size operations were not uncommon) moved to an objective area by helicopter and occupied a position on commanding terrain from which it could observe enemy activity. From their observation posts the Marines watched for Viet Cong and North Vietnamese moving through the area. By maintaining a radio link to their headquarters, the Marines were able to engage lucrative targets with artillery fire and air strikes without revealing their position. This technique greatly extended the effectiveness of U.S. firepower by hitting the enemy in his own backyard. For example, the 1st Marine Division credited its Stingray patrols in the Da Nang sector for disrupting the enemy main forces as they moved into attack positions just prior to Tet.

Although the Stingray concept called for the patrols to remain clandestine, they went to the field prepared for the worst. A squad, accompanied by a corpsman and occasionally by an artillery forward observer, would take a considerable amount of equipment for the defense of their position. In addition to the squad's own rifles, the standard equipment included M-60 machine guns (occasionally, Marines even took .50-caliber M-2 heavy machine guns and 60mm mortars), grenade launchers, claymore mines, and sniper rifles as well as binoculars, spotting scopes, night vision devices, and, of course, radios. Such heavy firepower was virtually a necessity because the observation posts used by the patrols were, for the most part, lightly developed as defensive positions with concertina wire, lightly constructed bunkers, and fighting holes. There were only so many pieces of commanding terrain, and the patrols returned to these again and again.

Most patrols remained in position about four to six days, although some teams went out for as long as ten to eleven days. On the other hand helicopters might extract them much sooner than planned if the enemy detected the patrol. One team that paid the price for detection by the enemy was known as "Cayenne." On 30 May, Team Cayenne occupied a position on a narrow finger near the Tra Bong River, less than one kilometer north of the border between Quang Nam and Quang Tri provinces. The jungle surrounding the position had been burned away, revealing a gentle slope upwards to the north with steep drops to the south, east, and west. Five days and four nights passed without a single sighting of the enemy. At 2245 on 3 June, the Communists suddenly struck. A series of explosions rocked the observation post and, almost instantly, forty Viet Cong overran the Marines' positions. The 1st Reconnaissance Battalion lost contact with the team immediately following the initial report and called for help from a Douglas AC-47 Spooky.

"Spooky 11" arrived on station over Cayenne's position at 2340. At 2351 the patrol leader reestablished radio communications with battalion headquarters and requested an emergency extraction for himself and his wounded corpsman. He reported that the other thirteen Marines of Cayenne were either dead or missing. The 1st Reconnaissance Battalion called for the extraction as another AC-47 and a flare-ship responded to the call for help and arrived to support Cayenne. Just over fifty minutes after the request, two Boeing Vertol CH-46 Sea Knight helicopters arrived, supported by a pair of Bell UH-1E "Huey" gunships. With the flare-ship lighting up the battlefield and the Hueys and AC-47s suppressing the enemy fire, the Sea Knights moved in to pick up the patrol leader and his corpsman, completing the extraction at 0209. Only a quarter of an hour later, Team Cayenne, thought to have been destroyed by the enemy, suddenly came on the radio. Six Marines were still alive, but wounded, on the hill. In the darkness and confusion of the sudden attack the patrol leader had believed them lost. The rescue effort went back into motion, two helicopter gunships arriving on station at 0254, closely followed by another pair of Sea Knights. By

0334 the six wounded men were on board the helicopters and on their way to Da Nang. One of the Marines later died of his wounds.

AC-47s remained on station over the abandoned position for the rest of the night, shooting at fleeting targets. As each gunship ran out of ammunition another replaced it. At 0642 four CH-46s inserted a reaction force into the ruined position to search for additional survivors and collect the remains of those who had died. The reaction force found seven dead Marines and one dead Viet Cong in and around the position.

Fortunately, the experience of Team Cayenne was the exception to the rule. Most Stingray patrols occupied their positions for several days and then departed without serious incident, sometimes without even sighting the enemy. There was even occasion for the grim humor prevalent in combat. 1st Lt. Philip D. Downey, leader of Team Night Scholar during an insert atop Loi Giang Mountain, three kilometers southwest of An Hoa, turned in this report of a sighting on 10 June:

20 VC with 10 bathing beauties. 10 women were bathing with 6 guards. Black PJs, khakis, and towels; packs, rifles, and soap.

Called F[ire] M[ission], resulting in 3 VC KIA confirmed and 5 VC KIA probable. Unable to observe women after this due to bushes, but patrol felt the water frolics were over.

Stingray patrols were capable of inflicting enemy casualties far out of proportion to their own size. Team Elf Skin occupied a position on a narrow ridge overlooking the Arizona Territory and the Vu Gia River from 10 June to 16 June. It recorded twenty-five separate enemy sightings which totaled 341 Viet Cong. From its concealed position the team fired twenty-four artillery missions for a reported tally of over forty enemy dead.

Two weeks later, Team Parallel Bars took up a position at the peak of the dominant Hon Coc Mountain, six kilometers south of Go Noi Island. Just after noon on 25 June it saw about one hundred VC moving west along a narrow finger outside the hamlet of An Tam (1), just southwest of

Go Noi Island. An artillery mission using "Firecracker" ammunition accounted for more than thirty reported enemy dead. A little over three hours later another group of about eighty Communists moved west along the same finger, in the same direction. That group, too, appeared to be leaving Go Noi Island. The Marine patrol leader contacted an observation aircraft on station over the area and arranged for an air strike, this time killing about another thirty of the enemy. At 1815 the same day, Parallel Bars spotted another group, sixteen Viet Cong, also moving west one hundred meters west of the previous sighting. Another firecracker mission fell upon the enemy, but it was too dark for the team to observe the results. Incredibly, at 0800 the next morning the team sighted a fourth group of twenty-seven Viet Cong moving along the same finger, but about nine hundred meters farther southwest than the first three groups. Parallel Bars called for fire still again, and reported killing five more VC.

Stingray patrols supported all major operations. Teams occupied positions in or near the area of operations and coordinated their activities with the responsible infantry unit. As an operation ebbed and flowed according to intelligence reports of the enemy's activities, the Stingray patrols moved to new observation posts to maintain support of the infantry. Even while some teams were supporting major operations, others remained far beyond the TAOR of any friendly unit, directing artillery and air strikes on Communist forces moving to and from their bases. For 1968, III MAF claimed that Stingray operations had resulted in more than thirty-eight hundred enemy killed.

Still, some questions remained among infantry and reconnaissance Marines as to whether III MAF was making the best use of its reconnaissance assets. This was especially true in the 3d Marine Division. Lt. Col. William D. Kent—commander of 3d Reconnaissance Battalion until early July 1968—several years later expressed his concerns that the reconnaissance patrols were "fighting" the NVA rather than "watching them," thereby losing "a lot of long-range intelligence." He believed there was an overreliance on radio intercepts and that the North Vietnamese "were smart enough not to talk." Kent commented that this was especially true in the NVA offensive in the Dong Ha sector at the end of April and the beginning of May 1968. He believed the system awarded "pats on the back for KIAs," but not for obtaining the elements of combat information.

Both Lieutenant Colonel Kent and Major General Davis, the former deputy commander of Provisional Corps and new 3d Marine Division commander, were influenced by the tactics of the 1st Air Cavalry Division. According to Lieutenant Colonel Kent, after the relief of Khe Sanh in mid-April he began exchanging patrol leaders with the Army units and sending some of the reconnaissance Marines to the Army schools. The Air Cavalry employed rapid helicopter insertions of small reconnaissance teams of four to five men to explore a given terrain, often using decoy aircraft to keep watching enemy forces off balance. Combining "Red" (usually gunships) and "White" (aero scout) teams (the combination informally called Pink Teams), the Air Cavalry could make a rapid reconnaissance and either call in the "Blues" (the aero infantry) or move on elsewhere. The methodology of the Pink Team was to have the aero scout fly low in an attempt to observe enemy activity or to draw enemy fire. The gunship would then react as was appropriate while awaiting reaction from the Blues.

Lieutenant Colonel Kent observed, however, that the reconnaissance Marines also had things to teach their Air Cavalry counterparts. According to Kent, the Marines taught them how to call in supporting arms, especially fixed-wing air strikes, and, surprisingly enough, map reading. He stated that his patrol leaders explained to him that for the Air Cavalry, "land navigation was not a big thing. . . ." They told him that the Air Cavalry reconnaissance troops "didn't have to read maps. They depended on the airplanes. There were airplanes up there all the time."

In any event, encouraged by General Davis, the 3d Reconnaissance Battalion began, as Lieutenant Colonel Kent observed, to "loosen up and do more snoopin' and poopin'." While still using ten-man Stingray teams, the battalion also started deploying smaller teams of four or five men, very often out of friendly artillery range. Using both walk-ins and helicopter inserts, the smaller patrols were out to obtain information rather than fight. According to Col. Alexander L. Michaux, the 3d Marine Division operations officer (G-3), the teams were sent out and told "not to call in fire, or anything. . . . Just find them and tell us where the NVA are. We'll fix them with a battalion." Lt. Col. Donald R. Berg, who relieved Lieutenant Colonel Kent in July 1968 as commander of 3d Reconnaissance Battalion, noted that when he took over the battalion, three of his companies were attached to other units. By mid-September he had the three companies returned to his command and carrying out reconnaissance missions. In December, General Davis observed that he had from fifty-eight to sixty active reconnaissance teams, of which forty to forty-five were in the field at any given time. Within artillery range he employed the Stingray patrols, while the smaller patrols, designated "Keyhole" missions, operated usually farther out with the mission of watching and reporting on enemy troop activity. Like the artillery firebases, the 1st Marine Division also adapted the 3d Division reconnaissance techniques in Operation Taylor Common at the end of the year.

3d Reconnaissance Battalion
11 July 1968–12 December 1968

	Jul	Aug	Sep	Oct	Nov	Dec	Total
Patrols	133	147	143	165	158	105*	851
Duration	2.13	2.45	2.36	3.19	8.60	3.89	3.77
Size	6.09	6.61	6.72	7.22	7.10	6.50	6.71
Sightings	45	54	78	71	55	20	323
Enemy	288	778	508	289	314	114	2291
Contacts	20	52	52	34	31	22	211
F/Missions	16	28	39	64	64	22	233
Rds Fired	416	1203	914	1742	1363	249	5887
Air Strikes	5	14	5	24	3	5	56
Enemy KIA	22	63	102	25	23	13	248
Enemy Captured	0	0	0	1	0	0	1
Weapons	2	5	8	0	7	1	23
Frndly KIA	4	1	5	1	3	1	15
Frndly WIA	26	5	20	4	6	8	69

*Includes 31 teams deployed in the field as of 12 December 1968.

18

Marine Corps
Reconnaissance Activities:
1969

The departure of several Marine support units from Da Nang to Okinawa, in June 1969, signaled the beginning of the Corps' withdrawal from the Vietnam conflict and the assumption of a greater share of the fighting by the South Vietnamese. In the remaining months of the year, the 3d Marine Division and elements of the 1st Marine Air Wing would follow. After five years in Vietnam's embattled five northern provinces, the Marine Corps' commitment was coming to an end. This chapter describes the effect on those Marine reconnaissance teams remaining in country and the commitment by III MAF to support reconnaissance assets as the need for Stingray operations not only continued but increased.

The key to successful operations lay in timely, accurate information about the enemy. In Vietnam, the guerrilla nature of the struggle made timely intelligence even more essential, and at the same time more difficult to collect and evaluate. By 1969 the Marines' intelligence effort had evolved from an initial reliance on conventional techniques into a multifaceted, highly sophisticated intelligence gathering system that combined traditional air and ground reconnaissance methods with a number of new technological advances.

The majority of intelligence obtained by III MAF and its subordinate units was derived from air and ground reconnaissance. Marine Observation Squadrons 2 and 6 served as the airborne eyes of the 1st and 3d Marine Divisions. Each month the squadron's UH-1E helicopters, OV-10As, and Cessna O-1 and O-1g light aircraft flew hundreds of observation missions. In addition, Wing helicopters provided a platform for the airborne personnel detector, detector concealed personnel, and side-looking airborne radar. The mixed complement of RF-4Bs, Phantom IIs, EA-6A Prowlers, and F-3d Skyknights attached to Marine Composite Reconnaissance Squadron 1, also flew numerous conventional and infrared photographic survey missions. When the 1st MAW (Marine Air Wing) was unable to fulfill requests for photographic missions, the 7th Air Force and Army aviation companies provided support. Rapid, expert interpretation and dissemination of aerial photographs was accomplished by III MAF's G-2 Photo Imagery Interpretation Center (PIIC), which included an automatic data processing system and a direct teletype link between III MAF and XXIV Corps. In addition, photo interpretation teams were assigned to tactical units to assist in the planning and execution of combat operations.

Although small-unit infantry patrols continually provided information, the division's organic reconnaissance battalions generated the bulk of ground intelligence. In January 1969, III MAF reconnaissance forces consisted of two reconnaissance battalions and two force reconnaissance companies. The 1st Reconnaissance Battalion supported 1st Marine Division operations and the 3d Reconnaissance Battalion supported the 3d Marine Division. Attached to each battalion was a force reconnaissance company. The original doctrinal purpose of force reconnaissance companies was to operate in an amphibious operation under the landing force commander (III MAF), providing preassault reconnaissance and long-range reconnaissance after landing. In Vietnam, the force reconnaissance companies were originally used for deep reconnaissance under III MAF control. But by 1969 the 3d Force Reconnaissance Company had been totally absorbed by the 3d Reconnaissance Battalion during its support of operations undertaken by Task Force Hotel. Although attached to the 1st Reconnaissance Battalion, the 1st Force Reconnaissance Company remained a separate entity.

Realizing the need for reconnaissance information beyond that provided division commanders by their respective reconnaissance battalions, Lt. Gen. Herman Nickerson Jr., long regarded as the godfather of long-range reconnaissance planning, shortly after assuming command of all III MAF in March, directed that the force reconnaissance companies be returned to the control of III MAF. 1st Force Reconnaissance Company became the first, beginning deep patrol operations for III MAF in June, followed by the reconstituted 3d Force Reconnaissance Company in October.

Although deep reconnaissance missions were conducted by units of the Army's Special Operations Group within I Corps, the information provided did not meet the specific tactical needs of III MAF. As a result of III MAF's desire for more coordination as well as coverage of areas not targeted by other operations, III MAF reassumed control of the 1st and 3d Force Reconnaissance companies, which then were placed under the direction of the newly created Surveillance and Reconnaissance Center (SRC) established in October 1969. Under the SRC, the force reconnaissance companies were assigned to perform deep reconnaissance to determine the location and current usage of enemy base camps, storage sites, and lines of communications; fix and identify enemy units tentatively located by sensor devices and agent reports; provide specific targeting and bomb damage assessment for B-52 Arc Light strikes; execute POW recovery missions; execute wiretap operations; and emplace sensors across enemy trails and in other critical areas.

Initially based at An Hoa Combat Base and then at Da Nang, Maj. Roger E. Simmons's 1st Force Reconnaissance Company concentrated its efforts during the first half of the year in support of Task Force Yankee and 1st Marine Division operations. Conducting missions in areas surrounding Charlie Ridge and enemy Base Area 112 to the west of An Hoa, patrols, usually inserted and extracted by helicopter, attempted to locate enemy troops, base camps, and storage areas. In addition they spotted targets for artillery fire, assessed bomb damage, and occasionally engaged enemy forces. During January 1969, for example, the company ran 116 patrols, sighting 1,339 enemy troops and killing 88, while sustaining seven killed and 37 wounded. The company also directed 88 artillery fire missions and ran 25 air strikes. Following transfer to III MAF, the company shifted operations to the far reaches of Quang Nam and Quang Tin provinces, and as a result the number of patrols gradually declined, totaling only five during December.

The 3d Force Reconnaissance Company, based with and essentially absorbed by the 3d Reconnaissance Battalion at Quang Tri, supported 3d Marine Division operations, conducting 20 patrols and observing or engaging 62 enemy troops while suffering one Marine wounded during January 1969. With the redeployment of the battalion and the division in October, the company was brought up to authorized strength and control was passed to III MAF. The company relocated next to the airfield at Phu Bai Combat Base. During the remaining two months of the year, 3d Force Reconnaissance Marines concentrated on patrolling the demilitarized zone and the newly created western reconnaissance zones of Quang Tri and Thua Thien provinces, focusing on the A Shau Valley and surrounding terrain.

At the beginning of 1969, Lt. Col. Larry P. Charon's 1st Reconnaissance Battalion was overstrength, possessing five "letter companies" and the 1st Force Reconnaissance Company, instead of the normal four companies.*

In support of Task Force Yankee and the 1st Marine Division, the battalion performed a variety of missions: furnishing teams to support regimental search operations; securing fire support bases and artillery observation posts; and training scuba divers to check bridges within the division TAOR for demolitions and to search waterways for obstructions

---

*Lieutenant Colonel Charon was succeeded in February by Lt. Col. Richard D. Mickelson, who was in turn replaced in October by Lt. Col. John J. Grace.

and weapons caches. However, the principal function of the reconnaissance battalion was to patrol the western fringes of the TAOR. Operating in six-man teams composed of an officer or NCO patrol leader, a radioman, three riflemen, and a Navy corpsman, battalion Marines normally spent half their time in the field and the remainder preparing for the next operation or participating in refresher training.

Reconnaissance patrolling, by 1969, had become somewhat standardized. Each team member packed food, water, ammunition, and equipment to sustain himself for up to six days in the field. The radioman carried the AN/PRC-25 and extra batteries, while the team corpsman took charge of the medical supplies. After several hours of rehearsals and briefings, helicopters lifted the team to its assigned operating area. Upon insertion, a radio check was made with the aircraft, radio relay, and company command post, and then the team departed the landing zone, following a prearranged route. Carefully noting and then reporting details of terrain and enemy activity, or calling in artillery and air strikes, the patrol attempted in most cases to avoid contact. At the end of the assigned mission, or when the patrol was discovered or attacked, helicopters extracted the team. On return each member of the team was debriefed and all reports of the patrol were reviewed and then distributed to the appropriate regiment or battalion.

Patrolling during the year by 1st Reconnaissance Battalion Marines resulted in a steady stream of sightings and engagements. During April, for example, the battalion conducted 177 patrols, sighting 2,746 enemy troops and directing 88 artillery fire missions and 31 air strikes. During the month, battalion Marines killed 177 at a cost of seven dead and 39 wounded.

Like the 1st Reconnaissance Battalion, the 3d Recon Battalion, under the command of Lt. Col. Aydlette H. Perry Jr., was also overstrength as 1969 began, having five letter companies plus the attached 3d Force Reconnaissance Company under Maj. Robert W. Holm. Supporting Task Force Hotel and the 3d Marine Division, 3d Battalion Marines performed the same types of mission as those assigned to 1st Battalion. Concentrating their efforts in the DMZ, in western Quang Tri, and in the piedmont west of Quang Tri City and Dong Ha, meant that "every indication of enemy activity," General Davis recalled, "was explored by the insertion of reconnaissance teams."*

Generally, two types of patrol missions were conducted by reconnaissance Marines within the 3d Marine Division TAOR. As General Davis explained:

"Under the artillery fan established at the time, we would use Stingray techniques with eight to ten men in a team, seeking the enemy, and seeking opportunities to deliver fire upon them. Well-out, smaller teams—four to five men—going on the basis of secrecy: only to observe, stay out of sight. If the enemy is encountered, they attempt to escape. These are not normally reinforced unless we are able to insert artillery at the same time. Under the artillery fan, normally they would be reinforced if the enemy presented an adequate target. On contact, the team hangs in and fights it out or if it's a small contact and they start to take casualties, we might extract them. However, if it's a large contact and under the artillery fan and the opportunity presents itself, they are reinforced in order to attempt to destroy the enemy force in its entirety."*

Using Stingray and deep-reconnaissance techniques, 3d Reconnaissance Battalion in May, for example, conducted 194 patrols during which 68 contacts with enemy troops were made, resulting in 80 enemy killed and the loss of four Marines killed and 31 wounded. During the same period, battalion Marines directed 60 artillery missions, 35 air strikes, and conducted 14 scuba missions.

Although the primary purpose of reconnaissance patrols was to gather information and direct artillery and air strikes, and not to fight, recon teams often found themselves involved in intense combat. Firefights erupted from ambushes, chance meetings with small enemy units, or efforts to take

*U.S. Marines in Vietnam, 1969. History and Museums Division, USMC.

prisoners. One such encounter took place in March in the southwestern corner of Quang Nam Province.

Shortly after noon on the twenty-third, a team from 1st Force Reconnaissance Company (radio call sign Report Card), consisting of two officers, seven enlisted Marines, and one corpsman, was inserted by helicopter near the Song [river] Thu Bon, southwest of Antenna Valley. The following morning the team moved up a trail where it was to set an ambush in an effort to snatch a prisoner. Once in position it became apparent that the trail was one of the enemy's main routes for moving supplies from western base camps through Antenna Valley into the An Hoa basin. During the first half hour in position a group of approximately thirty-two enemy troops passed two to three meters in front of the team's ambush. Waiting for an enemy officer or NCO, the team let most pass. The last, dressed in full utilities, a pith helmet, boots, and "strutting along holding his rifle at port arms," appeared to be a good target and was ambushed. As the Marines dragged the enemy soldier into their ambush, they heard movement down the trail, both north and south of their position. Pulling back five meters into deep elephant grass, the team engaged two enemy soldiers, killing both. Then six more appeared to the front. While taking those under fire and endeavoring to move down to a streambed, the patrol was hit from all sides by approximately eighty to one hundred enemy troops.

For thirty minutes the team fended off probes by the large enemy force until two Huey gunships arrived; the Marines used small arms only when an enemy soldier was actually sighted, otherwise they employed grenades and the M-79 grenade launcher. The fighting continued for another two-and-one-half hours while the gunships were on station, then suddenly stopped. Searching the area around their position before being extracted, the patrol counted ten enemy dead by Huey machine gun fire. "I learned," team leader 1st Lt. Wayne E. Rollings later reported, "that with a small unit, if you keep good security, 360, that you can hold off a very large force that outnumbers you considerably, and suffer very few casualties. We had no casualties." Although the patrol did not get its prisoner, who was killed by an enemy grenade during the fight, they did leave behind twenty-two NVA dead.

Two-and-one-half weeks later, Lieutenant Rollings and seven men were again on patrol. "The name of our reconnaissance patrol was Lunchmeat, and with 150 North Vietnamese soldiers surrounding us, that's just how I felt, like a piece of lunchmeat in a sandwich." The mission assigned Rollings's patrol was to reconnoiter a trail and ridgeline four kilometers southwest of An Hoa.

Near noon on 10 April, Rollings and his team were inserted into the area and began checking the ridgeline for enemy activity. Shortly after dusk the following day they spotted thirty-five to forty lights moving in a northeasterly direction, approximately eight hundred meters from their position. Before the team could move they heard movement to their front and rear. "We hurriedly set up a defensive perimeter in some dense undergrowth on the side of the trail," Rollings noted, "and called in Spooky [Air Force C-47 aircraft equipped with miniguns]."

With the enemy moving ever closer, Rollings called an artillery mission on a base camp spotted earlier in the day with the hope of forcing the NVA to call off the search, and then radioed for Spooky to make a pass. As Lieutenant Rollings continued:

His first burst landed about four hundred yards from us and I began to direct him in. He warned me to tell him when he was hitting within fifty to seventy-five yards of our position and that he would then start working out toward the enemy from there. But the enemy would still be between us and his fire so I waited until the outer fringe of his fire, which had a twenty-five-yard radius, was within five yards and then told him to start working away from us. I didn't tell him how close his fire was to us, because I knew he wouldn't have gotten close if he couldn't mark our position.

Patrol members counted more than thirty instances when they heard screams and groans as artillery and miniguns scored hits. In one instance, Rollings related, "we saw ten NVA get to within forty yards of our position before 'arty' caught them with a barrage that finished them all off."

At first light the patrol got word to move out, but within one hundred meters of its position it encountered twenty NVA troops. Spooky again was called for and the Air Force's C-47 began working in from the rear while the team hit the enemy from the front. "We had them sandwiched between us. After about a half hour, the NVA . . . took off." The patrol continued to search the area, but without success, and was extracted on the thirteenth with one minor casualty.

Other teams were not so lucky. On 4 June a patrol from Company D, 3d Reconnaissance Battalion, fought the battalion's most severe action of the year and lost. The team (call sign Flight Time) consisted of six recon Marines. Helicopters inserted the patrol, which carried two strobe lights for illumination, at 0930 on 2 June near Hill 471, overlooking the Khe Sanh and Lang Vei, in western Quang Tri Province. The team's arrival went unopposed and the Marines moved northward from the landing zone toward the high ground, finding evidence of recent enemy occupation in the area. The following day, after setting up its harbor site for the evening, the team observed five enemy troops in brown utilities and helmets, but did not take the troops under fire.

At 0250 the next morning the team began receiving small-arms fire and grenades from an enemy force of unknown size. Reporting one killed and five wounded, the team leader requested an emergency extraction and all available "on call" air. When the aerial observer arrived on station ten minutes later he saw that the enemy was within ten meters of, and surrounding, the team's position. He immediately requested that a reaction force be inserted to assist the team. At 0315 the observer expended his ordnance, heard a secondary explosion, and then lost all communication with the team.

The twelve-man reaction force arrived in the area at 0620 and reported sighting three, and possibly five, members of the team in terrain which looked as though it had been "hit by a flamethrower." On the ground the force found the bodies of five members of the team in an enemy trench and the sixth approximately ten meters down the hill. An on-site investigation indicated that the enemy had come up the northeast side of the hill firing grenades and small arms, and throwing satchel charges and bangalore torpedoes. The reaction force leader surmised from the burn marks on the ground and the bodies, and from the way in which the equipment was scattered, that the team must have been involved in hand-to-hand fighting before being overrun.

Enemy troops were not the only hazard faced by reconnaissance Marines when patrolling deep in mountainous terrain. In May 1969 a seven-man team (Centipede) from 3d Reconnaissance Battalion observed numerous tiger tracks while patrolling the steep, triple-canopied hills surrounding the Ba Long Valley. On two occasions during their four-day patrol a tiger came within ten meters of the team's position and had to be driven off with CS (gas) grenades. Among other nonhostile hazards were lightning, friendly fire, the rugged terrain itself, and equipment failure. Although reconnaissance Marines did suffer a number of noncombatant casualties, losses in most cases were a direct result of clashes with enemy troops.

With four years of experience behind them, reconnaissance Marines had, by 1969, developed tested techniques and equipment in order to supply their divisions with accurate and timely intelligence. To assure prompt artillery support when needed and at the same time prevent accidental shelling, special reconnaissance zones were established for each deployed team in which only the patrol could call for fire missions. The 11th and 12th Marines (artillery regiments) designated a battery or platoon of howitzers to support each team and assigned a liaison officer at the reconnaissance battalion's command post to assist in fire planning and coordination. To insure the rapid extraction of a team under fire or in a tenuous situation, the 1st Marine Aircraft Wing designated helicopters as part of a quick-reaction package that at times included division infantry forces to assist.

When not on patrol, reconnaissance Marines continually

trained for their exacting task. In addition to the initial indoctrination program for newly arrived personnel, which included instruction in the use of the AN/PRC-25 radio, map reading, first aid, rappelling from helicopters, observer procedures, and intelligence reporting techniques, the battalions conducted periodic refresher courses with special emphasis on weapons training, scuba diving, physical conditioning, and the use of new equipment such as extraction ladders. Selected personnel also were sent to the U.S. Army's Recondo School at Nha Trang for more specialized training at the hands of Special Forces veteran patrollers.

With the redeployment of the 3d Marine Division, Marine reconnaissance strength was halved, and what had been the reconnaissance zone of the 3d Battalion was passed to reconnaissance elements of the 101st Airborne and 1st ARVN divisions. Under the command of Maj. Alex Lee, the 3d Force Reconnaissance Company, by then a separate entity under III MAF, moved to Phu Bai and was tasked with patrolling the A Shau Valley. The 1st Force Reconnaissance Company and 1st Reconnaissance Battalion continued to concentrate on Quang Nam Province, although by December 1969 fewer patrols were assigned to deep missions in the western reaches of the province.

Although direct air observation and ground reconnaissance provided the bulk of intelligence, the artillery's system of observation and target acquisition also produced important information. Scattered throughout the division's area of responsibility were numerous observation towers which not only directed artillery fire but permitted surveillance of enemy movement. Supplementing the artillery's intelligence gathering capability were integrated observation devices and the computerized fire support information system.

Captured enemy documents and prisoners yielded additional information. To extract the intelligence, divisions relied heavily upon specially trained Marines attached to interrogation-translation teams, interpreter teams, and counterintelligence teams. Working within the division G-2 sections, the interrogation and interpreter teams, as their names implied, interviewed NVA and VC prisoners and suspected civilian detainees and reviewed all captured documents for information on enemy unit strength; designations; attack and withdrawal routes; staging, rally, and base areas; mines and surprise-firing devices' locations; and enemy combat effectiveness and morale. In September 1969, a typical month, teams attached to the 1st Marine Division interrogated 1,397 detainees, 18 of whom were classified prisoners of war, 45 as civilian defendants, 13 as returnees, and 1,321 as innocent civilians. During the same month the teams screened 3,107 documents for translation.

Electronic sensors provided yet another source of intelligence information. Products of the aborted demilitarized zone barrier project initiated by Secretary of Defense Robert Strange McNamara and abandoned in October 1968, sensors, by 1969, were being employed tactically throughout South Vietnam under program Duffel Bag.*

These "twenty-four-hour silent sentinels" not only aided economy of force but provided early warning of attacks on base camps and cities and contributed to the reduction of rocket attacks. "It appears," noted a MACV message, "that . . . sensor technology may be one of the more important developments to come out of the Vietnam War. At the present time, the only limitations on successful sensor-supported operations are the availability of sensors, and the degree of imagination, initiative, ingenuity, and resourcefulness of tactical commanders."

The Marines first used sensors during the siege of Khe Sanh in early 1968. At the same time, Air Force Igloo White aircraft—dedicated EC-121s in orbit over Laos—provided readouts from out-of-country sensors. The sensor information was relayed to Nakhon Phanom, where it was assessed

---

*The use of sensors within South Vietnam, nicknamed Duffel Bag, was one of four continuing sensor programs carried out by MACV in Southeast Asia. The remaining three were Igloo White, which involved the out-of-country use of sensors; Duel Blade II, the sensor-supported anti-infiltration system in and along the DMZ; and Tiger Jaw, the combined US/GVN border surveillance operation.

and targets passed to Khe Sanh and Dong Ha. Toward the end of the siege some local readout and assessment capability was given the Khe Sanh Marines. As a result of the experience at Khe Sanh, coupled with the onset of the rainy season in the Laotian panhandle, sensors became available for limited tests and evaluation in support of ground combat operations. Upon completion of the evaluations, code-named Duck Blind, in August 1968, it became apparent that sensors, originally designed to impede or substantially reduce infiltration from North to South Vietnam, could make significant contributions in surveillance and target-acquisition operations in South Vietnam.

A majority of the sensors employed by III MAF were the radio type, which transmitted information electronically directly to monitoring stations. The small, camouflaged, battery-powered devices could be dropped from aircraft or implanted by hand. Once in position the sensors reacted to minute physical changes in their environment. Seismic sensors, known as seismic intrusion devices (SIDs), responded to ground vibrations such as human footsteps. Magnetic sensors, or magnetic intrusion devices (MAGIDs), detected moving metallic objects, and infrared sensors (PIRIDs) reacted to heat emanating from bodies, vehicle engines, and campfires. Acoustic sensors picked up sound. Once activated the sensors sent a signal to a receiver, from which the operator could determine the location and probable nature of the object. Acoustic sensors transmitted the sounds they detected directly to the monitoring stations.

Sensors were generally planted in groups, or "strings" as they were more commonly termed, along enemy infiltration routes from the mountains into the lowlands. A typical string, designed to detect movement, consisted of several seismic and a few magnetic and acoustical sensors. Once they were activated, the monitoring station operator could request an artillery fire mission, alert a nearby ground unit, or simply record the time and direction of movement for later analysis. Seismic, magnetic, and infrared line sensors also were employed around fixed installations such as fire support or combat bases. The Da Nang barrier contained 106 such sensors, and plans called for the future implantation of an additional 775. By mid-1969 each division had over 100 sensors, maintained and monitored by the division's G-2 staffs.

Whether obtained by sensors, air and ground reconnaissance, or a paid agent, intelligence information had to be quickly evaluated, correlated, and transmitted to units in the field to be of any value. In order to facilitate this process, III MAF established the Surveillance and Reconnaissance Center at Da Nang in late 1969, under Assistant Chief of Staff, G-2, Col. John S. Canton. According to Colonel Canton, the center was to "physically and functionally integrate and coordinate all intelligence collection means in I CTZ, thus reducing the time lapse between the initial collection of intelligence information and the dissemination of processed intelligence to tactical commanders." In addition to directing deep-surveillance missions of the force reconnaissance companies, the SRC "monitored all intelligence collection in ICTZ. This ensured round-the-clock, timely and reliable communications of perishable intelligence data to using units, thus producing a quantum increase in the immediate utilization of intelligence assets."

"In this war, like no other war in the past generation," noted Col. Anthony J. Skotnicki, "we never worked under a lack of information. We actually acquired so much intelligence information we couldn't handle it." Despite advances in processing and organization, there remained "a considerable amount of difficulty in manually recording it and manually extracting it in order to put it together into useful intelligence."

=== 19 ===

"The Older We Get the Better We Were!"

by Col. Richard D. Mickelson, USMC (Ret.)*

1969

Col. Richard D. Mickelson, USMC (Ret.) served as the commanding officer, 1st Reconnaissance Battalion, from 8 February to 30 October 1969. His view of the employment of Stingray and of the employment of recon teams from 1st Recon Battalion in support of the 1st Marine Division's mission to "protect the Da Nang complex" sheds additional light on the complexity of that mission. With experience in reconnaissance operations since 1954, when he was the commanding officer of 2d Amphibious Recon Company, Colonel Mickelson enjoyed an extensive reconnaissance background. His first tour of duty in Vietnam began in 1962, as a member of a Military Assistance Advisory Group (MAAG), assigned to a Vietnamese Airborne Brigade. Assigned as the Marine Corps Liaison Officer to the US Army Special Warfare Center at Fort Bragg, North Carolina, in 1963, "Mick" participated in specialized training with the 82nd Airborne Division and tested HALO (high-altitude low-opening) parachute techniques and the Fulton Skyhook Extraction System. Assigned, next, to the Central Intelligence Agency to

---

*Commanding officer, 1st Reconnaissance Battalion, 8 February 1969–October 1969.

manage paramilitary ground equipment for clandestine operations, he became involved with the conduct of running surveillance teams out of Laos and Cambodia against the Ho Chi Minh Trail. Returning to duty with the 1st Marine Division in 1968, Mickelson was assigned as one of the operations officers in the G-3 Section, where he again became familiar with the territory. His observations and comments as the commanding officer of 1st Reconnaissance Battalion are a valuable "primary source" of information.

I realize your current research is pointed toward the (historical) development and employment of Stingray tactics during the Vietnam war. I believe, however, that it is essential in your research to know something about your sources. Accordingly, I'll give you more information than you need or, perhaps, want. This is done very deliberately as we all tend to bring our individual biases to the table of history. Individual biases, as you are well aware, are not only the result of personal experience but also reflect organizational biases, which in this case are those from within our Corps. Much of this was brought home to me following my retirement from the military, when I was involved in teaching the management of organizational behavior.

I have deliberately omitted the names of certain individuals as it opens up a new ball game. Also, please bear in mind that what follows was done with little or no research and is only my reflections.

Reconnaissance: the act of obtaining information of military value, especially regarding the positions, strength, and movement of enemy forces.—Standard Dictionary.

My first exposure to the reconnaissance game was in 1954–56 as commanding officer, 2d Amphibious Reconnaissance Company, Force Troops, Fleet Marine Force, Atlantic (2dPhibReconCo). As you know, the amphibious reconnaissance battalions of World War II fame had, by my time, disappeared and subsequently resurfaced as company units, one on each coast. We were under the administrative control of the

Commanding General, Force Troops, Atlantic (ForTrpsLant) and the operational control of the Commanding General, Fleet Marine Force, Atlantic (FMFLant). Force Troops at Camp Lejeune, North Carolina, actually Camp Geiger, was only interested, as I'm sure you are aware, in the accuracy of the unit diaries, disciplinary/reenlistment rates, condition of motor transportation and communication equipment, and the like. The brigadier general and his staff at ForTrps could not have cared less about (our) training or operational employment. It is interesting to note, however, that the Marine Corps hadn't changed that much over the years. I'm not personally aware of any commanding officer of an independent company/battalion, who, during this peacetime environment, was relieved for tactical error or a training (injury) incident. On the other hand, to bilge a commanding general's or inspector general's inspection could be, and has been, the "kiss of death" for many former commanding officers. On the flip side, FMFLant, at Norfolk, Virginia, was too far removed to worry about one small reconnaissance company except for one or more amphibious exercises per year.

This was pretty heady stuff for a young, inexperienced captain with little infantry and no reconnaissance experience under his belt. There was an exchange of ideas and training philosophy between my counterpart on the West Coast and the 2d Marine Division's recon company commander. The Test Unit, which had come into being on the West Coast, was of little assistance for understandable reasons.

Our mission at the time was primarily **data collection only**. It called for a limited raid capability, and as a result we possessed organic 60mm mortars and light (.30-caliber) machine guns. Maintaining a degree of proficiency with these weapons, although mandatory, was time consuming. Our mission statement was a holdover from the days of Marine amphibious battalions. I felt, as did many others, that the employment of a small company (-) coming from either a submarine or a destroyer for an amphibious raid was rather remote. The training emphasis was, as a result, oriented toward seeing and not being seen. During this time frame there were, to the best of my knowledge, no disparate factions within either the reconnaissance or intelligence communities. Staff officers with reconnaissance experience at either ForTrps or FMFLant levels were all products of the very same environment. Air-to-ground radios were not organic in those days. **Ashore, radio silence was strictly maintained.** On force-level amphibious exercises, the radio company at ForTrps invariably worked the aggressor role. Prior to D day they had only recon elements to work against. It didn't take a brain surgeon to realize that they could locate us in a heartbeat if we spent too much time on the radio. On the larger exercises, FMFLant would dictate that radio silence would be maintained until our return to the transport vessel (making the rapid dissemination of timely information impossible). Our reconnaissance teams traveled very light, carrying only individual weapons and a minimum of equipment. The ability to move with speed was paramount. We were literally on our own! If we became engaged in a firefight with imminent threat of death or capture, scattering and reassembling at a known rallying point was an option. Often referred to as "quail tactics," this was obviously a court of last resort. Rule # 13: Every night you'll be told where to meet if surrounded by a superior force. Standing Orders, Roger's Rangers, 1759.

In this type of environment there was no attempt to bring back our dead. Seriously wounded also presented a grave problem. Although we did have Navy corpsmen, there was no such thing as a medical evacuation plan. The prospect of evading the enemy for two or three days, then negotiating a heavy surf line at night, was a tall order to fill even without wounded Marines to worry about.

Our primary means of transportation at the time was the submarine. For training purposes we relied upon the USS *Sea Lion* (ASSP 315) homeported at Norfolk. Her counterpart on the West Coast was the USS *Perch* (ASSP 313) homeported in San Diego. Basically, the "amphibious submarine, personnel" (ASP) had been modified by turning the boats' torpedo rooms into berthing spaces that could accommodate approximately eighty Marines and proved to be excellent for training purposes. (Talk about a captive audience!) Procedures for operating with these boats had been developed over a period of time, beginning with the combat cargo officers who were assigned the first couple of years. Also, the manual MCS 3–5, *The Employment of Submarine Transported Landing Forces,* was a great "how to" guide. It is interesting to note that we in the Corps have made a science out of reinventing the wheel. While the tools may change, the doctrine remains.

In my time with 2ndPhibRecon we never operated ashore following D day. There just wasn't enough real estate available for us to use! The only opportunity I had to get my reconnaissance into the field was at Fort Bragg, North Carolina, operating as aggressors against Special Forces students. This proved to be an ideal training environment, as we could utilize organic motor transport and communications and set up a combat operations center, and this is where we first experienced the complexities of working with helicopters. I might add that during this time, I completed the Special Forces Officers' Course at Fort Bragg, which aided me during my next assignment and several others to follow.

I was relieved in the spring of 1956 and ordered to the Landing Force Training Unit, Atlantic (LFTULant) in Little Creek, Virginia, as they needed a reconnaissance officer to teach amphibious entry techniques to Army Special Forces units. Over the next three years I spent the majority of my time as the OIC (officer-in-charge) of the Reconnaissance Section. We also trained Marine reservists and ships' detachments, tailoring our courses to meet a unit's particular needs. For example, Special Forces soldiers were not interested in learning techniques of hydrographic survey or land navigation. They came to learn submarine and ship-to-shore operations. The force reconnaissance company came into being during this period. My observation of them was that they spent most of their time jumping out of airplanes and swimming out of submarines. Don't get me wrong, I, too, enjoy doing those same things. However, many new people were coming into the reconnaissance game and I felt that they had begun to lose sight of the basics.

Following a tour on independent duty I reported to the 3d Marine Division on the island of Okinawa, in 1961, and was immediately assigned as the operations officer (S-3) of 3d Recon Battalion. By this time I had been promoted to the grade of major and had the most recon experience of any officer in the battalion. We were fortunate, as our letter company commanders were well experienced, one even having commanded 1stPhibRecon. They pretty much wrote their own training schedules to meet their needs. During the next six months I was with the battalion, we deployed on both company- and battalion-size operations. Although working within a division was a new experience for me, nothing was to happen that changed my philosophy concerning the employment of Marine reconnaissance assets. It was still **data collection** and occasional **screening** of division flanks.

My tour of duty was split in 1962, and I was ordered to the Military Advisory Group (MAAG) in Vietnam. Initially assigned to the Operations Division as an Evaluations Group, Vietnam (JOEGV), which reported to the Department of Defense via the newly created Commander, U.S. Military Assistance Command, Vietnam (COMUSMACV), JOEGV crossed all service lines evaluating new equipment and concepts of employment. It was an interesting six months and I particularly enjoyed my association with the Vietnamese Airborne Brigade (not the least my opportunity to get back on jump status).

In early 1963, I was ordered to the U.S. Army Special Warfare Center at Fort Bragg as the Marine Corps liaison officer. With instructional duties in all three of their major courses—the Special Forces Officers Course, the Counterinsurgency Warfare Officers Course, and the Psychological Warfare Officers Course—I was able to cross all boundaries. As the lone Marine in an Army environment, I was given what can only be described as royal treatment! Not only was I back on a jump status, but the opportunity to participate in specialized training was frosting on the cake. During my tenure with the

Army, I completed the Special Forces Jumpmaster Course, the 82d Airborne Division Jumpmaster Course, and the HALO Parachute Course, and was the thirty-second person picked up by the Fulton Skyhook Extraction System, the same recovery system featured in the movie *The Green Berets*. I also received both senior and, subsequently, master parachute ratings, with authorization from Headquarters Marine Corps (HQMC) to wear those parachute badges. As you know, "badges" are important in an organization as large as the U.S. Army, and with my Vietnam experience, to include Vietnamese parachute wings, I was accepted as one of the family within the U.S. Army.

I departed the Special Warfare Center, by then named the John F. Kennedy Center for Special Warfare, during the summer of 1965. I left with a deep and abiding respect for the Special Forces soldier. Additionally, I had learned a great deal about working with guerrillas/irregulars, insertion/extraction techniques, communications, and the like. I had also been exposed to the Army's long-range patrolling techniques, and the Air Force's Special Air Warfare Center, at Eglin Air Force Base. *My basic philosophy concerning Marine reconnaissance was only reinforced.*

One month after being assigned to the staff at the Basic School, located at Quantico, Virginia, I was called to HQMC and told not to unpack my bags. Two months later, following a background investigation and several security clearances, I was reassigned on military detail to the Central Intelligence Agency. My billet was with Special Operations Division of the Plans Directorate (clandestine services if you will). I was involved with the management of military/paramilitary ground equipment for the clandestine services. I chaired the Panel on Weapons, Sabotage, and Harassment Devices and was a member of the Communications and Photography Panels. Back on jump status, and with a promotion to lieutenant colonel, I felt as though I had been turned loose in a candy shop. As you know, the agency is very compartmentalized. My particular job, however, crossed all lines within the Plans Directorate. Whether the African Division desired a chrome-plated .45-caliber revolver with ivory grips, or the Southeast Asian Division needed a 75mm pack howitzer, the requests came across my desk together with the justification. The job involved a considerable amount of travel (worldwide) concerning the development, field testing, and employment of ground-related equipment.

In Southeast Asia we were running surveillance teams out of Laos and Cambodia against the Ho Chi Minh Trail. Again, it was **see and not be seen**! From insert to extraction, there was rarely any communication between a reconnaissance team and home base. The team traveled light and there was no medical evacuation plan or plans for any supporting arms. This decision was understandable when one must consider the countries we were operating within and the irregulars, Hmong for example, who helped us accomplish these missions. Other than equipment requests I did not have very much contact with the Studies and Observation Group (SOG) in Vietnam. Although briefed both in Washington, D.C., and in Saigon as to SOG's methods of operation, I had no first-hand experience with them.

I departed the Central Intelligence Agency in the fall of 1968 with mixed emotions. It had been a great tour and they had asked me to extend, but as tempting as it all was, I felt that it was time to return to the Marine Corps. I had literally been away almost seven years!

Ordered to the 1st Marine Division in Vietnam, I arrived in the fall of 1968 and was assigned as one of the operations officers with the division's G-3 section. Although I'd hoped to command an infantry battalion, it was in retrospect a great assignment. I had worked for both the G-3 and G-3A along the way. I also discovered that in getting familiar with the territory I had numerous friends and acquaintances within the Americal Division, 101st Airborne Division, Special Forces, and operatives working for the Central Intelligence Agency. This association served me well as I went along in my assignment.

Some recon observations as G-3/OpsO. . . . There were many misconceptions concerning the proper employment of reconnaissance assets among both the division staff and commanders. This was due in part to the ever-changing mission statement of the reconnaissance battalion over the preceding years. The methods of employing the reconnaissance battalion in the Vietnam environment, particularly in the early years of the war, also contributed to the problem. Last but by no means least was the fact that Marine reconnaissance units by their very nature reflect the personalities and the philosophies of their commanders.

The "screening task" of the reconnaissance battalion's mission statement, as I recall, had originated in the late 1950s. When employed in this particular role, reconnaissance patrols were turned into infantry patrols. The patrol size increased, crew-served weapons appeared, and the load of the individual Marine increased dramatically. Although the screening task disappeared in subsequent years, it remained stuck in the minds of many of our senior officers.

The fragmentation of both the reconnaissance battalion and its companies, especially in the early Vietnam years, was commonplace. The same can be said about the force reconnaissance companies. It was not uncommon for the reconnaissance unit, assigned in direct support, to be used as a "point man" for the infantry. "Walk in" was the primary means of team insertion, either passing through infantry lines—a dangerous maneuver, particularly at night—or by dropping off the line of march. Glorified infantry at best. Compounding this problem was the gross lack of understanding by infantry regimental and battalion commanders of the reconnaissance mission and capabilities.

The philosophy and personality of the commanding officer of a separate battalion or company has a far greater impact on his unit than that of the infantry battalion or company commander. This has been registered in my mind since PhibRecon days and was only reinforced again on this tour in Vietnam. As you are so acutely aware, *corporals and sergeants are truly the backbone of the reconnaissance game*. Have you ever been on a patrol where the personality of the patrol leader didn't come into play?

The Stingray concept was being employed during this time frame, although, as I recall, it was coming primarily from recon observation points or positions (OPs) rather than recon patrols. More on OPs later! The major problem was battle damage assessment (BDA) missions. The emphasis on "body count" in Vietnam was appalling and it went all the way up the chain of command. I'll give you a prime example.

Let's say a recon OP observed a battalion-size enemy unit moving quickly through the valley floor below. This was normally a nighttime occurrence and detected with the aid of night observation devices (NODs). This sighting resulted in calling in an artillery mission(s). For the sake of discussion let us say that the artillery rounds dropped right on the enemy unit, causing major disruption, and little or no movement was observed for the remainder of the night. How about the BDA? Was it two, twenty, or two hundred enemy dead or wounded? This was difficult, at best, to estimate. Even with a ground patrol inserted the following morning, either by helicopter or walking off the OP, results were inconclusive. Was the mission successful? You bet it was! However, "body counts" were invariably inflated and we learned at the division level, both in G-2 (Intelligence) and G-3 (Operations and Training), to take them with a large grain of salt.

On 9 February 1969, I assumed command of the 1st Reconnaissance Battalion (+), the beginning of my tour in the reconnaissance community. Of the fifteen officers fortunate enough to command this battalion between 1965 and 1971, I was the eighth in line.

At that time the battalion had a fifth letter-company with 1st Force Reconnaissance Company as an attachment. Additionally, we often had one or more recon platoons from the Special Landing Force (SLF) battalions. Operating procedures for the SLFs, when working within the division's tactical area of responsibility (TAOR), was to "chop" (send) their recon platoons over to ReconBn at the time they came ashore. This made for, needless to say, one big recon outfit!

As I recall, our strength was about 970 men, including Navy personnel. At peak strength we had 46 officers and 54 staff noncommissioned officers in the battalion. Add one SLF platoon and we easily had over a thousand men. Fortunately, I was blessed with a great staff and it did not hurt that at division the G-1A and the sergeant major were old recon hands. The bottom line was that not many Marines with either recon experience or training were siphoned off the pipeline. Just prior to joining the battalion I learned that both the battalion executive officer (XO) and the S-3 officer were due for rotation. I was in a position to handpick their replacements. My selections were unsung hitters, older than most majors, consummate professionals with whom it was my privilege to serve.

The 1st Marine Division's mission of protecting the Da Nang complex was rather static in nature compared to our counterparts to the north. The reconnaissance battalion's cantonment, known as Camp Reasoner, its home for several years, had constantly been improved. It certainly could not be described as primitive. I recall joining a new mess sergeant who told me after his first day, "This is better than the mess hall I left in Quantico." I would be foolish to say that the cantonment area was not a morale factor, even in an "all volunteer" organization. I had inherited one of the highest reenlistment and lowest disciplinary rates within the 1st Marine Division. To the best of my knowledge the battalion had only one man "over the hill" during its entire stay in Vietnam. This is not to say that we did not have our problems, but that is another subject.

A bit of my own philosophy concerning personnel, especially as it pertains to staff/support people: Reconnaissance experience be damned! Although it was always welcomed, I was far more interested in having the best-qualified people available to assist me. As an old farm boy from North Dakota, I had learned early on that "you have to have horses to pull the plow." My reasoning went back to my PhibRecon days, when an officer could lose his job for failing a motor transport inspection. I really believe that some Marine reconnaissance units, over the years, "lost the bubble" when they insisted that virtually all recon personnel be able to pass something akin to the Ranger school physical fitness test prior to joining a recon unit.

I recall Division informing me that they had a fine young engineer lieutenant who desired to extend his tour if he could be assigned to recon battalion. I grabbed him up in a heartbeat! He was not only a fine officer, who quickly absorbed the recon training, but he brought us much-needed engineer expertise. The same could be said for any staff function. My adjutant, for example, was a "mustang" first lieutenant who had spent his entire enlisted career in administration. He could not have passed the Army's airborne physical fitness test if his very life depended on it, but the division adjutant regarded him as being one of the finest personnel administrators in the division. He worked well with the companies, and the entire battalion benefited from his presence. Along the same line, one of my problems was a parking lot full of radio vehicles which had to be maintained, although not tactically utilized. My communications officer and motor transport officer, with no recon experience between them, came up with a great solution. They assigned the vehicles at the company level for all first-echelon-level maintenance and training. They placed compatible radios on the company-manned OPs and they were utilized as a company radio admin net. Another problem that quickly went away! I guess what I'm trying to say is that while we could train most anyone to be a reconnaissance man, there was no capability to train a motor transport chief. Enough said on this subject. . . .

The reconnaissance battalion was averaging approximately twenty patrols in the bush at any given time, while in addition manning five OPs. This meant that the individual Marine, at the company level, would average two patrols each month and spend one week out on an OP. The recon plan for any given week would be developed in conjunction with the division G-2. We had one dedicated air package each day which consisted of four CH-46 helicopters, one CH-47 Chinook transport helicopter, and two UH-1 (Huey) helicopter gunships. The Hueys were later replaced by the AH-1 as quickly as the Cobras came into the inventory. As the troops would say, "Four trucks, a tractor, and two guns." We used the CH-47s, which were capable of handling a sling-loaded water trailer or radio vehicle, primarily for resupplying the OPs. We often had two air packages available, especially following periods of bad weather, which was not at all unusual during the lengthy monsoon season.

A secret to success, one not enjoyed by infantry units, was the morning briefing. The daily air package would normally arrive before 0700. They would shut down their aircraft and the pilots would join the team leaders inside our S-2 hootch. A briefing followed concerning the day's sequence of events, priorities, insertion/extraction sites, alternate landing sites, and so on. The pilots, more often than not, recommended changes that would invariably speed things up. The bottom line was that when the birds left the pad, everyone was working off the same sheet of music. This resulted in few, if any, operational discrepancies! I'll never forget the staff secretary of the 1st Marine Division Air Wing calling one morning to inform me that the CG desired to attend the next day's briefing. Upon arrival he informed me that he had come to learn our secret. He went on to say that in the past month we had shot up more of his birds than the rest of the division combined. Yet, no operational discrepancies were either being filed or received and his people were even standing in line to fly our missions. The secret to success, of course, was the morning briefing session. Also contributing was the fact that we fed helicopter crews hot chow on the pad and were quick with citation recommendations/confirmations. Again, luxuries the infantry units were not in a position to afford. Overall, the helicopter squadrons that supported us were excellent—some better than others. It was very simply a matter of experience. Our recon Marines were very perceptive. If you were down at the pad when the air package arrived on any given morning, you would hear comments like, "Hey, it's Lady Ace, we've got it made today!"

We are too busy sawing to sharpen the saw!
                                        —Author unknown

One of our well-known retired general officers, and a former boss of mine, has always maintained that "you only command two echelons down." In other words, your real influence only stretches so far. Upon joining 1st Recon Battalion, I felt that there were four areas I could directly influence. The first was to "lighten" the individual recon Marine's load. They looked like overburdened infantrymen. It is interesting to note that even today, 1997, at least four current R&D projects are pointed toward lightening the load of the reconnaissance Marine. The second was to reduce the length of our patrols. Tired Marines can easily become careless Marines. The third was to halt the practice of "ghosting." This was having a corporal or sergeant listed as the patrol leader with a new staff noncommissioned officer or new commissioned officer going along for the ride. The senior man was now always listed as the patrol leader and given the admonishment that only a fool will not take advantage of the experience available. It was not unusual that the team's corpsman had the most experience in the bush! We had, however, lots of one month's worth of experience and ten months on the job. Last, but certainly not least, was **the emphasis placed on training**.

A word about radio call signs. As you are perhaps aware, the reconnaissance battalion was assigned more individual call signs than the rest of the entire division combined. Although these changed periodically, we had so many call signs that we always retained many of them, month after month. Individual teams, accordingly, grew attached to their particular call sign. When I joined the battalion, they even, in many cases, had the call sign painted on the team's hootch. I met a good deal of resistance initially in constantly switching call signs. Even I would rather have remained "Swift Scout 6" than becoming "Snow Flake 6," but so be it! The attachment to call signs slowly but surely disappeared.

Another challenge was educating regimental commanders as to the role of reconnaissance assets in support of their infantry operations. I have previously mentioned the fragmentation of the reconnaissance assets in the earlier years and the problems this caused. This led commanders into thinking they had to have a recon company in direct support on any named operation. This first surfaced during Operation Oklahoma Hills in March 1969. Fortunately for me, I'd worked for the regimental commander on different occasions and there was, I believe, a mutual respect for one another. I explained that in "direct support" he would have perhaps four teams available at any given time. He would put them in, take them out, and go get them if they should get into trouble. In "general support" he would get as many teams as the situation dictated, and the battalion would be responsible for the teams' insertion(s). Further, we would place a reconnaissance liaison officer on the regimental staff and debrief at his headquarters if the situation was warranted. He bought all this and it set a precedent for all subsequent operations with his regiment.

When a task force was formed, normally with a brigadier general in command, I turned to 1st Force Reconnaissance Company to act as the "eyes and ears" of the command. In early 1969, Task Force Yankee was formed and it serves as a good example. 1st Force Recon was placed in direct support and the Marines did a superb job. As background, my predecessor, Lt. Col. Larry P. Charon, had maintained a separate identity with 1st Force Recon as part of the battalion, but with a minimum of effort I was able to sever the umbilical cord. This subsequently paid great dividends. In June 1969 we "chopped" (transferred) 1st Force to the III Marine Amphibious Force Headquarters (III MAF) under the command of Lt. Gen. Herman Nickerson. Up north, 3d Force Recon Company had been totally assimilated into 3d Reconnaissance Battalion. As a result, III MAF had to wait until August before the company could be reconstituted and was ready for operational employment, until the command of Maj. Alex Lee.

(I will, however, always have a soft spot in my heart for 1st Force Recon Company. I made the last parachute jump of my career with the Marines of 1st Force, just prior to sending them off to III MAF.)

Two other incidents which set precedents early on are

worth mentioning. The first involved inserting a reconnaissance team into an area that we knew, from our own reporting, was swarming with North Vietnamese Army (NVA) units. Both III MAF and the 1st Marine Division intelligence folks were demanding additional confirmation on enemy activity. My analogy to the commanding general was that "we can look through the bars of the cage and see the tiger. . . . Now you're asking me to go inside the cage and get bitten just to prove he's there." I was told, in so many words, either you do it or we'll find someone who will. My recon teams went in that morning, were compromised within ten minutes, and we spent all day trying to get them out. Fortunately, with no loss of life! However, some men were wounded and we had several birds full of bullet holes. The bottom line was that there were no more "demand" insertions from on high. I should add that this was not the result of my dynamic personality. The III MAF Surveillance and Reconnaissance Center (SRC) was activated and they took control of the two force reconnaissance companies. As a result, we were able to concentrate all of our efforts within the 1st Marine Division's TAOR.

The second incident involved tactical decisions on behalf of the commander. We were forced to temporarily evacuate an observation post due to the proximity of a scheduled B-52 Arc Light mission. The plan was simply to pull back along a ridgeline and then return to the OP once the scheduled mission had been completed. To make a long story short, they were in contact in the early afternoon and I jerked them out with an air package that was deadheading home. The division G-2 went absolutely ballistic for abandoning an OP without his knowledge, and placed me on report! The division chief of staff, after listening to the G-2, asked me for my side of the story. I told the chief it was a simple matter of **who** was commanding 1st Reconnaissance Battalion. It was a tactical decision on my behalf, and division had been concurrently informed. Further, I was ready to go to the "oleo man" to get this matter resolved. The chief of staff simply said, "Colonel, go back and command your battalion!" I should add, we returned to the OP the following morning without incident. To the best of my knowledge no hard feelings resulted and the incident was never mentioned again.

A bit more on 1st Recon's OPs. For the most part our OPs were strategically located and it was here that we ran most of our Stingray operations. With the coming of the integrated observation devices (IODs) we became much more sophisticated. On the "hot" OPs we maintained a forward observer team and, occasionally, a forward air control team. We also had to reinforce the OPs, as the enemy knew damn well where the fire was coming from! They were consistently probed and on more than one occasion we "had them in the wire." This reinforced my feeling concerning the vulnerability of a single patrol on a Stingray mission.

Another personal philosophy concerning reconnaissance patrolling. . . . Akin to the old free-fall parachute adage, "when in doubt, whip it out," mine was "when in doubt, get them out!" If a reconnaissance patrol in contact with the enemy could not manage to break off that contact by late afternoon, my instructions were to go in, get them, and bring them home. There is nothing good about trying to conduct a nighttime extraction under fire. And, as Vince Lombardi used to say about the forward pass: "Only three things can happen and two of them are bad." Seriously, life is too precious. Live to fight another day was my motto! Compounding the problem was the CH-46 helicopter. To say the least it was not the ideal bird for employing recon assets, but it was all we had except on very rare occasions. Accordingly, I felt we were somewhat restricted.

During my tenure with 1st Recon Battalion, we ran well over a thousand patrols. Although some of them could be considered milk runs, the vast majority were not. We ran successful wiretaps on four occasions, which III MAF considered quite a feat. We had several prisoner snatches, too. On one occasion a recon team was observing one of our infantry battalions moving in trace in the Arizona Territory, a notorious VC/NVA staging area west of Da Nang. Moving parallel to them was an NVA unit estimated to be at company strength. Coming up on the infantry battalion's tactical radio net, the team apprised them of the developing situation. The battalion commander was then able to swing into a blocking position and proceeded to decimate an NVA company without sustaining any friendly casualties. In my opinion that was reconnaissance at its best. I'm also pleased to report that we were the first, to the best of my knowledge, to employ both the "ladder" and the "special purpose insertion/extraction" (SPIE) gear operationally.

Another factor in our favor was the Marine Corps' lenient policy on extensions during the Vietnam War. As I recall, for a six-month extension an individual would receive a thirty-day leave. For most this was spent in Australia with a fast trip home, toward the end of the leave period, to visit Mom and Dad. Additionally, the CG gave me the authority for a very liberal rest and relaxation (R&R) policy. The bottom line was that "deserving" Marines could get two R&R trips per thirteen-month tour of duty. A great incentive and morale booster to say the least, to those men who so willingly laid their lives on the line. It also meant that an individual three months into his extension was eligible for R&R. Combine this with "out of country" jump school and scuba school, and it was no wonder that morale within the reconnaissance battalion was high. As previously mentioned, our cantonment area was one of the best, and except for the occasional rocket attack it was safer than being in San Diego. The result was that the battalion was laced, particularly on the staff side, with experienced young noncommissioned officers who had spent more than their fair share of time in the bush, on patrol. As a patrol leader, when you were on the radio with any watch stander in the battalion COC, you were speaking to someone who had walked in the same footsteps. Not surprisingly, our well-trained and seasoned noncommissioned officers were invaluable in the training role. There was little or no slacking off in professionalism, as there was always the threat of being returned to the States. My successors reported that in the 1970–71 time frame the extension policy was terminated with the drawdown of personnel. Understandably, the experience level dropped alarmingly.

Back to the Stingray concept. . . . I think you are beginning to gather that I avoided it like the plague! Not so at all. However, there were conditions that had to be met. I firmly believe that when we placed people in harm's way, we also had an obligation to support them. When a reconnaissance patrol "initiates" contact they are really in harm's way. **I believe they had to know that we stood ready to support them!** This was especially true when we operated outside the artillery fan and during periods of marginal flying weather. Compounding the problem were two significant factors. First was the emphasis on maintaining radio contact, and second was bringing home our dead, both foreign to my early recon background! I cannot tell you how often we sent out OV-10 (Broncos) to reestablish contact with a team that was temporarily off the air for one reason or another. There was no escaping this, as the enemy had the capability, and used it, to monitor our radio nets in the division COC.

As previously mentioned, with a number of patrols operating in the bush, we always had one, and often two, dedicated air packages working for us. With a patrol in trouble, this meant diverting one's assets. And, anytime we requested an additional air package it had to come at someone else's expense. Accordingly, I avoided Stingray missions for the individual patrol unless conditions were ideal. As a footnote, in later years, with the troop drawdown, Stingray patrols were commonplace. I have spoken with one of my successors who had four Stingray teams in contact at the same time. This raises the hair on the back of my neck. An experienced patrol in contact and with wounded, requesting an emergency extraction, doesn't need to be second-guessed, much less be informed that there can be no extraction "today." I don't think I was overly cautious in my approach. I prefer to call it assigning acceptable risk.

I cannot say enough about the young Marines/corpsmen who joined the reconnaissance battalion. The overwhelming majority came right out of the training pipeline without the benefit of any formal reconnaissance training. Once assigned to the battalion they volunteered to remain, assimilated the training, and quickly, for the most part, became productive members of the command. It has been said that you do not command a reconnaissance unit, be it a patrol, company, or battalion, but rather serve with it. There is some truth to this statement. Lou Holtz recently said in briefing a backup quarterback, "I don't expect you to push the team, just get in the seat and drive."

We had a very good group of staff noncommissioned officers and, as is usual, they were the backbone of the recon battalion. Those with prior reconnaissance experience were invaluable in both the training and leadership role. I was particularly pleased with those Marines with no prior recon experience!

I've already given you my outlook on personnel; however, I do have another story to relate concerning personnel. Upon taking command of the battalion I learned that my sergeant major was due for rotation home to the States. The division sergeant major informed me that there was no one on the horizon with any recon experience and no one available he really wanted to send to me. However, if I was willing to wait a couple of weeks, he had a "real water walker" who would be coming into country. When my new man arrived he informed me that he had never served or desired to serve in recon; what he really wanted was to go to his old outfit, the 1st Marines. Following some discussion concerning the needs of our battalion, I asked him to give us a week, with the proviso that I would have him reassigned if this remained his desire. Three days later he informed me that he wanted to stay. The only Marine I ever had to convince that his home was with recon! To say he was very effective would be an understatement.

Our young lieutenants for the most part were excellent. They, as a group, have been *much maligned* by many writers of the Vietnam era. Most of them arrived in Vietnam with only what they had learned at the Basic School for experience. But many tend to forget just how good the Basic School is at training our new Marine officers. In Korea, I learned as a young lieutenant fresh out of the Basic School that as soon as your troops discovered that your primary concern was their welfare, you were home free as a troop leader. Nothing original, you understand, although this point of view was emphasized to all incoming officers. It has been most gratifying as the years roll by to observe their progress. Their success is obvious in civilian pursuits and, for those who remained in the Corps, evident by the number who reached field grade (major, lieutenant colonel, colonel) and general officer rank.

A few words, if I may, on **command**. I insisted that all of my officers must "get their feet wet." However, a company commander, or platoon leader for that matter, cannot spend all of his time in the bush, as he has responsibilities beyond a single patrol. By the same token a battalion commander cannot spend his time riding every emergency extract, much as he would like to do so. I had a hazardous duty flag on my official record when I arrived in Vietnam, resulting from my tour with the CIA. As a result I would get my derriere chewed by the CG every time I rode in a gunship or on an insertion/extraction bird, even though he fully realized that it came with the territory. Who was it who said that "desecration was the better part of valor"?

A few parting shots on Stingray tactics. I believe my approach was valid considering the environment I found myself in during 1969. When you look at the mission of the reconnaissance battalion, the number of people we maintained in the bush, and the assets we had available to support them, the choice was an easy one.

In my opinion the force reconnaissance companies were in the best position to employ Stingray tactics conducted by the individual patrol. Most importantly, they were inserted into those areas where the division assets were not going to patrol, regardless of what was uncovered.

In 1969 we were all aware that the nation's commitment to the war in Vietnam had ended. Plans for the drawdown of forces were being implemented months prior to my arrival. It would be foolish to say this did not have an impact, because it certainly did. To get the job done with the fewest casualties possible was my plan of the day. For the record, I held the battalion for eight months with a change of command on 12 October 1969. Thus ended my reconnaissance odyssey with the Corps in Vietnam.

It has been twenty-eight years since I commanded the 1st Reconnaissance Battalion in Vietnam, and in many instances it seems like only yesterday. Upon occasion it still creeps back into my dreams. Reflections are difficult, especially without the benefit of historical research as my memory dims with the passage of time. Our casualties were relatively few in number when one considers the magnitude of our operations or compares them to those of an infantry battalion. They all, however, had a great impact and there is no escaping the responsibility for the Marines and Navy corpsmen who were killed or wounded during my tenure. They willingly went in harm's way on whatever missions they were assigned. I'll never forget flying out to a hospital ship with the CG to award a young Marine, who had lost his right leg, a Bronze Star and a Purple Heart. His first words, as I came up to his bedside, were, with tears running down his cheeks, "Skipper, I'm sorry I let you down!" Memorial services, although a vital necessity, were never easy. I recall one of my officers, years later, telling me that he never would forget my parting words at these services. This I had not remembered. He reminded me, "You always said, 'We must put this behind us and look ahead, as the helicopters arrive tomorrow morning at 0700.' "

In retrospect I should have been more insistent upon recognizing my young Marines and corpsmen. I don't recall ever being turned down on an award recommendation. To the contrary, I remember division actually upgrading my recommendations on two occasions. I was queried by the CG more than once over the sparse number of award recommendations that came out of the battalion. The majority of our missions were surveillance in nature and did not involve frequent contact with the enemy. I felt, as did my company commanders, that we were just doing our job. In looking back, this I would change!

Along this line, there are numerous other factors that could be discussed. However, in the final analysis I only attempted to fine tune the excellent organization that I inherited.

The Book of Ecclesiastes 3:1 informs us, "for everything there is a season, and a time for every matter under heaven." The biblical writers however do not specifically address a time for the future or a time for the past! I have been discussing the past, but what about the future? The demise of the reconnaissance battalion has diminished capabilities at the division level. To whatever level it will return still remains to be seen. At the force level, with the coming of the surveillance, reconnaissance, intelligence group, the capability remains. There is a need for longer tours of duty within the reconnaissance field due to the never-ending need for complex and specialized training. This, too, must be recognized! We might do well to look at the Australian Special Air Service (SAS) in this regard. I crossed paths with the SAS on three different occasions throughout my military career. They were serious professionals, both regular and reserves, who tend to spend a career in the business.

Some additional food for thought. . . . The future of Stingray-type operations will not rest solely with reconnaissance-type units. If we look at the configuration of today's Marine rifle squad, the sophistication of weaponry/delivery systems, communications equipment, position locating devices, etc., the possibilities seem endless. It may well be that we in Vietnam were only the wave of the future! I hope that my observations and comments will be of help in your explanation of the Stingray concept.

— 20 —

Vietnamization and Redeployment Reconnaissance Operations: 1970-1971

At the beginning of 1970, III MAF reconnaissance forces consisted of the 1st Reconnaissance Battalion and the 1st and 3d Force Reconnaissance Companies. The two force reconnaissance companies were controlled by III MAF, and 1st Recon Battalion was under its parent 1st Marine Division.

Vietnamization, the U.S. policy initiated by President Nixon in 1969, was the phasing out of U.S. forces and the turning over to the South Vietnamese of responsibility for prosecution of the war. The policy included maximizing U.S. military materiel assistance to help strengthen South Vietnam and intensify ongoing pacification programs. U.S. strategists hoped that South Vietnam could successfully oppose North Vietnamese forces without U.S. support.

Although U.S. leaders hoped South Vietnam could be prepared to defend itself, that goal was secondary to getting out of the war with "honor," as President Nixon characterized it.

By now, reconnaissance patrolling had become a well-developed skill, but one practiced without much of the needed coordination and support necessary to conduct successful Stingray missions. And that was a problem; no one wanted to become that last Marine killed in the Vietnam War.

The 1st and 3d Force Reconnaissance Companies, directed by the III MAF Surveillance and Reconnaissance Center, conducted patrols deep in enemy base areas, usually beyond the 1st Marine Division TAOR. Based at Phu Bai, the 3d Force Reconnaissance Company, commanded by Maj. Alex Lee, concentrated its efforts on the A Shau Valley, a major communist infiltration route and assembly area in western Thua Thien Province. Patrols from this company, usually inserted and extracted by helicopters from the U.S. Army's 2d Squadron, 17th Cavalry, ventured far into the mountains to locate enemy units, base camps, and storage sites. They spotted targets for artillery fire and B-52 strikes and occasionally fought small communist units. During January 1970 the company observed or encountered 159 enemy and killed 26 in eight separate engagements with losses of only one Marine killed and 14 wounded. The company also directed 38 artillery fire missions.

1st Force Reconnaissance Company, working from Da Nang, conducted long-range patrols in Quang Nam and Quang Tin Provinces. During January this company saw much less action than the 3d. The company completed 13 patrols, sighted 12 enemy, and killed one, with no casualties.

During February and March 1970 the Keystone Bluejay redeployment reduced force reconnaissance strength, and the III MAF–XXIV Corps exchange of roles ended separate force reconnaissance operations. The 3d Force Reconnaissance Company ceased combat activities in February, although the unit, almost at zero strength, remained in Vietnam until July. With the breakup of the III MAF Surveillance and Reconnaissance Center, both the cadred 3d and the still active 1st Force Reconnaissance Companies were placed under the operational control of the 1st Marine Division. 1st Force Recon Company, attached to Lt. Col. William C. Drumwright's 1st Reconnaissance Battalion, continued operations as a division reconnaissance unit.

At the beginning of 1970 the 1st Reconnaissance Battalion was over strength, with five letter-companies instead of the usual four. Company A, 5th Reconnaissance Battalion was also attached, but it redeployed during Keystone Bluejay. The battalion performed a variety of missions. It furnished teams to support infantry search and destroy operations, secure firebases, and locate targets for artillery raids. Scuba divers from the battalion checked bridges in the 1st Marine Division TAOR for underwater demolitions and searched streams for submerged cave entrances and weapon caches. Detachments from the battalion also protected four of the IOD observation posts.

Patrolling the western fringes of the division TAOR was the reconnaissance battalion's principal function. In those generally mountainous areas the enemy could move less cautiously because of the cover provided by the jungle canopy. Operating in six-man teams, reconnaissance units monitored movement over the network of trails that linked the rugged base areas to the fertile lowlands surrounding Da Nang. Each team included an officer or NCO patrol leader, a radioman, three specially trained riflemen, and a Navy corpsman. During most of 1970 the battalion had forty-eight such teams available for duty. Normally about half the teams were in the field, scattered from Elephant Valley to the far reaches of Base Area 112. Teams not patrolling or on other assignments protected the battalion cantonment near Division Ridge, underwent refresher training, and prepared for their next mission.

Reconnaissance patrolling had become a well-developed skill. Each team member backpacked sixty-five to seventy pounds of food, ammunition, and equipment to sustain him for as many as six days in the field. Helicopters lifted the teams to their assigned operating areas. After insertion, teams worked their way along streambeds, followed enemy trails, or "broke brush" across country, carefully noting and reporting details of terrain and enemy activity. Some teams tried to take prisoners or, using the Stingray concept of operations, concealed themselves where they could direct artillery and air strikes on enemy troops and base camps. At the end of their assigned five- or six-day missions, or when they were discovered and attacked by the enemy, helicopters extracted the teams.

Patrolling resulted in a steady stream of small contacts. During June 1970, for example, the 1st Reconnaissance Battalion conducted 130 patrols, sighting 834 Communists, and directed 120 artillery fire missions and 25 air strikes. Reconnaissance battalion Marines were credited with 198 enemy killed and the capture of three individual weapons, at a cost of two Marines dead, fifteen wounded, and nine nonbattle casualties. For the individual reconnaissance Marine, this level of activity entailed a grueling routine. Lieutenant Colonel Drumright, the battalion commander, reported:

"These kids . . . work very hard. You put them in the field five days; they're out of the field three. Their first day back is cleaning gear. Their second day, they train. . . . They go through throwing hand grenades again, scouting and patrolling, [and] immediate action drills, which is being able to get that first shot off the fastest, and . . . we do night work with them. So they never really have a day off."

The primary purpose of reconnaissance patrols was to obtain information, usually through surveillance of enemy movement. Frequently reconnaissance teams directed artillery and air strikes on VC/NVA units while avoiding contact with them, but teams often found themselves involved in close combat. Some fights erupted from ambushes set by teams or from efforts to take prisoners; others were meeting engagements with small NVA or VC elements.

In the first months of 1970 many contacts resulted from an aggressive counterreconnaissance effort begun on orders of NVA General Binh, the Front 4 commander. At Binh's direction North Vietnamese regulars and main force Viet Cong formed fifteen- to twenty-five-man teams to protect their base areas. Some of these teams carried captured M-16s and wore American clothing and camouflage paint to confuse Marines during firefights. The counterreconnaissance units watched for helicopters inserting Marine recon teams and signaled the Marines' arrival with rifle shots, then tried to close in and attack the Marines before they could leave the landing zone.

The Marines responded to these enemy tactics by making false insertions, often complete with helicopter gunship and fixed-wing landing zone preparations, before actually putting in a team. To avoid forewarning the enemy, some insertions were made without LZ preparation fires. As a result of these varied measures most reconnaissance teams were able to move out of their landing zones before the enemy arrived. The Communists then tried to track the Marines across country. These deadly games of hide-and-seek frequently culminated in firefights and emergency extractions. Due to Marine small-arms proficiency and the availability of lavish air and artillery support for teams in contact, the enemy invariably suffered many more casualties in these engagements than they inflicted.

On 14 June 1970 a team from Company E, 1st Reconnaissance Battalion, fought the battalion's most severe patrol action of the year. The team, call sign Flakey Snow, consisted of five enlisted Marines, a Navy corpsman, and two South Korean Marines assigned as patrol members as part of a combined allied reconnaissance training program. Helicopters inserted the patrol at 1122 on the fourteenth in the southwestern Que Sons about five miles west of FSB (fire support base) Ryder. Although deep in the mountains, Flakey Snow's first area of operations was a level region with no jungle canopy, but a secondary growth of small trees, bushes, bamboo, and sharp-edged elephant grass. The team's arrival was unopposed and it moved northward from the landing zone along a wide trail that showed signs of recent heavy use. After an uneventful hour, the Marines crossed a small stream and turned eastward on an intersecting trail. This trail, also obviously well traveled, ran toward a hill where the patrol leader, Sgt. Frank E. Diaz, planned to spend the night.

Clouds closed in and heavy rain was falling. About 1220, Diaz called a halt along the trail to wait until the rain stopped. There the Marines heard heavy machine gun and automatic weapons fire. Although no bullets seemed to be coming toward them, the members of Flakey Snow formed a defensive perimeter with only the elephant grass for cover and quietly readied their weapons. As they did, two Viet Cong, both armed with AK-47s, came walking up the trail "right into us," Diaz recalled. The Marines shot and killed both of them but the firing gave away their position. Diaz at once reported by radio that his team was in contact.

Contact quickly became heavy. From positions north, east, and west of the Marines, an enemy unit, later estimated to be at least fifty men, opened fire with 12.7mm machine guns and automatic weapons. The Marines, with their backs to the stream they had just crossed, hugged the ground and returned fire with M-16s and their one M-79 grenade launcher. Whether the enemy was a counterreconnaissance unit or simply a large force encountered by chance was never established, but it was obvious that they were determined to overwhelm Flakey Snow. "They really wanted to get us," Diaz reported later, "for whatever reason they had in mind." The enemy began rushing the Marine position in groups of three and four, firing and throwing grenades. Some closed to within thirty feet of the Marines before being cut down. Bodies piled up in front of the patrol. Diaz had his men pull two or three of the closest into a barricade. One American Marine was mortally wounded and another was hit in the shoulder by grenade fragments. A Korean received a severe leg wound. "All this time," Diaz recalled, "we could hear people moaning and groaning on both sides. . . . The enemy just kept coming, and we just kept shooting and shooting."

Diaz called for an aerial observer, and an OV-10 arrived over the patrol at 1245. The aircraft at once began strafing the enemy positions, causing some secondary explosions and more "loud crying and moaning." At 1300, Cobra gunships arrived on station and added their machine guns and rockets to Marine firepower. The closeness of the enemy to Flakey Snow prevented the use of artillery, but according to Diaz the gunships were "really accurate and a great help in getting us all out of there." In spite of this punishment the determined enemy hung on. Their fire slackened as the helicopters made their strafing passes, but then resumed.

At 1345, CH-46s from HMM-263 arrived to extract the team, but the wounded could not be hoisted out, so the pilot of one of the Sea Knights, Maj. Peter E. Benet, executive officer of HMM-263, managed to land close enough to the team, with the nose of his aircraft hanging over the stream and the rear wheels on the bank. Benet's copilot, 1st Lt. Peter F. Goetz, reported that as the helicopter settled in, "we had to cut down through the elephant grass with our blades, the elephant grass was so high."

Diaz at first thought that the helicopter had been shot down. Then he saw the tailgate opening and began moving his men toward it while he and the reconnaissance battalion executive officer, who had jumped out of the gate with a rifle, covered the withdrawal. Under continuing enemy fire the reconnaissance Marines scrambled on board carrying their injured and dying. A few enemy tried to rush the withdrawing team but Diaz and the extraction officer gunned them down. Lieutenant Goetz, monitoring the helicopter's radios, saw another enemy soldier "pop up, right about our eleven o'clock, with an AK. . . . It was really fortunate that one of the Cobras was passing over us at the time and spotted him and blasted him with some rockets."

At 1353 the helicopter lifted off with all members of Flakey Snow. Diaz and his men had only a magazine of ammunition left between them and a single M-79 round; the helicopter crew had expended all the ammunition from its two .50-caliber machine guns. At the price of one American Marine dead of wounds, another slightly wounded, and a South Korean Marine severely injured, Flakey Snow had killed at least eighteen enemy in front of the patrol's position. An unknown number of enemy had been killed or wounded farther away, either by small arms and grenades or by OV-10 and helicopter guns and rockets. Sergeant Diaz reported that "the firefight was so intense, and the fire was coming from so many directions, that the enemy themselves had killed their own people, trying to get to us."

While no other fighting during 1970–71 equaled Flakey Snow's in severity, reconnaissance teams continued to meet aggressive enemy counteraction, either from chance contacts with regular units or special counterreconnaissance teams. On 3 September a six-man patrol from Company C inserted in the mountains just south of Elephant Valley came into contact with at least fifteen to twenty enemy who tried to surround the team. After a firefight in which the Marines killed three enemy and suffered one man wounded, the team was extracted only fourteen minutes after insertion. As soon as the extraction helicopters departed, the 11th Marines fired 225 105mm rounds into the landing zone, and fixed-wing jets also struck the area.

Artillery bombardment and air strikes on LZs were a standard 1st Reconnaissance Battalion tactic after an extraction under fire. The way Lieutenant Colonel Drumright saw it, under those circumstances a reconnaissance team acted on the enemy the way "a little bucket of honey" acted on bees. He explained, "The bees, they'd swarm all around. And then you'd pull the bucket of honey out and you'd work the area over, and then you get all the bees that don't run off. . . . You get them out of their caves. They have to come out of their caves to fight."

By late 1970 the enemy had become much more cautious about attacking reconnaissance teams. Instead, their counterreconnaissance forces began shadowing Marine patrols, following them, and signaling their location with rifle shots. The NVA and VC would engage a patrol only if it approached an important base camp or cache. The enemy occasionally used dogs to track the Marines. Reconnaissance teams sought to evade the enemy by night movement; they would establish a night position about sunset, then quietly shift position after dark. To temporarily kill the enemy dogs' sense of smell, the Marines often scattered CS crystals on trails and around night positions.

Combat frequently erupted when reconnaissance patrols unexpectedly burst into occupied camps. To protect their hideouts from air strikes, artillery bombardments, and infantry sweeps, the enemy began locating them in the dense vegetation below the crests of the reverse slopes of ridges. They rarely left discernible trails into those positions. To increase their chances of finding such camps, reconnaissance teams often hacked their way through the vegetation on the slopes rather than following the easier natural routes along crests or streambeds. "Breaking brush" in this way, teams occasionally walked into camps while enemy troops were still in them. When that happened a team would attack immediately, moving quickly through the camp, shooting at any enemy they saw, and throwing grenades into huts, bunkers, and caches. According to Lieutenant Colonel Drumright:

"Our guys could outshoot theirs. They could throw a hand grenade further. They could think a little faster. They used a . . . technique of just going right through the camp throwing hand grenades into every hole and bunker you could find, usually about two or three going through the camp, and the other two or three covering. . . . Then they'd move back out of the area and try to saturate the thing with artillery and air."

Patrolling deep in the mountains had its hazards even when no enemy were encountered. In May a tiger attacked a 1st Force Reconnaissance Company patrol leader while the patrol was in its night position, dragged him off into the bush, and killed him. In September a 1st Reconnaissance Battalion patrol lost two men killed and two others seriously injured in an accident during an unopposed extraction. The battalion suffered its most severe noncombatant loss on 18 November when its commander, Lt. Col. William C. Leftwich, and nine other reconnaissance Marines died in a helicopter crash in the Que Sons. Lt. Col. Bernard E. Trainor, who had previous reconnaissance experience, then commanded 1st Reconnaissance Battalion until its redeployment in the spring of 1971.

With five years of experience behind them, the division and wing had developed well-tested techniques and equipment for inserting, supporting, and extracting reconnaissance teams. To assure prompt artillery response to calls for fire and at the same time prevent accidental shelling of friendly units, the division established a special reconnaissance zone for each deployed patrol in which only that patrol could direct fire missions. The 11th Marines usually designated a battery or platoon to support each patrol and stationed a liaison officer at the 1st Reconnaissance Battalion CP to assist in fire planning and coordination.

The 1st MAW's quick-reaction helicopter package, Mission 80, could be used for emergency extraction of teams, among other tasks. Reconnaissance units had developed standard procedures for teams involved in a contact from which they could not extricate themselves. Normally the first step would be to call in the nearest OV-10 to locate the unit and provide initial suppressive fires. The wing would then dispatch two Cobra gunships and two CH-46s to lift the Marines out. While the Cobras worked the enemy over, to within twenty-five yards of the reconnaissance team if necessary, a CH-46 maneuvered to an LZ or lowered a special extraction device. Final authority to pull out a team in trouble rested with the 1st Reconnaissance Battalion commander. "When it happens out there, it happens very quickly," Lieutenant Colonel Drumright reported. "And the key . . . is to very quickly get the OV-10 and start the gunships out and make up your mind . . . whether to leave them in or take them out." Some of the most skillful patrol leaders could maneuver their men out of a contact and continue their missions, but the battalion usually followed the more prudent course of immediately withdrawing an engaged team and reinserting it later.

A new piece of equipment, the special patrol insertion/extraction (SPIE) line, made it easier and safer for teams to go in and out of small mountain and jungle landing zones. To put teams in or take them out of sites where a helicopter could not land, the Marines had previously used a 120-foot ladder lowered from the tail ramp. Because of its weight the ladder was hard to maneuver in narrow spaces, and in hot weather at high elevations helicopters often had difficulty lifting it in this "thin" air with Marines hanging onto it. In those situations the SPIE, a strong nylon line, proved to be a practical alternative. Much lighter than the ladder and more compact when stowed in a helicopter, the line could be dropped quickly through small openings in the jungle. Reconnaissance team members, who wore a special harness, then hooked themselves onto the line, and the helicopter lifted them straight up and flew back to base trailing the Marines behind it. If necessary, Marines could fire their weapons while attached to the SPIE rig; many found it more comfortable to ride in flight than the ladder.

To train reconnaissance Marines for their exacting job, the 1st Reconnaissance Battalion conducted periodic eleven-day indoctrination courses for all newly arrived personnel. The course, supervised by the battalion S-3, included instruction and practice in the use of the PRC-25 radio, map reading, first aid, rappelling down cliffs and from helicopters, air and artillery forward observer procedures, and combat intelligence reporting. New reconnaissance Marines also practiced scuba diving and rubber boat handling. Weapons refresher training and physical conditioning received emphasis throughout the course. According to Lieutenant Colonel Drumright, "It was strictly scouting and patrolling, and learning to shoot first . . . and straight . . . and to throw a hand grenade. Learn to hide. Learn to move. Get him in physical condition so he can outwalk the enemy." The course ended with the planning and execution of a practice patrol in a safe area.

Under an agreement between the 1st Marine Division, Quang Da Special Zone, and the 2d ROK Marine Corps Brigade, the 1st Reconnaissance Battalion conducted three-week training courses for ARVN and Korean troops. During 1970 the battalion instructed 230 members of the ARVN 1st Ranger Battalion as well as the reconnaissance companies of the 51st Regiment and the Korean Marine Brigade. Vietnamese and Korean graduates of the course then participated in Marine patrols, one or two men to a team. The South Korean Marines who took part in the Flakey Snow fight were trained under this program. Both Korean and South Vietnamese reconnaissance troops learned quickly and performed well with the Marines.

The battalion also trained combat-operations-center and communications personnel for the Allies, in the hope that the South Vietnamese, in particular, would eventually carry out their own independent reconnaissance effort. Repeatedly the 1st Marine Division pressed Quang Da Special Zone to begin deploying all-Vietnamese patrols in a reconnaissance zone separate from that patrolled by the Marines. The South Vietnamese continually refused, pleading a lack of manpower, helicopters, and radios. They preferred to continue combined patrols with the Marines. The South Vietnamese did not have enough helicopters to support the kind of wide-ranging reconnaissance program the Marines carried on. For the reconnaissance missions they ran they relied on foot patrols from fixed bases. Marine commanders recognized that the Vietnamese would be limited to such short-range operations after the Americans withdrew.

The Keystone Robin Alpha redeployments drastically reduced Marine reconnaissance strength. During August 1970, 1st Force Reconnaissance Company stood down and left for the United States, leaving a subunit of two officers and twenty-nine enlisted men attached to the 1st Reconnaissance Battalion. The reconnaissance battalion itself deactivated Company E in August, and in September companies C and D left Vietnam. These withdrawals halved the number of available reconnaissance teams from forty-eight to twenty-four. The 1st Reconnaissance Battalion, then under Lieutenant Colonel Leftwich, turned over protection of three of the four IOD sites to the infantry regiments and reorganized its two remaining letter companies. Each company would consist of two three-team platoons and one four-team platoon. With these rearrangements, Leftwich planned to have all twenty-four teams available for operations and an average of twelve teams in the field at a time.

With fewer teams available and with operations in the mountains restricted by the fall-winter monsoon, the reconnaissance battalion concentrated much of its patrolling in areas closer to the populated lowlands. As part of Operation Imperial Lake, beginning in early October, the battalion saturated the Que Son Mountains with patrols, keeping eight to ten teams continuously in the area. These teams worked closely with infantry quick-reaction forces in an effort to deny more territory to the enemy while using fewer Marines. Smaller saturation operations covered Charlie Ridge and eastern Elephant Valley.

Instead of being inserted and extracted by helicopters, most of the teams participating in saturation patrolling worked from platoon patrol bases in the mountains. The 1st Reconnaissance Battalion set up the first of these on 5 October on Hill 845 in the Que Sons. Three teams used the hill as a CP, radio relay station, and resting place. Remaining for thirteen days, they fanned out on foot on assigned patrol missions. One team usually rested at the patrol base, constituting a reaction force, while the other two were deployed. From then on the battalion maintained a patrol base continuously in the Que Sons and periodically established bases on Charlie Ridge and in Elephant Valley. When weather often restricted helicopter operations, once inserted into their patrol bases, teams could remain longer in the field and reinforce each other in the event of a major contact. The teams also gained an advantage of surprise, since no helicopter activities, except for those involved in setting up the patrol base, signaled the reconnaissance Marines' entry into the enemy's operating areas.

Under Lieutenant Colonel Trainor's guidance the battalion continued that pattern of operation later in 1970 and during the first months of 1971. Its patrol base on Charlie Ridge became part of Operation Upshur Stream late in January. On both Charlie Ridge and in the Que Sons, infantry platoons took over the protection of reconnaissance patrol bases, while reconnaissance teams did most of the patrolling during Upshur Stream and Imperial Lake. Lieutenant Colonel Trainor observed that his reconnaissance teams usually had the "advantage of the initiative." He later wrote that during his command tenure "no team was ever ambushed; on the contrary it was the teams that did the ambushing."

During late 1970 and early 1971 reconnaissance sightings of enemy troops and reconnaissance-inflicted enemy casualties grew steadily fewer. This decline reflected both reduced Marine reconnaissance activity and the shift of most patrolling to areas closer to Da Nang. The low level of action also indicated an apparent decline in enemy strength and aggressiveness. In December 1970 the 1st Reconnaissance Battalion sighted only 162 NVA and VC during 56 patrols, called ten artillery fire missions and three air strikes, killed 23 enemy, and captured nine weapons. In the same month the battalion lost three Marines wounded in action and seven nonbattle casualties. Action continued at this rate during January and February 1971.

On 14 March 1971 the battalion began its Keystone Robin Charlie redeployment. On that day the Headquarters and Service Company and Company B ceased operations. After a farewell ceremony on the nineteenth, those units left Da Nang on the twenty-fourth with the battalion colors, bound for Camp Pendleton. Company A of the battalion, the reconnaissance element of the 3d MAB, continued operations until 28 April, when it extracted its last two deployed teams from Sherwood Forest, west of Da Nang, and from Elephant Valley. On 1 May the company stood down; by the thirteenth the last reconnaissance Marines left Vietnam.

=== 21 ===

My Thoughts about Stingray Operations in Vietnam*

Stingray excited us more than anything else we were doing. It had begun with a vaguely worded idea in a concept paper devoted to operations in the undefined future. The authors postulated that the Marine Corps units fighting in the last decade of the century might employ search-and-attack teams to bring artillery fire, naval gunfire, and air strikes down on the enemy, rather than attacking him head-on with infantry and armor in the classic manner. We believed in the ability of small units to make a positive contribution to winning battles, one that would be greater than their cost in men and material.

Using Stingray techniques, reconnaissance teams could take advantage of the growing ability of the aviation and artillery arms to provide accurate and responsive fires, and by so doing directly account for the destruction of large numbers of the enemy. It was our view that laser-guided precision munitions and laser-target designators were items that should receive expedited development so that force reconnaissance units in the Republic of Vietnam could use them against the NVA.

While carefully considering Stingray, we concurrently studied combat operations of the Navy's SEAL teams, the

*Interview with Lt. Col. Alex Lee, USMC (Ret.), Commanding Officer, 3d Force Reconnaissance Company, 1969–70.

operations of the Army's various long-range/Ranger elements, and the Marine reconnaissance units in Vietnam. [1st Lt. "Bucky"] Coffman and I were firmly in the camp of those who sought to take advantage of the presence of reconnaissance units in areas normally controlled by the enemy. Neither of us believed in the silent observation philosophy. We wanted to insure that the teams would be prepared to inflict losses on the enemy—large losses!

Stingray, however, was just one of a multitude of missions that reconnaissance teams might be ordered to undertake. If ordered to employ this tactical concept, the teams would need the ability to call artillery fires and direct air strikes, thereby killing large numbers of the enemy quickly. For team survival, any offensive action of this type would be followed by immediate disengagement. Stingray was controversial because many Marines felt that reconnaissance [teams] should merely look and listen, leaving combat action to regular infantry units. Our view was that they could do either, or both, as the situation and the leader in tactical command might determine. We saw effective use of technology as a way for the small element to become a serious threat to larger formations.

LT. COL. ALEX LEE, *Force Recon Command*

Background

The entire concept that eventually came to be known by the formal name of Stingray began for *me* during the period 1960–64 while I was assigned to an entity that had as its title an enigmatic, odd, and unclear nomenclature. We were called Code 121, The Weapons Planning Group. This group was created by Mr. Richard T. Gray and funded throughout by covert money passed down via the Pentagon to the station in California where we were headquartered. Mr. Gray's real name was never mentioned, nor did I ever learn it, despite working for the man for several years and seeing him on ten or more social and professional occasions in later years. Mr.

Richard Gray shared with many men we worked with in the turbulent 1960–64 period a "color" name for simplicity. On various occasions we, too, used names like Mr. Brown, Mr. Black, Mr. Green, or Mr. White as we visited openly and/or covertly in numerous countries around the world.

Code 121 was both an operational and an analyzing entity that went overseas to perform specific combat tasks, collect intelligence, perform other operational tasks levied on us from above, and act as an operational analysis unit. Code 121 created its own operational analysis component, in which some of the operational people also doubled as analysts. In this mode we carefully examined ideas and created different combat scenarios based on scientifically proven possibilities and predictions.

In plain English, as operational analysts we took all the "off the wall" ideas that anyone in the military or scientific community brought to us or could postulate as raw ideas and then ran them out to their logical end results. We examined the future of many aspects of warfare, with a heavy emphasis on all aspects of special operations. When employed overseas we might, using some newly developed piece of equipment, engage in small-unit combat operations. Upon our return the results of those operations would be integrated into our views on the impact of the scientific ideas embodied in the tested equipment and on any future improvements in that particular piece of equipment.

All members of Code 121 were either civilians or military personnel stationed at the U.S. Naval Ordnance Test Station at China Lake, California. This unique base—in shorthand, USNOTS—is one of the greatest technological sites in the United States inventory, and will never, ever, get its "just due" for all of the contributions it has made to the weaponry needed to get the job done in combat. At China Lake one finds the actual melding of operational input with sophisticated scientific thinking. In the development of China Lake, the Navy was actually able to create an area where free thinking was encouraged and where scientists could come to see things from the operational perspective.

It was there that Dr. William McClain came up with the idea for the Sidewinder missile, testing his hypothesis using a board of circuitry that he had pieced together in his own garage. Successes like the Sidewinder missile were standard fare at USNOTS.

We were a small, tight team with our own budget and outside support coming secretly to us from Washington, D.C., via the base command and technical structure. In theory we worked on projects developed locally and created in Washington by our cover control, the Defense Advanced Research Projects Agency (ARPA). Often that was true, but we also responded, in the main, to other agencies of the U.S. government when so tasked. In addition to the military operational types assigned to Code 121, we also had some first-class scientific practitioners. We had a detonation physicist, a high-level mathematician, an aeronautical engineer/electrical engineer (a man who was operationally qualified), and at USNOTS we had immediate access to any scientific discipline we might need. There were literally several hundred Ph.D. holders in the main laboratory, all of whom were immediately accessible, if needed. Our level of priority was sufficiently high to set aside *any* other work, at *any* time—seven days per week!

Although we were a small group (less than twenty individuals), we were approached almost daily by other sections of the base to comment on their particular ideas and help analyze the possible future for those ideas. It was through this type of give-and-take that I was first introduced into the scientific world of lasers, Doppler radar, tropo-scatter communications, freeze-dried and irradiated food, night vision devices (image orthicon intensifiers and all the infrared devices), rip-stop nylon, triangular bullets (the "tround"), fuel-air explosives, steel-shanked boots, and every other possible item that a host of scientific disciplines could bring to the table.

Weapons planning group consistently worked sixteen-hour days as the norm when we were in town and longer days when deployed to faraway places to find answers to questions raised by the president or someone close to him—answers that others would be less well prepared to seek out. We had no charter, no table of organization, and it seemed no limit to the missions that might pop up for us to be asked to accomplish. It was a difficult yet challenging time in our lives.

At the same time we actually did do some "weapons planning" work as part of our daily routine. Mr. Gray had decided that we should examine small-unit combat power from the ground up and determine how science could be applied to make small units much more capable. We began by doing a full examination of everything fighting men carry or wear—in cold weather, in temperate climes, and in the tropics. This was a complete examination that began with the naked man, moving then to:

his underwear

his socks

his basic clothing—all climates

his load-carrying system—all aspects (fighting/survival loads)

all items carried in and on that system—all!

his water needs and means of carrying it

his nutritional needs

his shelter needs—all climates

his navigational needs—maps, compass, RDF, everything!

his communications needs—hand/arm signals to satellite comm

his protection needs—flak gear, helmets, insoles, eyewear, etc.

his firepower—knife, pistol, rifle, to small atomic demolitions, etc.

his "called in" firepower capabilities—air, arty, naval gunfire, etc.

his mobility needs—afoot, by sea, air, undersea, and land

his physical limitations—aural, visual, olfactory, etc.

All of that study was accomplished in-house and by traveling all over the world, collecting data from the British, the

French, the Germans, the Israelis, the Australians, the Pakistanis, the Indians, the Gurkhas, the Chinese, and the Vietnamese, who, at the moment, were fighting a very real war. All of that information was compiled into constantly growing files. For example, we even had some of the data the Nazis developed during their "experimental" work on human physical limitations compiled in the death camps of Europe. This particular data was supposedly unreachable, held under seal in some archive, yet we had it three days after Mr. Gray suggested that we should look at what they did and what they had recorded. The documents arrived by a small jet, accompanied by a translator who stayed with us until we were satisfied that we had received all there was to get. He then took the documents and departed.

The overseas search for data was coordinated with a search through all of the facilities and military forces in the United States doing work in areas related to any of the aspects noted above. To give a flavor of the kinds of data our research turned up, I cite the two following examples:

1. The 81mm mortar: The U.S. Army was very proud of its arsenal in Watervliet, New York. There they had worked out some special steels that would reduce the ninety-eight-pound weight of the mortar tube by more than 26 percent. While that was nothing to sneeze at, we did our numbers, too, and noted that the 81mm mortar was part of a system that had a tube, base plate, bipod, sight, aiming stakes, night lights, and wire, and came with one hundred rounds of ammunition. The total of which weighed more than twelve hundred pounds. Cutting twenty-four to twenty-five pounds off just the tube would not be a great help to those who had to carry the *entire* system forward toward the enemy!

2. Around this same time the machine gun controversy was all settled, by others, and U.S. forces wound up with the new 7.62mm M-60 machine gun. The weapon fired the new lighter NATO cartridge and it was claimed that this reduced the load of the infantryman. The developer (Springfield Arsenal) created a new type of ammunition can which was

smaller and easier to carry than the can that held 250 rounds of the old .30-caliber machine gun ammunition. Of course, the can only held 200 rounds versus the 250 found in the old can. The result was that each machine gun team, with four ammunition carriers, now had 1,600 rounds to work with in combat—instead of 2,000 rounds. They were carrying exactly one pound less in weight per man (14.5 pounds X 2, as opposed to 15 pounds X 2 per man) while bringing 400 fewer rounds onto the battlefield. It was both frustrating and maddening to hear about that kind of **"progress"** over and over and over again!

Of course, the opinions we held about these "forward steps" did not in any way alter the statements made by the developers of these items. They spoke grandly of the wonderful changes they had wrought. Operational analysis is, of course, a form of the application of common sense as well as mathematics, and for many developers both are to be avoided at all costs! While we had a direct line into the office of the secretary of defense and to the director of the Defense Advanced Research Projects Agency and, for that matter, to the president, we never had the slightest sense that our findings and opinions about these matters were given any consideration at all.

The only time we really had an impact on a grand scale was with the rifle controversy when the AR-15 was tested by the U.S. Army. In the Pentagon it was felt by some that the testing (which failed the AR-15 flatly) was the subject of some form of cheating. We were asked to perform the same tests at USNOTS and to then forward the results to the director of ARPA. Of course, we found that the AR-15 was fully qualified as a candidate weapon for the war in Vietnam. Later, at Fort Benning, Georgia, we learned the name and the billet of the officer who had personally bent the test weapons before they went to the firing line for the competitive tests with other candidate weapons. Based upon our findings, that officer was shifted from weapons test work to civil affairs duty in the Republic of Vietnam. We had a thousand AR-15s shipped to the Republic of Vietnam and issued to the Airborne Brigade, tested them in combat, and then wrote our reports. The AR-15 grew up to become the M-16 that continues in use as the current U.S. service rifle.

Almost every day we worked at USNOTS we were asked to look at some scientist's idea, or examine some bit of scientific data developed in another project area, with an eye to its possible application to small-unit ground operations in combat. I'll cite three examples of this type of work to clarify how this aspect of our daily lives worked:

1. The X-115 Helicopter Trap Weapon:

One day we were asked to take a look at a project designed to create a new bomb to open up landing zones in the jungle. At USNOTS they chose to try to make a continuous rod warhead—i.e., one that on detonation would spread a connected rod bundle out from the center of the blast to forty feet. As a continuous, horizontal rod, it would "mow down" the jungle and let the helicopters land. We were asked to look, and we directed that they get large bamboo, stand it upright and set off the weapon. Once testing was completed and they proved that the rod concept worked, one of us took it to Admiral Harry D. Felt, in Hawaii (CINCPAC), and received permission to go to Vietnam and try it out. The result was the full evaluation of the bomb in combat for the Vietnamese Army's helicopter operations.

2. Fuel-Air Explosives (FAE Bomb):

When this idea was brought to us we had them examine the Korean War archives and build very precise replicas of Chinese Communist bunkers. Much to their credit, the Army Corps of Engineers had superior data and drawings from the Korean experience. We told them to populate the bunkers with goats, and then evaluate the results. (Goats are as tough as nails—like people!) Over the following years the use of overpressure, created by FAE, was refined as a killing agent for dug-in troops.

3. Laser Technology:

In 1959 or 1960 the people at one of the big East Coast science centers (it may have been at the Massachusetts Institute of Technology or Harvard, I forget which) used a large ruby laser to bounce a light beam off the moon. The result was *accurate*, and I mean *really accurate* (1.5 meters plus/minus) measurement of the distance between the earth and the moon. The USNOTS scientists came to us and presented most of what they knew about lasers, asking if any of this made sense to us (those who were in the area for the moment), and we came up with different ideas and brainstormed them for the scientists. Eventually, from those initial meetings came the formalized plan to develop a laser designator and a laser spot tracker (later the tracker was mounted in the A-4M aircraft) to be used to drop bombs with great precision. Laser rangers of all types (tank sights, artillery forward observers, mortar observers, reconnaissance teams, infantry patrols, etc.) were discussed and we endorsed the idea of lasers for ground combat with great fervor. The ideal of small units with hand-held designators was always foremost in our discussions because that sort of combat is what we were always focused on. It was, de facto, Stingray-friendly as an idea!

So, it should be obvious that my personal involvement within the basic concept behind the type of combat activity that became known as Stingray had a solid foundation long before the code name was ever used to identify this use of small forward-deployed fighting elements to direct fires against larger enemy forces.

Another interesting aspect of my service with Code 121 was my access to the secret and top secret files of the other services. For a portion of my time in Code 121, I made a conscious effort to obtain copies of anything that might prove to be of interest to the Marine Corps command structure—be it operational concepts or research and development information. I was cured of this penchant, with great clarity, one day when I stopped in at Headquarters, United States Marine Corps (HQMC) and handed a copy of a top secret "Army eyes only" study on the future of air mobility to a Marine two-star general. In that study the U.S. Army had postulated that it was inherently their role to develop the use of helicopters in such a way as to lead to the eventual disbanding of the Marine Corps in the military structure of the armed forces. I believed that this might be of particular interest at HQMC. Sadly, it was my actions in obtaining the document—not the contents of the document—that the general found interesting. He threatened to have me arrested and be made the subject of an Article 32 investigation (something like a civilian grand jury) for a general court-martial for my acquisition of this item from the U.S. Army. Fortunately, clearer thinking by other generals who got involved did finally prevail, but it was such a hostile response that I never again visited HQMC with data that came to my hand during my tour at USNOTS.

In Code 121 we created a volume known as the Black Book, and in that book we set down all our findings and analysis—separated into the natural spread of such things. For example, there was an explosives section, a communications section, a tactics section, an equipment section, and so on. Each section reported our views and study work and each had detailed and specific recommendations. Every recommendation was couched in terms of the coming conflict in the Republic of Vietnam—laying out for the reader alternative ways to fight the war that appeared to us to be just over the horizon for the United States. We were preparing one copy for the president, one copy for the director of the Central Intelligence Agency, and one copy for the secretary of defense when President Kennedy was assassinated in Dallas, Texas. The new president had little or no real interest in learning anything or even listening to any recommendations from us. By early 1964 it was quite clear that Code 121 was no longer going to be in the "loop" and we began to disband. By July we were all gone, and Mr. Gray and the only three volumes of the Black Book that were printed—ever—went to Washington, D.C. I have no idea into whose hands they finally fell, but I do know that the new secretary of defense, Mr. Robert Strange

McNamara, never took time to give us his attention, and after Mr. Kennedy was gone we never had access to the president again.

Marine Corps Operational Philosophy

All through the early years of the 1960s there was in the Marine Corps a very serious conflict within the reconnaissance community. This conflict was between those Marines dedicated to silent information collection and those who saw a "commando" role for the reconnaissance community. This debate raged both in the actual reconnaissance community and among the senior officers who would be using the intelligence and operational products of the Marine Corps's reconnaissance units. All of this has been discussed in other forums and need not be detailed here. However, that internal quarrel had a very deleterious effect on some of the first uses of the reconnaissance units in the Republic of Vietnam.

In 1965 the 1st Reconnaissance Battalion and the 1st Force Reconnaissance Company were deployed to the Republic of Vietnam under commanders who held to the silent collection of information doctrine. Regardless of conflicting views, the reconnaissance outposts often used indirect and aerial firepower on enemy troops they had sighted. Thus, the facts of the conflict soon forced the commanders to see that reconnaissance teams would always be likely users of aerial and artillery firepower—both for the basic infliction of casualties on the enemy and for self-protection. In each case this was not welcome news to the commanders who sided with the information-collection-only crowd, and some of them continued to resist and/or misunderstand the overall concept for years.

During 1965 and 1966, while the Marine Corps was building up its forces and fighting every day in the Republic of Vietnam, there was a study group in Washington, D.C., and at Quantico preparing a very large, very formal document on the future of Marine Corps warfighting techniques. I suppose it was created under the auspices of the Operations (G-3) Division at HQMC, but everyone seems to have had a hand in submitting parts of the overall work. The document had a long and impressive name, but in verbal shorthand it was known by everyone as MARCORPS–85, and it had in it something contributed by nearly everyone. It postulated the battlefield of 1985 and suggested how future battles might be fought and won. It set forth many possible amphibious warfare scenarios and clearly established concepts as to how these future operations might be conducted.

MARCORPS–85 was very strong in the aviation sections, as it should have been. A strong point about aviation is the ability of aviation experts to fully quantify many of the variables expected to apply to future aircraft. Identifiable things such as lift capability, speed, fuel consumption, and the range of aircraft being planned years into the future can be used in studies like MARCORPS–85 with very good effect. Infantry combat is much more difficult to predict, and despite all the years of Robert McNamara's idiotic yatterings about assigning a quantification to nearly everything the combat infantryman does from tying his boots to farting in the wind, ground combat remains one aspect of warfare that will not easily bend down and be made subservient to the number crunchers.

The study examined many aspects of science and technology and provided "informed" opinion with regard to the effect of those technologies on warfare twenty years into the future, the year 1985. Many aspects of warfare as you and I knew it in 1969 and 1970, while in 3d Force Reconnaissance Company, were not even mentioned in the rather vague text, yet at the same time some things were set down with careful specificity. For example, the study stated as a *fact* that force projection ashore would be conducted by 1985 from platforms (ship decks) fifty miles at sea. At first there were no objections raised to such firm guidance, and theoretical amphibious operations always began with the fifty-mile standoff from shore. Later, Marines like Lt. Col. Gerald Polakoff asked "Why?"

and there was no answer. It appeared at the time as if the fifty-mile figure had simply grown magically onto the page. Some Marines refused to question the distance, accepting it as written. However, with men like Lieutenant Colonel Polakoff available, the proper questions finally were asked and everyone in the research and development world of the Marine Corps was forced to justify various force-projection ranges when they used them in their requirements justifications or in doctrinal theorizing.

Interestingly enough, the MARCORPS–85 study did contain the seed kernel of what we all wound up knowing as Stingray operations. The authors of this study opined that small units might well have a very disproportionate ability to affect the battlefield of the future. They postulated fighting entities known as "search and attack teams" that would range deep into areas nominally dominated by enemy forces and then engage those forces with superior firepower. This may sound reasonable to most, but there was a large contingent of senior Marine officers who found the concept to be absurd at best and a preposterous waste of assets at worst. Their opposition was couched in the normal concepts of cost ratios and fretful concern about asset availability for so many small units operating across the battlefield in quasi-independence. Implicit in their objection was the fact that they desired to avoid changes in doctrine that might mean a more fragmented battlefield, with small-unit commanders possessing both authority and the flexible ability to use that authority. These were not evil men, but men who saw the Korean War, with its "main line of resistance" (MLR) and its "main supply route" (MSR), as the way major ground units should deploy and fight. They also saw reconnaissance as fit only to man the "combat outpost line" (COPL) and conduct small patrols or similar forays forward of the MLR, or to protect the MSR.

Of course, while the officers who opposed the use of reconnaissance units to call fires or in any other way engage, harass, or attack the enemy were discussing those matters and pressing their views on all who would listen, all the terms and concepts changed. The Marine Corps dropped the MLR concept and, with that, the MSR and COPL vanished, too. The new view was to make the elements along the "forward edge of the battlefield" (FEBA) more flexible by assigning them a "tactical area of responsibility" (TAOR) instead of a particular frontage on a defined boundary between "us" and "them." The COPL vanished as a concept and, with a widely dispersed unit each working its own TAOR, so did the MSR. It was no longer possible to consider units as having a contiguous frontage where our forces engaged those of the enemy in a struggle over terrain. Instead, the battlefield was deemed to be en route to becoming much more fluid, and with that fluidity would come a role for the search-and-attack teams.

One of the most vocal proponents of a far more active role for reconnaissance units—including what we call Stingray— was the late Col. Patrick G. Collins, USMC. As a captain in 1965 and 1966, he was a reconnaissance company commander and later operations officer of the 1st Reconnaissance Battalion in the Republic of Vietnam. On his return to the United States in 1966 he was constantly ready to discuss his own fully developed concept for "active" reconnaissance. By 1967 the now-Major Collins's mind was made up. He believed that the war in the Republic of Vietnam should be fought by small, tough, and violently aggressive units of about sixty men each. Those units would be established deep within the jungle, far from the coastal enclaves, for a period of about sixty fighting days. For all of the two months, or more, of active combat deployment, the units would operate from hidden base camps. They would operate in squad size— twelve to fourteen men—teams that would spend their time actively looking for trouble, finding the enemy, and calling firepower down on them. Major Collins considered survival of the sixty-man units as being based upon careful avoidance of larger enemy forces, and the rapid response of air and ground units when a team was engaged by more powerful enemy units.

When, and if, the enemy did corner the unit and try to bring them to battle, Major Collins offered the view that this was what you wanted—now fixed-wing air and artillery could smash the enemy force that the Marines had been hunting. For Major "Patty" Collins that was not far from the (probably bogus) tale of the Marines at the Chosin Reservoir in Korea, who supposedly said that with the 1st Marine Brigade surrounded, they were finally happy because "now they knew exactly where the North Korean and Chinese forces were." Major Collins always stated that the teams could and should expect to win the final battle because of our inherent Marine Corps firepower advantage. Use of firepower, air, or artillery as an adjunct to reconnaissance operations is Stingray work, and Major Collins held the view that only the reconnaissance units were really qualified to operate in the enemy's backyard, where they could hurt him by calling in killing ordnance.

Any concept that dispersed small units all over the landscape, each in the throes of its own battle, brought forth many powerful, more doctrinaire officers to oppose it. Even as early as 1966 the overpowering fear of the bad publicity inherent in the possible destruction of just one of these small units by North Vietnamese or Viet Cong forces chilled all but a very small number of the Marine Corps' general officers. They could, of course, lose sixty men in a regimental fight in just one afternoon, but those men fell among other Marines and there would be little chance for that many Marines to suddenly be overwhelmed and killed while far from their comrades. It was the separation from major units as much as the potential for loss that upset the officers and caused them to oppose any use of reconnaissance—or for that matter, infantry forces—in detached small elements that might be snuffed out by the Viet Cong or North Vietnamese.

Throughout the war in Vietnam, internal strife over the proper use of reconnaissance assets in the Marine Corps continued. Clear, articulate thinkers such as Lt. Gen. Herman Nickerson Jr. understood the potential of using reconnaissance elements as a way to deliver significant firepower against the enemy. He had begun to espouse his views on the matter as early as 1959 when, as a colonel, he was instrumental in making sure that the force reconnaissance companies came into being as units of the regular Marine Corps. As a commander he could clearly see the need for someone to bring fire down on enemy forces when they were detected, and in his view it was natural for the reconnaissance elements to do this because, as he said repeatedly, "they are already out there."

Lieutenant General Nickerson encouraged, very strongly, the use of all reconnaissance elements in the Stingray fashion in 1966 when he was commanding general of 1st Marine Division, and he expounded the same tactics when he returned again to the Republic of Vietnam in 1969 as commanding general, 3d Marine Amphibious Force. As overall commander of the eighty-five thousand plus Marines in combat, he directed that the mission of the reconnaissance units, both at division and force level, include the delivery of firepower. While this had been, for quite some time, the tacit view and a fairly representative employment pattern of the reconnaissance elements, it was General Nickerson who set it in concrete for all Marine units deployed in Vietnam.

Combat Operations in the Republic of Vietnam

During 1965 and 1966, I was serving in the 2d Battalion, 7th Marine Regiment (2/7). At that time it was quite normal for the reconnaissance battalion of the division to either assign a reconnaissance platoon as "attached" to a battalion or, at least, to place one in "direct support." Our platoon of reconnaissance Marines was the 2d Platoon, Company C, commanded by 1st Lt. Dalzell Williams. His recon platoon could field either two or three teams in support of missions from our battalion, and/or missions generated far up the chain at division headquarters. For the most part the platoon spent its time at the whim of others, but at times it was quite responsive to the requests of the Marines of 2/7.

The commander of the division reconnaissance battalion in 1965 was strongly supportive of the view that all reconnaissance elements should observe the enemy but not engage him. While that concept was altered occasionally, nonengagement was the original point of view, and we in 2/7 fully understood that if we wanted to exploit enemy sightings, we had to do it ourselves. Lieutenant Williams began the practice of slipping 2/7 a copy of his patrol reports when there were sightings in or near our area of operations. As our year of combat in 2/7 scrolled by, this personal practice by Lieutenant Williams became of increasing value.

During the spring of 1966, Lieutenant Williams became more and more frustrated by the fact that the higher headquarters took no action against Viet Cong Chu Luk forces (regulars of the interprovincial battalions and regiments) that his teams located. He and his recon teams would risk their lives to obtain the information, and nothing would happen. He came to 2/7 with a series of patrol reports and asked if we wanted to exploit the sightings; he was not permitted, on a regular basis, to engage the enemy units with air, artillery, or naval gunfire. Occasionally, the restrictions were lifted, but in most cases he was ordered merely to observe and report. That frustrating situation was altered by the battalion commander of 2/7, Lt. Col. Leon N. Utter.

In April, May, and June 1966, Lieutenant Colonel Utter ordered and directed several company-size operations in our tactical area of responsibility. The operations were not known as Stingray, but were conventional aerial assaults into areas where the reconnaissance platoon had located the enemy. In each case there were air strikes and artillery preparation before our Marines were committed, and the enemy normally melted into the countryside.

One of these missions, however, was moderately successful. I happened to be in command of Colonel Utter's Company F at the time, and we reacted with speed and violence to one of Lieutenant Williams's recon team sightings. At dawn the company conducted an aerial assault into a village area where dozens of Chu Luk or Dia Phoung (local provincial battalions of the Viet Cong) fighting men had been seen. We had a sharp firefight, killing fifteen to twenty VC on entry (after the preparation fires) into the village and took control of 132 local people—almost all old men, women, and children—who did not flee. Having no restriction of the kind that hampered Lieutenant Williams, we directed both air and artillery on the Viet Cong elements who had left the area when we landed, some of whom we could see climbing ridgelines two thousand yards or so to the west. We engaged them with firepower off and on for almost an hour. While it was not classic Stingray, we did use firepower to deal with those enemy troops—not our bayonets. Having firepower at hand saved us from chasing the enemy into the jungle and closing with him for hand-to-hand fighting.

Late in the day I began sending all the Vietnamese people we had in hand back to the rear by helicopter. The accompanying Vietnamese Army intelligence people had classified the civilians as "Viet Cong sympathizers" (VCS), a term that meant they had come from an area outside the control of the government of the Republic of Vietnam and as such were likely to support our enemy with food, lodging, medical assistance, and intelligence on U.S. Marine and Vietnamese Army movements. The helicopters came and went, hauling the civilians away. In the meantime I had one platoon set up an ambush in the village while the rest of Company F withdrew to the east and set up a perimeter in a depression with a thick earthen berm around it. The depression may have been a manioc field or perhaps a place where water buffalo were kept; however, it was clearly not being used for anything at that time other than a helicopter pad for my rifle company. When the helicopters stopped flying and all the VC were gone, we waited in complete silence for things in the village to develop.

Just before dark, Viet Cong troops began walking back into the village. They came openly, thinking that all the Marines had just flown away in the helicopters they could see heading toward the coast. The leading men of the returning Viet Cong unit, with their rifles at sling arms over their shoulders, were about to step on the machine guns of the ambushing platoon when the staff sergeant in command signaled his men to fire.

The resulting carnage was sudden and chilling because we knew that if the tables were turned, we could find ourselves in the very same situation. It reaffirmed in us the need to be extremely careful to remain vigilant at all times! Again, this success was not Stingray, but it was a combat result that came directly from the efforts of the reconnaissance teams to find the enemy forces and bring combat power against them. That type of small-unit action was repeated many times by the Marines of 2/7 and by other battalions of the 7th Marines. It was the view of Col. Oscar Peatross, commander of the regiment, that we needed to find the enemy by whatever means and hammer him when we found him, not just report his passing from point A to point B. Obviously, Colonel Peatross could see the value of Stingray tactics—he just was not able to alter the status quo for the reconnaissance teams, so he did the best he could and permitted his battalion commanders the freedom to respond to enemy sightings with applied combat power.

From 1966 to the end of the war, many significant small-unit actions were really the ground equivalent of Stingray. Long-range fire was not always the weapon used by the reconnaissance element. It sometimes was, instead, the "reaction force" concept that had come into being by the middle of 1966. In that concept every regiment had a rifle company or perhaps two designated as the reaction force, waiting in the regimental area to be quickly airlifted into battle. It would respond to units in trouble, to chance encounters with the Viet Cong or the North Vietnamese Army, and to those sightings of large-size enemy units by reconnaissance teams. Still, it was not classic Stingray tactics—despite the fact that combat power was applied.

Despite the opposition to Stingray-type operations, all through the first year of extended Marine Corps commitment to the war in Vietnam there were frequent uses of the Stingray concept. As one might expect, great successes and some very brutal failures occurred, wherein many men were lost when their observation posts or recon patrols were overwhelmed by powerful enemy forces. It is very important to note that

1st Marine Division and 3d Marine Division operated in vastly different areas. The 1st Marine Division was sent to Vietnam piecemeal, its regiments being at first attached to the 3d Marine Division while the headquarters remained outside the Republic of Vietnam. The 1st Marine Division was initially fragmented, its elements located from Qui Nhon in the south to the Chu Lai enclave to Da Nang. That was a direct result of Robert McNamara's "incremental" deployment approach, and it was not until the middle of 1966 that the 1st Marine Division was really a fully functional combat unit.

The 3d Marine Division was operating in the northern provinces of the Republic of Vietnam, where there were far fewer civilian residents and far more areas where fire could be quickly used against enemy forces. Stingray ideas had more acceptance in the north, both because of the greater freedom from the potential for civilian casualties and because it appeared logical to use firepower when facing the powerful forces of the North Vietnamese Army along the demilitarized zone (DMZ).

The Stingray attempts that failed in Vietnam had a very disproportionate effect on the thinking of senior Marine commanders. While they never turned a hair at the loss of ten or twelve infantrymen from a larger force, each day, they were horrified when a small reconnaissance unit was detected and assaulted with a sad conclusion by the enemy that the recon team had been attacking with air or artillery firepower. There are classic tales of recon teams that were "treed" by the enemy when they began to use their radios to call in fire. Men died as heroes in some of those encounters, but in the larger picture there were obvious portents for the future of using applied firepower in a timely fashion by the reconnaissance elements— as opposed to those teams just sitting and noting the enemy moving across their field of view. It is also very important here to separate the concept of Stingray—actively seeking to take the enemy under some sort of "force multiplying" firepower—from the use of air, artillery, or naval gunfire in the last-ditch emergency mode, when the recon team is fighting for its very life. In many cases cited as failed examples of the

Stingray concept, the team had actually resorted to calling for indirect fire in order to survive. The difference remains in the *intent* when the team went into the jungle.

In the second year of the war there were many more active participants in the Stingray concept. Of note was the activity of 1st Lt. Andrew Finlayson—call sign Killer Kane. This outstanding officer was very successful in the use of the Stingray technique—he went into the jungle to find the enemy and then hammer him with firepower. Lieutenant Finlayson was a textbook example of the mindset that Stingray requires. He had no desire to ever fight the enemy with his small team. Instead he saw his team as just another one of the long fingers of the U.S. Marine Corps, a finger probing the enemy's heretofore untouched sanctuaries. Killer Kane not only made his team known to *Time* magazine and the American public, he was also the subject of considerable discussion on the radio nets of the Viet Cong and North Vietnamese Army. The intelligence files of the time include radio battalion intercepts of North Vietnamese senior leaders placing a price on the head of Lieutenant Finlayson and his fellow recon Marines.

When 1st Lt. Andy Finlayson used the Stingray methods he had a far, far greater effect on the overall conduct of combat operations than any other eight-man unit. He used air and artillery as a way to multiply the combat power of his small, well-trained team many, many times over. Had there been hundreds of similar teams deployed throughout the jungles of Vietnam it might have been possible to make the infiltration of personnel, supplies, and equipment by the North Vietnamese Army *prohibitively costly*. At least, it is clear to me that had hundreds of such teams been operating deep in areas dominated by the enemy, they would have seriously disrupted the enemy's ability to move freely and/or concentrate for assaults against the coastal enclaves and population centers. Without a doubt Lieutenant Finlayson was a superior example of just how the Stingray concept could have had a significant effect on the operational power brought to the battlefield by the deployed Marine Corps forces. Of course, concomitant with that effect is the fact that all teams are not going to be successful, and commanders who use the Stingray concept will be forced to face the fact that reconnaissance teams will occasionally be found and overwhelmed by a determined enemy. When that happens, and it will, the commander has not only dead Marines to consider, but he will very likely have some who are missing or captured. The fate of those captured from Stingray teams will be the most horrible outcome that the overall commander must contemplate. In wars like that in Vietnam there is very little quarter given, and the enemy force that takes a Stingray Marine captive will probably kill him very slowly and brutally over a long period of time. No prisoner of war status is likely—ever.

By the time 1968 arrived, bringing with it the Tet Offensive and the siege at Khe Sanh, the Stingray concept was being used throughout the two Marine divisions. Reconnaissance teams and Marine rifle company patrols were operating in the aggressive mode, calling fires immediately on discovering enemy forces. There are, in fact, a number of well-documented instances wherein an entire rifle company operating on an aggressive combat patrol used air and artillery firepower to engage the enemy they discovered—instead of the tried-and-true "close with and destroy" tactics of Marine infantry. Of course, there were still some who did not agree with those ideas, but for the most part they were not in a position to return the reconnaissance elements to the passive observation-only mode.

At Khe Sanh, the entire combat base and the U.S. Marine units situated on the nearby hills, 881 and 881 south, always used firepower to the maximum. Few patrols were sent outside the combat base or down from the hills because the enemy was always there in great strength, and the patrols would be engaged and destroyed without any value being achieved from the combat exchange. In fact, two or three abortive patrols were run, all of which had very heavy casualties because the North Vietnamese Army had thousands of men in and around the Khe Sanh area.

Reconnaissance teams were often used from the coastal

enclave to help support the Khe Sanh combat base by seeking to learn enemy movements concentrating for assault. Those recon teams were all "locked and loaded" in total readiness to engage North Vietnamese units with indirect or air-delivered munitions. The hills and valleys around Khe Sanh combat base could be called a "target-rich environment."

While one might not originally see the use of B-52 Arc Light carpet bombing missions as being a Stingray application, it was for Marine Capt. Misrah "Harry" Beig. After all, he had a small unit—six thousand Marines—engaged against a large enemy unit of twenty thousand to thirty thousand men. He wanted to take an active role against the enemy forces who had infested the combat base and he prepared his case well. He wanted to use firepower to multiply the effect on the enemy force of the presence of the Marines in that defensive position.

Captain Beig was the target information officer and he kept himself and his data in the intelligence section of the command bunker of the 26th Marine Regiment. That bunker was deep, close to the Khe Sanh airstrip. He kept known targets, ones that he wished to strike, on more than 2,500 individual cards (one for each particular grid square in which he had an interest) and on the maps as well. He studied those cards every day and from them developed his personal theories about the intentions of the enemy. Because of that intense study he was the individual responsible for the movement of the "bomb line" (an imaginary line on the map short of which Air Force, Navy, and Marine bombing aircraft may not drop a bomb that is not delivered as a response to a controller on the ground—for fear of causing friendly casualties in and near the combat base).

Captain Beig, later assassinated in Bangkok (the escape door on his floor was nailed shut and a fire started by arsonists on both sides of his room), was a student of the enemy and his tactics. He had determined that the North Vietnamese Army knew (from spies in the Republic of Vietnam) exactly where the bomb line was and had chosen to move the major ground forces and indirect fire weapons of those forces inside that line. That choice made the enemy's mortar pits and ground forces immune to the B-52 Arc Lights and moved them away from most bombs dropped by attacking fighter bombers. Only bombs called down under the direct control of the forward air controller (FAC) could be dropped inside the bomb line.

When Captain Beig had completed his analysis of the battlefield, he knew where the North Vietnamese had their forces and where their mortars (which hammered the base every day with 82mm and 120mm fire) were located. To help complement his cards and map studies he used observer reports, countermortar radar, seismic data (provided by the AN/PSR-1 Personnel Seismic Intrusion Devices [PSIDs] that I brought to Khe Sanh in February 1968), sensor technology reports from Nakhon Phanom in Thailand, and good old common horse sense to reach his logical conclusions.

Harry Beig was a student of the North Vietnamese leadership, too. He read their doctrine and studied their application of that doctrine to the battlefield. He believed that the salvation of the Khe Sanh combat base lay in dealing realistically with the method the NVA were using to "hug" the base with close-in forces that could not be effectively engaged with heavy bombing because of the standard, pro forma establishment of the arbitrary bomb line. With enthusiastic and never-swerving energy, Captain Beig pressed the commanding officer of the 26th Marine Regiment, and anyone from higher headquarters who happened to visit Khe Sanh during the siege, to have the bomb line removed. Finally, after much careful considcration, General Westmoreland and his staff in Saigon gave permission to the 26th Marines to move the bomb line closer to the combat base.

Captain Beig and the colonel commanding the regiment settled on a new bomb line. The new line followed identifiable terrain features about 750 meters from the main trenches of the combat base. This brought the bomb line almost two thousand yards closer to the dug-in Marines, and exposed to attack all the North Vietnamese positions Captain Beig sought to hit. With this most welcome decision made, the call went out for a very big B-52 strike.

When the air strike was delivered it consisted of six B-52 aircraft in two cells of three aircraft each. Those six aircraft would bring with them nearly six hundred 500-pound and 750-pound bombs, all of which would be dropped in carefully spaced rows across the North Vietnamese units. Delivery was scheduled for the very middle of the long, dark February night. A late hour was chosen in hope that the North Vietnamese would be up and out of their bunkers, manning their mortars, and making themselves more vulnerable to the rain of bombs coming to them from Anderson Air Force Base on the island of Guam. The aircraft were to pass parallel to the runway at the combat base, dropping their ordnance in the normal long string, parallel to the long axis of the dug-in units. The impacts would fall across the terrain, like a parade, in front of the eastern aspect of the entrenched Marines. The B-52 flights arrived precisely on schedule and began their run well over thirty thousand feet above the muddy battlefield.

In the dark we could not hear the bombers up there above the broken cloud layers. Only the calm, almost laconic reports on the different radio nets from the direct air support center (DASC) gave us any indication that they had begun their bomb run. Two flights of three B-52s were inbound and we waited, knowing that if they made any significant error their bombs would fall on us instead of the North Vietnamese Army. It was a tense few minutes prior to drop time!

Suddenly, without so much as a whisper from the aircraft above ever reaching our ears, the sky was filled with the sound of roaring death. The 500-pound bombs poured out of the dark, clouded sky with absolute precision. The bursts moved in a steady walk from our right to our left in front of the trench line where we were standing. The explosions were pounding us with shock waves, and the top two or three rows of sandbags were jumping straight up in the air as much as a foot off the parapets of the trench, some of them falling into the trench line and others falling to the outside. Marines bent double in the trenches with their fingers in their ears and their mouths wide open as they tried to minimize ear damage from the repeated shock waves. Soon the bombers were gone, but secondary and tertiary explosions continued for six more hours as the North Vietnamese Army lost its stockpiled ammunition, its mortars, and an unknown number of its fighting men. Fires raged in the North Vietnamese gun pits for hours as their powder increments and standby ammunition vanished into the night sky.

Was it a Stingray mission? Perhaps, because when analyzed it differs little from those missions called by 3d Force Reconnaissance Company in 1969 and 1970. Like a reconnaissance patrol, we had a unit that was not capable of aggressively attacking the larger force with its own firepower. The Marines were, however, able to use the power they could call down from the sky to help create a military catastrophe for enemy forces arrayed to menace them in their defensive positions.

Also, during the time I spent at Khe Sanh we used some ideas generated at the development center in Quantico, Virginia. One that had particular top-notch results was the integration of night vision devices with moving-target radar. With a radar looking down a long finger that led into the defensive position, we installed a tripod-mounted AN/TVS-4 night vision device at a listening post about forty meters down the hill and to one side of the radar field of view. When the radar detected movement, the night vision device operator scanned the area and confirmed the presence of the enemy. Since we had two sites, cutting the angles to the target from both provided a very exact location of the enemy, and all the mortars and 105mm howitzers could hit them with time-on-target (TOT) fire for effect without any prior ranging rounds needed. Again, the application may not be pure Stingray, but it was an extremely effective use of firepower by Marine rifle squads in the forward fighting holes to aggressively attack the North Vietnamese.

Marine Corps Development Center, 1966–69

During the period from late 1966 to mid-1969, I was the ground reconnaissance officer at the Marine Corps Landing

Force Development Center (LFDC) at Quantico. This billet was situated in the Intelligence Branch of the LFDC; however, it was not limited to intelligence-related activities. Because we were involved in developing equipment for reconnaissance units, we had no choice but to examine every item as it related to operational tactics and techniques. 1st Lt. C. C. Coffman Jr. was my assistant in that billet and we shared office space with Col. Gerald H. Polakoff (the branch chief); Lt. Col. Alfred M. Gray (electronic warfare and special communications); Maj. Hugh L. Scott (special communications); and two other officers who did individual equipment work. These two officers did their work at the very margin of incompetence, and we called the pair "buckles and shoes," a sneering reference to their limited abilities and utter lack of humor. It was a cramped space, with twice as many men in the room as it could comfortably hold. There was considerable hostility present, and tensions often ran high because the workload for those of us who were in Lieutenant Colonel Polakoff's branch was roughly ten to fifteen times that carried by "buckles and shoes." Regardless, the two always found time to complain about how hard they worked and how they found working in the same office with the loud, boisterous, and difficult Major Lee and the even louder and more boisterous 1st Lt. C. C. "Bucky" Coffman something that they hated.

The Intelligence Branch was an element of the Ground Combat Division of LFDC, a division headed by very bright, forward-thinking infantry colonel Ted Metzger. Fortunately for Colonel Metzger and those of us in the Intelligence Branch, the LFDC was commanded by one of the most brilliant officers in the Marine Corps, Maj. Gen. Alan J. Armstrong. General Armstrong was an aviator who could relate with ease to the ground elements of the Marine Corps because he really listened, asked detailed questions, and studied everything that came to hand with great care. The general was a leader without peer, one who gave his subordinates the freedom to excel because he issued "mission type" orders that did not tell anyone how to do their job—his guidance and orders merely set forth the objective of the effort and we were left to be creative as to exactly how we would go about completing the task.

With regard to Stingray and its basic concept, the LFDC was a unanimous hotbed of support for the idea and for the technical equipment needed to make it work. From Major General Armstrong on down, we all agreed that in the future, small recon and infantry units would have a much larger role to play on the battlefield through the controlled delivery of accurate firepower. The general made sure that the Communications Branch and the Aviation Division and our Ground Combat Division always melded our efforts toward an improved capability for Stingray operations—by whatever name it was known, the concept was accepted and made a part of our everyday thinking.

Within LFDC numerous projects related to Stingray operations were begun and expanded during my time as the reconnaissance officer. In our branch alone, more than a dozen efforts were under way that would be of considerable value to the end users in a Stingray mode of combat. Some examples:

A. Laser Illuminator.

The project was virtually 100 percent Stingray related. The idea was for the recon team carrying the illuminator to be able to place the laser marker on a target for the A-4M to attack after the laser spot tracker built into the aircraft had detected the illuminated area on the ground.

B. Laser Range Finder.

With a laser range finder a small unit could precisely determine their own location as well as that of enemy forces. With such very precise measurements available, first round fire-for-effect could be expected—after all, the artillery already knows very accurately where *it* is, and it is only the poor navigational ability of infantry units that makes the use of "ranging rounds" necessary.

C. Position, location, and reporting system.

This was the predecessor of the modern 1990s satellite navigation systems. We were testing the idea of obtaining very precise unit location from satellites as early as 1967 in Bermuda, using synchronous satellites over Brazil and base stations in Schenectady, New York.

D. Sensor Technology.

A side issue to the use of sensors was the fact that when you put them into the ground by hand, you know where they are with great accuracy. When the sensor detects enemy movement, you can place accurate fire on them immediately. We did this at Khe Sanh with exceptional results.

E. Night Vision Technology.

Working in concert with the U.S. Army's Limited Warfare Laboratory, we strenuously urged the improvement in night vision equipment, both the large tripod-mounted scopes and smaller handheld devices. The Stingray uses of such technology are obvious.

F. Handheld and other miniature radar.

These devices were seen as just another way to locate moving enemy forces with great accuracy so firepower could be delivered immediately.

G. Steerable parachutes and electronic homing devices.

We felt that with better parachutes the Stingray teams could be more easily infiltrated into areas normally dominated by enemy forces. The homing devices would permit later resupply of the teams by high altitude drops.

H. Swimmer Delivery Vehicles.

The Marine Corps actively participated in the development of swimmer delivery vehicles (SDV) for several reasons. With regard to Stingray, use of the SDV would place well-equipped troops ashore in a very stealthy manner, troops that could quickly become Stingray elements in an area where the enemy did not expect to encounter *any* Marine elements.

I. Sound Attenuating Microphones.

With a properly silent microphone a Marine could call for fire over his radio without the sound of his outgoing remarks being used by the enemy to find his unit and thereby endanger his survival. We saw this as Stingray and simple reconnaissance common sense.

J. Underwing Pod for the A-6 Aircraft.

One project on the drawing boards which received a fair bit of interest in 1967–68 was the use of underwing pods to deliver four-man reconnaissance teams by high-altitude drop. With two men under each wing, the A-6 would launch from a carrier and drop the four men from above twenty-five thousand feet over enemy terrain. While it was clearly feasible, and mock-ups were created from the design work, we did not care for the idea when we considered that we would be the men under the wings during catapult shots from the carrier deck.

K. Offset Bombing Beacons.

All work on beacons for computer-controlled delivery of bombs by aircraft (the A-6 was the aircraft in question) responding to the call of small units was obviously Stingray related. If the recon team could be accurate in locating its position and the area where the enemy was operating, they could destroy that enemy force using the beacon to guide the bomb drop.

There were probably 250 other projects under way in the center during the period I served at LFDC. The Artillery Branch worked on both munitions improvements and accuracy improvements, either one of which might have an impact on Stingray operations. The Communications Branch was in the middle of the backpack radio improvement cycle, and all the new radios were more reliable and farther ranging. In addition, burst-technology investigation related to the transmission of fire missions by Stingray teams in microseconds instead of minutes on the air. For that matter, improvements in clothing, shoes, and load-carrying capabilities for the Marine Corps as a whole would have an impact on Stingray capabilities. Therefore, you could say, without being too far off the mark, that the entire effort at LFDC had some relationship to Stingray.

From outside LFDC there came an impetus to dig deeper and press harder on those items that would make the small unit much more capable of conducting Stingray-type operations. In the Department of Defense a section of the Advanced Research Projects Agency was tasked to conduct a formal study designed to make small ground units more powerful. The title of the program was Small Independent Action Forces. Known by all as SIAF, it brought all manner of support money into LFDC and caused First Lieutenant Coffman and me (I was the designated SIAF action officer) to work even harder. Every aspect of the SIAF study effort related to Stingray because the goal was to make small units much more capable and more deadly to the enemy. SIAF had money to study enhanced training methods, insertion techniques, equipment mixes, combat-power multipliers, and the tactics to be used by small units. Of course, Stingray was one of the primary tactics examined and discussed throughout our work with SIAF. After all, if Stingray were to become part of the Marine Corps of the future, we saw the work done in 1966–69 as having an ever-increasing impact on the development of that capability.

On the tactical and doctrinal side of the Marine Corps Stingray effort, we at LFDC pressed steadily and with consistent pressure to see that the idea became a permanent portion of the Marine Corps doctrine. We wrote papers on the subject for submission to HQMC and provided input to those who were rewriting the Marine Corps' operational manuals. By 1968, it was our view that the question had been resolved—small units, in particular reconnaissance units, should always be prepared to employ the Stingray concept. Without doubt, many continued to oppose the overall concept of a battlefield with small-unit leaders conducting their own wars, but those who held important positions within the Marine Corps seemed to agree that Stingray was a logical extension of the

combat power of the Marine expeditionary forces. At the
same time the extreme cost of deploying and protecting such
small units was not discounted. Our aviator general, Maj.
Gen. Alan J. Armstrong, clearly understood the necessity for
innovative methods of dealing with the enemy, and his enthusiastic support helped us win the day at HQMC.

Stingray at Work in 3d Force Recon Company

In 3d Force we believed in Stingray and went to great
lengths to employ it against the North Vietnamese Army whenever we met them. We would have used bombs dropped from
barrage balloons if we thought that would work—anything to
make the recon teams more capable of killing the enemy!

I was involved in the development of Stingray in the manner
I describe and I used it myself in combat. I do believe that it
works and that money, time, and clear thinking should always
be applied to the problem of making the small units who will
do that work more powerful as well as more able to call in fire.
They need to have superb navigational capabilities, very precise ranging capabilities, more individual firepower, better
food, better clothing, better munitions, better communications, and better training. They also need a Marine Corps that
is willing to make available to them the support and protection
that will enhance their ability to survive when they are treed
and must shift from the delivery of ordnance on a distant
enemy to fighting for their very lives while they await extraction from the battlefield. I do, always, see a specific difference
between Stingray wherein the unit is hunting, and a small unit
(reconnaissance or whomever) using fire to cover their fright-
ened asses.

=== 22 ===

"We Have Something of a Problem Out Here. . . ."*

3d Force Recon Company 1969–70
and 1st Force Recon 1970

Today, employed as a maintenance chief at Marine Corps Recruit Depot at Parris Island, South Carolina, Mr. Charles "Tommy" Sexton is asked, from time to time, to speak to young Marine recruits and tell them about his experience as a recon team member in 3d and 1st Force Recon companies.

Assigned to 3d Force Recon Company in 1969 and 1970, Tommy was a primary radio operator. On 5 February 1970, his recon team was inserted by helicopter into the A Shau Valley to conduct a Stingray mission. Taken under fire by a company-size NVA unit, Tommy's team was nearly annihilated. For his actions that day, Tommy was awarded the Navy Cross.

I was born in Columbia, South Carolina, on 26 August 1948, and after graduating from high school in 1968, I joined the Marine Corps. I went through boot camp at Parris Island, South Carolina, and from PI, I went to advanced infantry training school at Camp Lejeune, North Carolina. My first duty station, after Camp Lejeune, was with the Ground

*Interview with Charles "Tommy" Sexton, 1998.

Security Force at Guantanamo Bay, Cuba, a place where Marines have been stationed for more than one hundred years.

There, as one of many Marines assigned to guard what we called the defensive line which separated Cuban soil from the U.S. naval base, I remember being on perimeter duty one day when a group of Cubans made a mad rush for the fence. A lot of Cubans were killed trying to get over the fence, and that was one remembrance which still sticks in my mind. The Cubans brought lots of townspeople out to the scene and said that we had shot these people. We hadn't.

They put us out there on that fence line—seventeen miles long. In front of us were barbed wire and angry Cubans and behind us was a huge, deep minefield consisting of fifty thousand land mines. We were each given five rounds—and only five rounds—of ammunition for our M-14 rifles. Three Marines were assigned to each of the bunkers positioned along the perimeter, and the only way out for us was to travel along the fence line back to safety. Our instructions were to pick up the telephone and call the sergeant of the guard if we felt there was a possibility of an attack, and there we were with five rounds of ammunition and miles of fence line between us and safety.

When I would sit out there on top of that bunker at night and think about the situation, I'd smile, saying to myself, this is one hell of a mess we're in and we don't stand a chance. If they overran us, we've only got fifteen rounds of ammo between us, a minefield behind us, and miles to safety. That was the first time I was placed in a difficult situation, but as I discovered, it was not to be my last.

With new orders, I left Guantanamo Bay, returned to Camp Lejeune, and reported for duty at Camp Pendleton, California, before going to Vietnam. We were standing in line going through processing when a staff sergeant told us to "count off," the way we had been taught to do in boot camp. He told all odd-numbered Marines to take a step to the left and all even-numbered Marines to step to the right. Then he said, "Congratulations! All of you who stepped to the right have just volunteered for Force Recon." That was my first introduction to recon. I went to communications school and on to additional reconnaissance training at Camp Pendleton. All of us who had "volunteered" were cross-trained. We practiced learning each other's jobs as recon team members so we could function at all of the different positions that made up a team. Other than team leader, the positions were point man, automatic rifleman, M-79 grenadier, team corpsman, and tail-end charlie—the last man in the team. By learning the responsibilities required in those positions we learned how a team was supposed to properly function. More important, I left Camp Pendleton feeling that I was well trained for my next assignment in Vietnam.

My first day in Vietnam, I reported in to 3d Force Recon Company, located next to 3d Reconnaissance Battalion in northern Quang Tri Province. The company was preparing to move south to a new base at Phu Bai, several hours away from Quang Tri by truck and closer to that infamous place known as the A Shau Valley.

As a new joinee I was told to report to a particular hootch where I would find my platoon sergeant, and he would tell me all that I needed to know. I found the sergeant sitting in the hootch, playing cards with some other NCOs. He told me to "go and get a can of diesel fuel and a lot of paper, and burn the shitters." He told me specifically to start with the officer's shitter. I was a little surprised at what he told me to do so I asked him to repeat his order. He told me, again, to get a five-gallon can of diesel fuel and then go burn the shitters.

I said, "Okay, Sergeant," and then I walked outside and, as instructed, I burned the officer's shitter to the ground. It was my first day in Vietnam and no one had told me about the way the outhouses were designed. Needless to say, after that, I was in charge of making sure that nobody else burned it down. But I did burn that sucker down to the ground. Today when I speak to recruits and drill instructors here at Parris Island, I say, "You've got to look at where the man comes from. You just can't take things for granted. They took it for granted that I knew what they were talking about when they told me to burn the shitter, and I did exactly what I was told to do. But, where I come from, once an outhouse was no longer usable we just dug another hole, picked up the outhouse and moved it, then filled in the old hole. No one had told me that the outhouses in Vietnam were built with old oil drums used to collect the human waste and paper so that once collected, the contents were burned away and the drums were placed back inside the outhouse. I did learn."

The point I try to make with these young recruits, and with their sergeants, is that anytime Marines give orders they need to remember where their men come from and make sure they understand what is being asked of them. A young Marine can't read your mind. He may have a picture in his mind but it may not be the same picture that's in your mind. What happened with me didn't hurt anybody, but it could have hurt someone. It was funny, but that's what happened.

I went through a lot more training after I joined 3d Force. They had a two-week course called RIP school, the initials standing for Recon Indoctrination Program. We knew that the 3d Marine Division was leaving Vietnam and returning to Okinawa, and that 3d Recon Battalion was pulling out of I Corps and leaving too. 3d Force was going to have to expand its TAOR (tactical area of operations) and we would take up the slack. Our training would be key to our survival.

By the first of February 1970, I had participated in more than a dozen long-range reconnaissance patrols, always as the primary radio operator. On the fifth of February our six-man recon team was made up of a Sergeant Smith, our team leader, and corporals Adam Cantu and Allen M. Hutchinson, lance corporals Daniel Savage and Giuseppe Ventresca, and me.

I found all of their names, together, when I went to the Vietnam Memorial Wall. That was an experience for me when I visited that wall. I stood in front of it and a very strange feeling, difficult to describe, came over me. I could instantly visualize who they were and what they were.

But I remember one patrol; this was after what happened on 5 February. (I was planning on getting married on a February fourth. Linda and I were going to elope. But we found out that we had to wait twenty-four hours before we could get a marriage license in South Carolina. She was going to Clemson University at the time. When the legal clerk told me that we could get married on the fifth, I simply refused. I said there just ain't no way that I would get married on the fifth. That particular date has a special meaning for me, and I've always been very careful on that day. (That story later.)

When I was with 1st Force Recon Company, I went out on one patrol with First Lieutenant Corbett, known as Sugar Bear. This was one of the few times a lieutenant went with us into the bush, and he was checking me out as a possible team leader. I was sitting and talking to him beside a trail and in the process of showing him where we were on the map and where we were going. About that time we heard a radio coming down the trail.

I was one of the last Marines over there who still carried an M-14 rifle, and during the entire time I was with 1st Force they wanted to take it from me, but I managed to hang onto it. Well, I opened up with my M-14 on the two NVA coming down the trail, and consciously tried to save one of them as a prisoner of war. I shot and killed the first one, who had a rifle, as he came down the trail. The second one, the radio operator, I stitched across the legs, but I also hit him in the stomach and side. I went up to the wounded man and the lieutenant came over and asked me if I thought he'd stay alive until the chopper arrived. I told him there was no way. So I went ahead and shot him and threw the ace of spades card on top of him. We saddled up to leave and the lieutenant said that he wanted us to use the trail, and we began to move out and at a fast pace. I mean we were flying down that trail—all six of us.

I came around a bend in the trail and we ran right into seven North Vietnamese soldiers also running down the trail. I was running as the point man and we were trying to break contact. I threw up my rifle and their point man threw up his rifle, but neither of us fired. I put my left hand down and motioned slowly for my people to back up, and he motioned for his six people to back up. As soon as we had all turned around we all took off running—them and us! Some people still don't believe this happened, but I'm here to tell you that it did. We sat there in our harbor site that night and watched and listened as the NVA moved around with flashlights looking for us, but we positioned ourselves on the side of a mountain and they beat the bushes trying to find us, without success. I sat there in the dark and tried to think about what had happened. It was something that could only happen in a movie. We didn't want to become engaged in a second fire fight, and the North Vietnamese certainly didn't want any part of us. I wondered if I had made a mistake by not shooting into them, but what was done was done.

Now then, here's what happened nearly six months earlier, on the morning of the fifth of February 1970, when I was in 3d Force Recon Company, and I'll try to describe the events that surrounded my being awarded the Navy Cross.

The day before, the fourth of February, a recon team from 3d Force Recon Company was flown out to the A Shau Valley by helicopter from the U.S. Army's 2/17th Cavalry. The recon team was inserted into its zone, but came under heavy enemy fire right away and had to be extracted. Several slicks (gunships) were hit, but none were shot down. Our team was inserted into the same general area, the following day, but at a different landing zone. Our mission was to discover why they had been hit so quickly the day before. Much to our surprise, the Army sent over the same helicopter pilots as the day earlier.

They were supposed to drop us off, but didn't. Instead they hovered over the LZ for several minutes to see if they were going to take fire. That's just too long to be stationary in enemy territory. Then they dropped down to a lower altitude and hovered again. They never did touch their skids to the ground. We were well beyond nervous at that point, so Sergeant Smith signaled for us to jump.

As soon as we got on the ground we had to establish radio communications between ourselves and our helicopter gunship support, but the insert helicopter didn't fly away, it stayed over our insertion point. As soon as we established radio contact with them we moved away from the LZ. We hadn't gone more than a hundred yards before we came to a four-lane highway in the jungle! It could not be seen from the air because the triple canopy covered it so well, but it looked like Interstate Highway 95. It was all hard-packed dirt, but we could see where two trucks, coming from opposite directions, could use the road. This information was immediately radioed back to the company's COC (Combat Operations Center) at Phu Bai, via our radio relay site, and we were told to move to higher ground and keep an eye on the road. Of course any road that wide was to be treated as a danger area, and we crossed it, one at a time, taking the usual precautions.

Just seconds after tail-end-Charlie crossed the road, several team members spotted NVA soldiers trying to maneuver around us. I saw several of them, and was next to last in the order of march. Then one of our men opened up on them at about the same time they began firing at us. It was that fast. They were on both sides of us and the volume of fire was terrific.

When the NVA opened up on the team, I was in a kneeling position and immediately began firing back. Suddenly I felt a round strike me in the chest. It sent me twisting to my left, and as I turned back into my original position I reached over to grab my knife out of its scabbard, only to discover that I now had half a knife.

The bullet that hit me had gone through the day-night flare taped to the sheath of my K-bar (knife), which was positioned upside down on my shoulder harness for quick release. The bullet had broken the steel blade of my knife in two.

The NVA were still firing at me and I remember wondering, how in the hell had I broken my K-bar? That was before I realized that all of my teammates had been hit and were dead. I put the broken K-bar back in the scabbard and fastened the snap back in place.

I reached out in front of me and grabbed Adam Cantu's body and took his K-bar off his fighting harness. That's when I began to cut the hand grenades from the fighting harnesses of my dead teammates. We had made a habit of taping the hand grenades to our ammunition pouches so we wouldn't lose them moving through thick brush, but a sharp fighting knife made a quick job of getting the grenades free from the canvas magazine pouches.

I began to throw the grenades at the closest points of enemy fire, giving myself precious seconds to use my radio and come up on the frequency of two Cobra gunships that we knew were flying in the A Shau Valley. I was able to contact them without difficulty and both of them headed toward my position. I radioed to them that I was surrounded, and that I was a member of a Marine force recon team with four men dead, one man wounded pretty badly, and myself trying to hold on. Sergeant Smith was badly wounded. All of them had been shot in the head, but Smith was still alive. He lived for several more days following the firefight, but died on board the U.S. Navy hospital ship *Sanctuary*.

Lance Corporal Ventresca was from Philadelphia. I sure would like to see him again, because I wrote him up for a Bronze Star, but I never found out if he received it. Ventresca had been hit in the head by an AK-47 round, and lived to tell about it. The bullet struck him just below the hairline, right above his eyes, but was deflected off his forehead, went under his scalp, and exited out the back of his head. Of course, I thought he was dead because his face was covered with blood and he didn't move. Ventresca didn't regain consciousness for more than an hour after being hit. In fact, I had called him in as being dead—killed in the initial seconds of the firefight.

I was on the ground for seven or eight hours before an Army Blue Team was sent in to get me, two dozen infantrymen with automatic weapons who had been staged at Camp Eagle as part of the 101st Airborne's reactionary force. I probably owe my life to them.

The Cobra gunships were shooting at the enemy, but their machine gun and rocket fire was impacting behind the maneuvering NVA. I couldn't tell how many NVA were around me, but I could certainly hear them moving through the brush to get closer to me. I told the gunship pilots that I was okay but that the rest of the team was dead, and to bring their rounds right in on top of the smoke grenades I had thrown out. They did exactly what I asked. The close air support was a great thing to witness, but it caused me something of a problem because their firing was forcing the enemy to move toward me, not away from me.

I was now down to one magazine and one hand grenade. At this time Ventresca regained consciousness. He sat up and listened to me. I told him to fire his M-16 in a particular direction, hoping that the sound of two types of weapons would delay the NVA from charging my tenuous position. It must have worked, because they didn't come any closer. That was a good thing, too, because I was saving that last hand grenade for myself and Ventresca. I had already made the decision that we would not be taken alive by the NVA.

The Army Blue Team came up on my radio and identified themselves. They said they were close to me but couldn't find me. I told them I would fire one round from my rifle into the air and they were to listen for the shot and move in on my location. I told them I could hear people moving around me in the brush and that I hoped it was them, so I fired the round and someone hollered out in English, "Hey, it's us!"

A group of soldiers encircled me. Their men moved quickly and took the wounded—Sergeant Smith and Lance Corporal Ventresca—out of area, moving to a medevac site. The leader of the group, an Army second lieutenant, threw out a smoke grenade to mark our position and then an Army slick came in overhead and dropped a sling down as they prepared to take out the wounded. The problem was, the lieutenant had thrown out his smoke grenade too close to Ventresca and he began to choke on the smoke. He had a lot of blood in his mouth from his head wound and he was coughing and choking badly.

Once we got the two wounded up and away the lieutenant turned to me and said, "Okay, let's go." I was surprised by this and replied, "No way. Not without the dead. We don't leave ours. They go with us." I meant what I said, and he knew I meant it because I still had my rifle in my hand and it was pointed straight at him.

He said, "Well, they're all shot in the head. I don't know how we'll get them out of here." I told him I'd take care of it myself. I pulled each man's T-shirt over his head and tied their arms and feet together with comm wire, then told the lieutenant to have his men cut some poles from a nearby stand of bamboo. His soldiers did as he ordered and they placed the bamboo poles between their feet and arms. It took two soldiers to carry out each of the three dead Marines. But I wasn't going to leave them behind.

I looked around the area and noticed that the soldiers had left all of the M-16s and our primary radio right where they had fallen. I was really pissed off because I had to gather up all the rifles and the radio myself. I moved up front to where this young lieutenant was moving with the men and, pointing to my dead teammates, said, "Lieutenant, they get the first chopper, and I'll go with them." He didn't dare argue with me.

When that first Huey came in we loaded the dead inside and I crawled in on top of them. There isn't much room inside a Huey and that was the only place available for me, but I didn't mind.

I began to think about what had happened. It was the first time I was able to really give thought to the events of the day. And, for whatever reason, my mind returned to that broken K-bar. I was worried about that damned knife because as Marines we are taught to protect everything we are given, and that knife was an important piece of my gear.

I pulled the K-bar out of its sheath and looked at it—the steel blade broken neatly in two. I wondered aloud, "How in the world did that happen?" And that was when I turned the sheath over and saw the AK-47 round sticking out of the leather. The helicopter door gunner, a sergeant, had been watching me and his eyes seemed to get huge. He spoke on the intercom to his pilot and told him what he was seeing. When we finally got on the ground the pilot came over to me and asked about what had happened. When I explained it all to him he just stood there and shook his head in disbelief.

I'll tell you something else that happened that day, something that I can only describe as spiritual, but which has remained with me all these years.

That morning began with a blanket of low-lying fog covering the ground all around the Phu Bai area, where we lifted off. By the time we were inserted into our recon zone in the A Shau Valley the sun was out and it was really a beautiful day. But the moment the NVA initiated their contact against us it started raining hard. It became very dark and poured for about three or four minutes. When the sun came back out all those young Marines who had been my team were dead.

I immediately thought about a passage from the Bible that I had heard when I was a little kid. That passage mentions something about the firstborn son being killed and that a black cloud would descend over the land of Israel when this happened. Then the sun would reappear and all would be well. I can't recall the exact passage, but the vision of that happening stuck in my mind so deeply that on the morning of the ambush when the sun was covered by darkness I was afraid, but when it reappeared I felt no sense of fear whatsoever. I knew I would be all right. I knew what I had to do, and I did it. During my debriefing session that afternoon I told them that I knew that once the sun had come back out, I'd be okay.

I do want you to know that I don't regret anything that happened to me while I was over there. I had a good time while I was there. I met a lot of great people and I learned a lot.

I came back from Vietnam after serving in 1st Force Recon Company. I flew back from Vietnam, went to Camp Pendleton, and was discharged at Camp Pendleton.

During the Vietnam War my brother had joined the Army, and I had a sister who had joined the Navy and another brother who had joined the Navy, too. Out of all of us, I think I received the best training. My brother went through his training at Fort Jackson here in South Carolina while I was in Cuba. He told the Army that he had a brother who was headed for Vietnam, which kept him from going. About two weeks later I got my orders for Vietnam.

Being with 3d Force Recon was the best of it. I met some

U.S. Army soldiers who were billeted near us in Da Nang. One night while we were on perimeter duty, which we shared with the Army, I asked two of them if they had test-fired their weapons. They said, "We just checked them out of the armory. We haven't test-fired them." I marched them down to our test-firing area (they didn't even have one) and we discovered that four out of their six M-16 rifles didn't fire. They had no idea what was going on around them. Their last training was basic training.

Working here in the Maintenance Branch at Parris Island, and being able to observe Marine basic training, I have witnessed a great many changes since the days when I was a young recruit. Some of these changes are, in my opinion, quite good, but many are not good, and I'll tell you why. I see many of today's young Marines interacting with civilians on board the depot. The civilians seem to take on a parent-child relationship with many of them. Many of these men and women are, unfortunately, products of broken families; no mother or father to have helped them along and through no fault of their own. These kids are looking for a father figure and they think the Marine Corps will provide that lost part of their lives for them. It will not and it should not. It seems like many of these kids have an excuse for their problems. Few of them want to take responsibility for their own actions.

I was talking with a gunnery sergeant just yesterday and he said, "Tommy, they aren't worried about face-to-face combat anymore. They saw us dropping bombs from thirty thousand feet up, on television during Desert Storm, and they just don't believe they'll ever have to face anyone man to man. The Marine recruits don't get hand-to-hand training anymore. It's been cut out of their training and it's a damn shame. If we are supposed to train like we'll fight, then we are in big trouble."

Most of the Marines I've talked to have never been in a fist-fight, and it will be too late to learn when the time comes. They just won't know what to do. The Army has already admitted that it made a big mistake by allowing women to initially train with the men. Their training has been a disaster, and the drill sergeants at Fort Jackson will tell you so. The Army won't admit it to the press or an investigative group, but men who have been in combat know what needs to be taught and who will be able to do the fighting. On the ground it will not be the women who will fight and win.

It will be small-unit leaders, led by men.

=== 23 ===

The Battle for Hill 510

By definition Stingray missions were conducted at significant distances from the closest friendly forces. For recon teams to have the constant ability to communicate at all times with higher headquarters, the employment of radio relay sites was often necessary. This is a factual account of the price paid to keep such communications open.

Marine force reconnaissance teams are not usually given the mission to set up defensive positions in enemy-held territory, but on 1 August 1970 two recon teams from 1st Force Reconnaissance Company, headquartered in Da Nang, were required to do just that. After being inserted by a CH-46 helicopter onto Hill 510, a former radio relay position in the Thuong Duc river valley twenty-five miles west of Da Nang, the teams were expected to set up a "292" ("two-niner-two") radio site on the hill and hold their position while five other recon teams from the company were inserted into the valley and spread out to search for the North Vietnamese.

What brought this unusual event to a dramatic climax had begun early in April 1970, when S.Sgt. Daniel P. Williams, a former recon platoon sergeant from 3d Force Recon Company, took his new team, Misty Cloud, out to patrol within the Thuong Duc corridor. Williams and his recon Marines made numerous enemy sightings and calls for fire from their vantage point, and later warned their superiors that the possibility of a confrontation between a six-man force recon team and a numerically superior force of NVA was inevitable. But Williams's warning and those of subsequent recon teams that later occupied and improved the defensive positions on the hill went unheeded.

During that first six-day mission in the valley, Misty Cloud sighted 145 North Vietnamese soldiers as well as numerous trails, hootches, campfires, and electric lights. The team's urgent requests for twelve artillery fire missions were answered by Marine gunners, resulting in ten NVA confirmed killed, an additional ten probable KIA, and fifteen secondary explosions. Then, using Marine fixed-wing air strikes as part of the Stingray mission, the team accounted for an additional five confirmed kills and nine secondary explosions.

During the entire patrol, Misty Cloud encountered frequent radio jamming. The jamming of the team's two PRC-77 radios by the North Vietnamese was not a new occurrence, and to stop the jamming required that the team's two radio operators switch between alternate frequencies. Because radio jamming had been experienced by many of the teams of 3d Force Recon Company during the time they operated inside the DMZ, along the Hai Van Pass, and throughout the A Shau Valley, Williams was aware of the best countermeasures. But this time the enemy's jamming was far more extensive. Even more unusual was the NVA's use of women to repeat the team's call signs, play Vietnamese music on the team's radio frequencies, and break up the Marines' transmissions by shouting Vietnamese political phrases, slogans, and curses.

Of far greater significance was an observation made by Misty Cloud when it called in a fire mission against NVA soldiers in the open. The NVA had begun to cultivate large garden plots. They had prepared many small, irrigated patches of land near the banks of two rivers and were observed tending the plots nearly every day. The importance of the gardens to the enemy was evident when a field caught fire from an exploding artillery round. As the resulting brushfire spread toward their cultivated fields, several North Vietnamese soldiers ran from the safety of their hidden underground bunkers and, braving the explosions, attempted to beat out the fire.

Because of the significant increase in enemy activity in and around the Thuong Duc river valley, plans were immediately implemented to set up a permanent radio relay site and observation post. Manned by only a handful of recon Marines and their accompanying corpsmen from 1st Force, the OP on Hill 510 was to become a regular target of NVA forces who considered the Thuong Duc Valley to be theirs.

Hill 510 was first defended by fourteen Marines and one Navy corpsman. Their mission was to establish and defend both the observation post and the 292 radio relay site, enabling the company's reconnaissance teams to transmit their reports and calls for fire to the hill for relay to Da Nang.

Map studies showed Hill 510 to be a heavily forested, rock-covered pinnacle high above the junction of two wide but shallow rivers which meandered eastward through the Thuong Duc Valley toward the port city of Da Nang. The height of the small hill made radio communications much easier and offered a commanding view of the surrounding hillsides and valleys while providing limited concealment from the watchful eyes of the North Vietnamese.

The area on Hill 510 we actually occupied was no greater than fifty feet wide and one hundred feet long with a gradual sloping finger running from north to south along the narrow ridgeline of the hill. Numerous hardwood trees, large boulders, and the uneven terrain did not allow for much of a helicopter landing zone, which meant that only three methods of insertion were available to the first group to occupy the hill: a tailgate insertion from a hovering helicopter, a special insertion/extraction (SPIE) rig, or by using an external ladder draped over the tailgate of the starboard door of a CH-46 helicopter.

Later, with the help of several chain saws, some well-placed C-4 (explosive material), a few quarter-pound blocks of TNT, and a great deal of muscle and sweat, a small patch of jungle on the hill's southern slope was cleared for an LZ large enough to permit only the difficult and delicate landing of one Marine CH-46 helicopter at a time.

Hill 510 was occupied and successfully defended until mid-July, when it was finally decided to abandon the site due to the rapid reduction in reconnaissance missions around Thuong Duc previously requested by the Marine Amphibious Force (MAF) commander, Lt. Gen. Keith B. McCutcheon. But even as 1st Force Recon Company was preparing to leave the Republic of Vietnam and return to the States, it was decided to place a large number of the company's recon teams into the Thuong Duc Valley in one last effort to locate and destroy the NVA, who were continuing to inch closer to Da Nang. This action was the beginning of Operation Imperial Lake, the final major Marine offensive of the Vietnam War.

On 1 August 1970, six recon teams from 1st Force Reconnaissance Company, code named Allbrook, Auditor, A Lu King, Date Palm, Hansworth, and Impressive, were inserted by Marine CH-46 helicopters onto Hill 510.

The normal complement of Team Hansworth was augmented by Marines from within the company along with two Australian SAS Rangers, bringing its strength to eighteen men. Their primary mission was to set up the radio relay site just north of the original OP site and to monitor radio traffic from the other five operational teams as they patrolled the valley below. It was a classic Stingray operation at its best.

After the other five teams had been inserted, they quickly left the safety of the hilltop and quietly slipped away toward their assigned reconnaissance zones, leaving the Marines of Team Hansworth to prepare and defend the radio relay site. Team Hansworth then split into two groups, the first group led by a second lieutenant, new to the company, named Prins, along with Lorens, Bradshaw, Hobbs, Falco, Valez, Clark, and McAndrews, taking the high ground. The second group, led by Cpl. Jim Holzman, along with Palmer, Smith, Arnold, Rodriguez, Baker, Ramsdell, and Oxford, would provide security around the LZ. The two Australians, members of a small-unit exchange program, accompanied Corporal Holzman's group. With Second Lieutenant Prins's group occupying the top of the hill, Corporal Holzman's men spread out to cover as much of the LZ as possible and create a defensive perimeter nearly one hundred yards below the military crest of Hill 510.

Team Hansworth was the first team to be inserted onto the hill since the area had been abandoned several weeks before. Holzman's men found several booby traps that had been set up by the NVA. The gooks had trip-wired "tomato can" charges inside camouflaged holes, and each booby trap contained enough high explosive to blow a man in half. Fortunately the rotor-wash from the insertion helicopter had blown away some of the dried vegetation used as camouflage, exposing the holes.

Claymore mines with white phosphorus grenades taped to their backs were placed around the perimeter. Holzman's group had the foresight to bring along one M-60 machine gun, several cases of fragmentation and illumination grenades, and one 60mm mortar with several cases of high-explosive (HE) and illumination rounds.

By the end of the first day the recon Marines on Hill 510 felt they were ready for whatever the night might bring, but oddly, the only unusual event that first night came from within the teams. The two Australian Rangers assigned to Corporal Holzman's group began to comment openly that they did not like what they saw and felt uncomfortable with the situation. They told Holzman that when they went to the bush it was their practice not to move at night and to shut down their radios once it became dark. They would go to sleep and wait for first light before turning their radios back on. Making matters worse for the Marines guarding the hill, the two Aussies finally stopped complaining and went off to sleep, only to begin snoring so loudly that Holzman had to kick them awake, ordering them to put on their gas masks in order to muffle their telltale noise. Holzman described the problems he was having with these two individuals in his situation report (SITREP) to the company's operations officer, and early the next morning a CH-46 picked up the two unwanted SAS troopers and carried them back to Da Nang.

The second day on Hill 510 was spent by both groups digging in. There was no moon on the second night in the field, and with the approach of nightfall the evening wind picked up and it began to drizzle.

Near midnight the two-man listening post located outside the lower perimeter reported hearing movement "in all directions and getting closer" to their position. Holzman radioed this information to Lieutenant Prins, located on top of the hill, and told him he was going to throw a couple of CS grenades in the direction of the approaching noise. Lieutenant Prins instructed Corporal Holzman to allow him and his men enough time to put on their gas masks, and then radioed back to the corporal to make his move.

Holzman slowly pulled the cotter pin on one CS grenade and let the spoon fly, igniting the grenade before he threw it. The NVA had crept up, in total darkness, so close to Holzman's position that they thought he was one of them and that his grenade was the signal to commence their surprise assault. When they stood up on line, Holzman threw his grenade and all hell broke loose around Hill 510 as an estimated force of more than fifty North Vietnamese soldiers attacked.

L.Cpl. Mike Hobbs, assigned at one of the listening posts, remembered, "As I sat totally motionless in my fighting hole, I heard a 'click' which sounded like a pair of pliers cutting my claymore wire, so I raised up very slowly and saw a helmeted NVA soldier crawling by me, less than five feet away. He probably felt a tremendous amount of pain as eighteen rounds from my M-16 ripped across his upper chest."

The first round the NVA fired was an RPG-7 (rocket-propelled grenade), but the grenadier had aimed it above Holzman's position to impact among the Marines at the top of the hill. The RPG round struck L.Cpl. Bill Clark squarely in the chest, causing a secondary explosion of the fragmentation grenades attached to Clark's fighting harness. That explosion showered everyone on the hilltop with blood, shrapnel, and pieces of flesh from Clark's body.

One of the assaulting NVA soldiers snagged a trip wire

connected to a hidden illumination grenade, and when it went off the light silhouetted another squad of enemy soldiers running straight toward Holzman's position at the far end of the LZ. Meanwhile, other NVA soldiers continued to crawl closer, throwing satchel charges and firing AK-47s.

Relying on the effectiveness of accurately thrown hand grenades to kill the approaching enemy, none of Holzman's Marines had yet fired a single round from his weapon. The NVA fired several more RPG rounds at the hilltop, wounding Lieutenant Prins in the neck with shrapnel and subsequently sending him into shock, and seriously wounding Lance Corporal Bradshaw.

As soon as the assault started, Corporal Holzman had radioed the team's situation to the company COC in Da Nang, requesting the services of a C-47 flare-ship and an AC-47 "Spooky" gunship.*

While the Marines waited anxiously for the aircrafts' arrival, Holzman and Cpl. Jerry Smith ran to the 60mm mortar, and as Smith aimed, Holzman began to drop high-explosive rounds down the tube. The impacting rounds slowed the ground attack, but the NVA continued to concentrate their rifle fire on the hilltop.

When the Spooky gunship arrived the pilot radioed to Holzman that he didn't have a clear picture of exactly where the recon teams were located, at which time Lance Corporal Oxford broke out his strobe light, made a fast run to a nearby two-man fighting hole, and placed the light inside a C ration box.

Satisfied that he had a good fix on the Marines' positions, the pilot put his aircraft in a pylon-turn and delivered urgently needed protective fire. When the flare-ship arrived on station, it dropped enough flares on its first pass to turn night into day,

---

*This particular "guardian angel" supply aircraft was modified to carry three GAU-2A minigun pods on its port side, twenty-four thousand rounds of ammunition, and forty-five parachute flares with a burning time of three minutes each. The crew consisted of a pilot/aircraft commander, copilot, navigator, and three gunners to shoot the guns and drop the flares.

and that was when the recon Marines on Hill 510 opened up with their M-16s and M-60 machine gun, delivering effective fire into the exposed NVA.

Even though some NVA were caught in the open, they continued their attack up the steep hillside. Holzman saw one of the charging enemy soldiers stop to pick up a claymore mine, then resume his charge up the hill, carrying the claymore in front of his chest. The soldier came straight on toward the Marines' trench line until Holzman squeezed down on the green hell-box, instantly vaporizing the suicidal soldier and showering his NVA comrades with chunks of burning white phosphorus from the grenade the Marines had earlier taped to the mine.

Lance Corporal Hobbs remembers, "Just after that gook was blown to pieces, Corporal Lorens crawled out to my hole and brought me the rest of Clark's ammunition. I had used up all of my own, when Lorens checked on me, and then asked if I had set off all of the claymores. I told him I hadn't and to get behind a nearby tree, and then I squeezed the two hell-boxes. I believe that my claymores detonated because the resulting explosions were very close and the sounds of enemy movement in the darkness around me stopped. That was really when the attack ended and the surviving enemy soldiers turned and ran screaming down the hill for the safety of the jungle."

With first light the team insured that the remaining ammunition was redistributed and then began to search the immediate area to determine who was alive, who was wounded, and who was dead. Cpl. Mike Lorens, assistant team leader of Lieutenant Prins's group, had immediately taken charge when his lieutenant had been wounded and managed to keep his group of Marines together after some were wounded and one was killed.

It was Jim Holzman who had to perform the grisly task of collecting what remained of Lance Corporal Clark: his head, right arm, and the combat boot containing his right foot. Holzman placed his friend's body parts in an empty wooden grenade box, which became a field-expedient casket.

Sometime after sunrise, Holzman learned that Hobbs had spent the better part of the previous day with Clark as the pair dug their two-man fighting hole. Hobbs told Holzman, "Clark and I were told to dig a hole for our listening post, just big enough to hold the two of us, and with each shovelful of dirt we would complain that Force Recon Marines didn't dig in, or wear flak jackets and helmets. But, without a doubt, that fighting hole saved my life."

Just before the attack, around 2330, Hobbs had told Clark to return to the top of the hill and get some sleep. Left alone in the hole, Hobbs had heard the movement of the enemy closing in around him at the same time that Corporal Holzman was preparing to throw his CS grenade. Hobbs had remained at his position until morning, when he felt it was finally safe to move, and that was when he discovered just how close the NVA had come to taking out his lone position.

"At daylight the area where Clark had been sleeping was covered with dime-size specks of blood. The ground around our listening post was littered with pieces of enemy clothing, pools of blood, and numerous drag marks. The NVA paid a very heavy price for trying to take us out. And they failed!"

When the Marines on the radio relay site got word that extraction birds were coming in, Holzman wanted to be absolutely sure that their landing zone was secure. While making his patrol around the perimeter with Lance Corporal Falco, the pair made the first of two unique discoveries: in preparation for their night attack the NVA had tried to encircle the entire landing zone with one-pound blocks of TNT. The charges needed a match to light the primitive fuses, and the Marines reasoned that the constant drizzle during the night coupled with their defensive fire must have prevented the TNT from being ignited. The second discovery was credited to Lance Corporal Falco's keen vision. While he and Holzman were checking the perimeter, Falco spotted an NVA soldier hiding in the brush, cradling his AK-47. Falco shot and killed the enemy soldier before he could get off a shot, turned to Holzman, and said, "Ya know, those little bastards just don't know when to give up."

One Marine CH-46 helicopter that came in to extract the Marines from Hill 510 took one group and the two wounded Marines to the Navy hospital ship USS *Sanctuary*, while the second bird returned to Da Nang with the remaining Marines and Lance Corporal Clark's remains. By the end of August 1970 the war in Vietnam was over for most of the Marines of 1st Force Recon Company. The memory of defending one lone hilltop, deep in enemy territory, in support of the company's Stingray operations was indelibly etched in the minds of those Marines who survived the experience.

— 24 —

"And the Beat Goes On"

A Recon Marine in
Operation Desert Shield/Desert Storm*

In 1998, S.Sgt. Jeffrey Buffa, USMC, was a student at
The Citadel. Having served with distinction as a recon
Marine with 3d Reconnaissance Battalion, during op-
erations Desert Shield and Desert Storm, I asked Staff
Sergeant Buffa to describe his role as team member
during the Gulf War.

The majority of my fellow reconnaissance Marines in
Charlie Company, 3d Reconnaissance Battalion, had watched
the movement of Iraqi tanks into the nation of Kuwait on television with only a small amount of interest. It seemed that the
invasion would be unlikely to affect any of the company's operations since where we were, on the island of Okinawa,
Japan, was nearly half a world away from the Middle East.

President Bush then decided that this act of aggression
would not stand, and the massive buildup of American and
coalition forces in Saudi Arabia soon began. Apathy turned to
frustration as it seemed that once again Charlie Company
would be held out of this new action. The frustration of many
Marines was born of an intense desire to do their duty. Few

*Interview with S.Sgt. Jeffrey H. Buffa, USMC, The Citadel, 1998.

of our Marines made any pretense about being "lifers" in the Marine Corps. However, if they were going to serve their country, they wanted to serve where they felt they could best contribute.

Contributing to the defense of the nation's interests meant going to Saudi Arabia, not standing idly by on Okinawa. The frustration broke with the arrival of orders detailing our reconnaissance company with "standing up" a reinforced platoon for immediate deployment to Saudi Arabia in support of the 4th Marine Regiment.

Every Marine wanted to go to war, and the jockeying to get a position on a recon team became intense. Due to our excessively busy deployment schedule, there had never been set teams within the company. The formation of reconnaissance teams had always been an ad hoc procedure at best. While this creation of recon teams "on the fly" seemed a poor way of doing business, it actually had a positive effect, as it did allow every Marine to operate under varying conditions with one another. Most of the Marines in our company became comfortable operating with each other on patrol. Operational patrolling procedures were company-wide, not team specific, allowing for the interchangeability of Marines within recon teams without losing any combat effectiveness. But the scramble for a spot on a recon team was on, and three six-man teams were to be formed to go along with a small headquarters element led by our company commander, Captain Cocoa.

Originally, when the orders to deploy came down from higher headquarters, I had been told that I would not be going along. Frustrated with the prospect of being left behind, I did little more than mope around the company area. At the last moment I was miraculously chosen to go as the captain's driver, replacing another Marine who could not deploy due to personal problems.

Our platoon left Okinawa in mid-August 1991 for Saudi Arabia aboard two separate ships. Platoon headquarters found itself aboard the USS *Dubuque*. Still functioning as the captain's driver, I found myself questioning if I would be ready to join a recon team should the opportunity present itself. I looked upon most of the other Marines within our platoon with a certain amount of respect, if not admiration. Many of those Marines were simply phenomenal operators and I could only hope to be up to the task of serving alongside them. My only fear of going to war was in failing my fellow Marines at the moment of truth.

This platoon of recon Marines was ready for combat due to the intense preparation of the company by its former commander, Captain Malay. Through sheer force of his personality and extreme hard work, this officer of Marines instilled in us the discipline, knowledge, and esprit de corps that would make our platoon a very effective fighting force. I have met many officers in the Marine Corps, but few of them were warriors. Captain Malay was a warrior, and the success of our platoon on the battlefield would be a direct reflection of his competence.

On 2 September 1991 the platoon headquarters section arrived at the port of Al Jubayl. The headquarters section was met by a group from the teams that had already been in country for a few days. The headquarters group was taken to a tent camp in the port area, but on the day of arrival the entire platoon minus the captain was reunited and transported to a place called Camp 15, where we would be billeted off and on until October.

After arriving at Camp 15, those of us attached to headquarters learned that the platoon had been reorganized and subsequently attached to A Company, 1st Reconnaissance Battalion. I found myself in Recon Team 2 under the leadership of Corporal Swanson. Serving in a recon team had been what I wanted to do from the time I first joined the Corps, and the intense pride at being allowed to do so was only tempered by my fear of not being up to the challenge. I also enjoyed the prospect of serving under the leadership of Corporal Swanson, a Marine whom I looked upon with a high degree of admiration. Corporal Swanson was an intelligent and highly professional recon Marine and I trusted him implicitly.

The platoon arrived at Camp 15, where we were billeted in small housing units. The camp had originally been designed as an oil workers' compound and it seemed to me to be quite comfortable. While most Marines live a spartan life, the time we spent at Camp 15 seemed as though we were living in the Hotel Del Coronado in San Diego.

Within a few days the situation changed and the teams were again reorganized. Initially I was apprehensive about the change, but soon found myself being comfortable with the shift in personnel. My new team was led by Sgt. John P. Jestel. Sergeant Jestel, or "Jay" as most of us called him, was a Marine with a reputation for working hard and playing hard. Often criticized behind his back for being less than serious, I found him to be a skilled combat leader. Our assistant team leader was Corporal Reuter, who complained loudly about Jay's perceived lack of solemnity but always insured that Jay was fully supported in every way for each mission the team went on.

The team's primary radio operator was L.Cpl. George M. Dykes III. Dykes had a penchant for cleanliness even though we had deployed to one of the dirtiest places on earth. George could always get "comm" though, and that was all we could ask of our radio operator. Lance corporals Blackwell and Mike McAvoy rounded out our six-man team. Blackwell was perhaps the quietest man I have ever known and McAvoy was one of the biggest party animals I have met. I found myself walking the point, carrying an M-249 SAW (squad automatic weapon) for this motley crew of recon Marines. I often think that we were a misfit team; however, our team of misfits was considered by many to be the best group one could go to war with.

Our initial days at Camp 15 were spent preparing for vehicle (mobile) patrols. As the eyes and ears of the division commander we were expected to be out in front snoopin' and poopin'; but we had spent all of our previous training time in preparation for fighting a war in the jungles of the Far East, not in the deserts of the Middle East. Marines have always been the masters of adaptation, and that is exactly what we did. We adapted to our current situation and quickly learned what we had to do to become an effective desert reconnaissance team.

While foot patrolling was to be our primary method of movement, the teams also had to learn how to conduct mobile vehicle patrols. Driving a Hummer during a reconnaissance patrol seemed to go against everything we had been trained for, but we did it and performed well in the process. Our patrols began almost immediately. A rotation schedule was created that allowed each company to do a weeklong stint at Fire Base Kershaw at Manifa Bay, followed by two weeks in reserve at Camp 15. The fire base was really a series of fighting positions, manned by recon teams, located next to a FARP (forward area refueling point). The glamor of manning positions at the fire base was underwhelming, but it got the recon battalion's assets that much closer to Kuwait.

Much of the time spent at the fire base was truly boring and frustrating. Recon Marines expect to be forward, observing, not sitting in a rear area watching the waves splash up against the shoreline on some forgotten beach. When our teams did get a chance to patrol, they made the most of it. Mobile patrols were often conducted with two teams supporting one another. On patrol, each team had two or three Hummers linked by radio communications. Sometimes the teams would be dispatched singly and on some occasions the entire platoon would be sent out as a single unit. There must have been some method to the assignment madness, but it certainly was beyond the understanding of this young lance corporal. Teams on patrol were expected to report any unusual activity conducted by the Bedouins in the desert. High headquarters felt that Iraqis masquerading as Bedouins might cross the border to conduct surveillance activities or strike with some type of a terrorist act. If an overt military attack occurred the teams were expected to dig in, allow the Iraqi forces to bypass our teams, then report on enemy activity from behind the lines. Our missions were to be, primarily, ones of surveillance. However, our teams had always been trained to take advantage of targets of opportunity whenever tactically advantageous. A "Keyhole" mission could, at any time, now turn into a "Stingray" mission. Of course, none of these missions were "textbook" in any sense, since we had never trained in the desert. Training missions conducted during Operation Desert Shield were crucial in allowing our teams to experiment, learn, and refine the techniques we would need in combat.

In late October, 1st Reconnaissance Battalion, in its entirety, moved forward to the division staging area, commonly referred to as the DSA, at Manifa Bay. Fire Base Kershaw had been overrun, and not by the enemy. Life at the DSA could be characterized as sheer boredom. Only meager attempts to make life in a tent more comfortable broke the seemingly unending struggle to maintain our sanity. The company first sergeant, First Sergeant Bustamonte, tried to keep his Marines motivated and ready as best he could under trying circumstances. While the division headquarters was a beehive of activity, I found myself always focused on the team rather than on my platoon, company, or even battalion. My team was my world, my reason for being, and I paid little attention to much else.

As the days went by, information on the future conduct of the war was disseminated to our teams. Initial war plans called for our team to move by foot to the forward edge of the minefields where the Iraqi defensive works began and probe for gaps within the minefields so Marines could safely pass through these barriers. To assist us in this effort a young combat engineer was assigned to augment our team. The combat engineer tried to put a good face on the mission, but he could not do it. The team quickly realized that it was to be used as nothing more than a seven-man mine probe, not as a highly trained surveillance team.

The team did not waver but instead began to prepare itself as best it could. A mock minefield was constructed within the DSA so all the teams could practice movement to, in, and away from the minefields. Our team began to formulate an SOP (standard operating procedure) that, though far from perfect, was the best instruction we could come up with to assist in the teaching of this difficult detail. Our SOP divided a recon team into one three-man and one four-man element once we had patrolled up to the edge of the minefield. The A-element, comprised of Jay, Mike, and the combat engineer, would move into the minefield and mark a lane for the first assault elements of Marines. The rest of us, in the B-element, would provide covering fire for the advancing A-element. Once the A-element had reached what we hoped would be the other side of the minefield, the B-element would follow through the marked lane, while the A-element provided cover.

This tasking was unlike anything we had ever encountered. No one liked the idea of crawling totally exposed into an enemy minefield, but that was what was expected of us and we were going to do it the best way possible. Jay walked us through his perception of how the team should operate during this mission, and then asked us all for our input. Together the team formulated its SOP and then generated contingency plans to account for anything that could go wrong during the operation. The team did its very best to prepare, but reality overtook the war-gaming, and just after Christmas our team was sent to the Kuwait-Saudi border to conduct more traditional surveillance missions.

We arrived at a Saudi border outpost, where we received a quick briefing on the current situation from a Marine gunnery sergeant who had been working there for some time, observing the Iraqi forces by utilizing a ground-located FIR (forward-looking infrared radar) system. A U.S. Army Special Forces operator working closely with the Saudi border guard also chimed in with a few words of wisdom about the situation we faced. It seemed that the biggest threat facing us was the crossing of the Saudi-Kuwait border by Iraqi soldiers hell-bent on surrendering to American forces. Higher headquarters detailed our mission as one of surveillance: should an attack by Iraqi forces occur we were to hunker down behind the advancing Iraqi lines and report on the enemy's actions as they bypassed our locations.

Sergeant Jestel's first order to his team was to construct a bunker located along the "berm." The berm was, in fact, two earthen berms which ran the entire length of the Saudi-Kuwait border, from which our team would operate should an attack on U.S. forces occur. We spent two days working hard to construct a team bunker out of discarded lumber and old oil drums. The bunker was just a few hundred meters from the Saudi border outpost, so we could get to it quickly if the need arose.

Just hours after we had completed our construction, on 15 January 1991, the war began for our recon team. Around 2030 that evening the company commander and our platoon leader, 1st Lt. Steven Ross, arrived to tell us that at 0345 on the sixteenth the air war would commence. Immediately the team began to prepare itself for combat. While little remained to be done in overall preparation, we still had last-minute checks to perform on our weapons and equipment. Then we moved into the bunker. A second recon team that had been colocated with us moved into its bunker, too. Other units that had been at the Saudi border outpost quickly left for the rear. The wait for the beginning of the war began.

At 0345 the night sky lit up like a Christmas tree as enemy AAA (antiaircraft artillery) fire tore into the night seeking out the coalition air forces. It was almost surreal to watch as streaking tracer rounds and burning missiles filled the night sky. As I peered out over the muzzle of the M-60 machine gun I was helping to man, I counted forty-two missiles launched from a single site inside Kuwait territory. The AAA and missile fire would not cease for a single moment for nearly three days!

As morning broke the team relaxed a bit, since we could now see that little of the static situation had changed on the ground to our front. We observed little movement by Iraqi forces.

We attempted to send DCT (data communications terminal) traffic to our company headquarters, but received no reply. Later we learned that every time our company headquarters sent radio traffic it was shelled by Iraqi forces that were DF-ing (direction finding) their position. So the company headquarters was less than enthusiastic about sending routine radio traffic.

We spent several more days in our bunker observing the enemy forces in the Al-Wafra forests. It was during that period that our team received credit for its first "kill." A message from higher headquarters had directed our team to observe at night any and all missile fire from the known Iraqi positions. If a missile launch was observed, it was to be noted and, if possible, its position was to be triangulated and reported to higher headquarters. This tasking had a high priority and was treated by the team as such. That night, the team observed multiple missile launches from a position only a few kilometers to our front and took a compass bearing from our position. Combining that with a bearing taken by a recon team located farther down the berm, Lance Corporal Blackwell roughly calculated the position of the enemy missile launcher and we immediately passed the information to higher headquarters. Some time later the team was informed by the commanding officer of 1st Recon Battalion, Lt. Col. M. L. Rapp, that our message provided the intelligence that launched a coordinated air strike which destroyed the enemy missile launcher. According to the colonel that was the first confirmed "kill" during the war resulting from the use of information gathered by a Marine reconnaissance team. That provided our team with an immense sense of personal satisfaction.

After a few more days, our team was shifted east to a new position. The 1st and 2d Marine Divisions were shifting areas of responsibility, and recon teams from 2d Recon Battalion would fill the positions we were leaving. Along with the rest of the platoon, our team was moved to a place called OP (observation post) 4, a place the team, and the rest of the platoon, would never forget.

Once the entire platoon arrived at OP-4, Lieutenant Ross divided it in half, and our team along with one led by Sgt. Michael "Stryker" Davis was placed to the north of the Saudi border building, near OP-4. The two teams spread out a bit, then dug in.

Our primary mission was to observe the enemy, and, if possible, bring supporting arms to bear on targets of opportunity. Opposite our location was an active Iraqi observation post. We observed the enemy and they observed us. Being

Marines, we felt that if we could see the enemy we should kill him. Cross-border movement by individual teams had been strictly forbidden, so we called for an air strike. Artillery and naval gunfire were both out of the question since neither range-fan was even close to covering the target, and an air strike was denied by higher headquarters because the Iraqi OP was not deemed a "priority target." For all the talk about Marine Air being there for Marines on the ground, the recon teams felt slighted at being less than a priority.

During the day our teams conducted mobile patrols along the berm, and at night we remained stationary at our positions and observed the enemy. It was like trench warfare; the enemy knew—or thought he knew—exactly where we were and we knew where they were, and neither side was authorized to engage the other. That situation was about to change.

In the middle of one night toward the end of January our teams were attacked with direct fire from Iraqi sappers. The Iraqis had moved into RPG (rocket-propelled grenade) range, let loose with a few rounds, and then hightailed it back toward the relative safety of their OP. Fortunately, the Iraqis were miserable at even basic recon operations. I can say this because they attacked the empty Saudi outpost building instead of hitting our two positions to the north and south of where our platoon's teams and headquarters section were located. Neither of our teams returned fire, deducing that if the Iraqis did not know where we were, we were not going to tell them. Coincidentally, during the attack Lieutenant Colonel Rapp happened to be spending the night with the HQ section. After his return to the rear, the Iraqi OP opposite us miraculously became a priority target and was bombed (and subsequently abandoned, as the platoon would later discover).

Prior to his departure, Lieutenant Colonel Rapp issued an order to have one of the teams occupy the Saudi outpost building. In my opinion, this placement of a reconnaissance team in a target known to be registered by the enemy defied all logic. Nonetheless the order was carried out. And, our team got the tasking. The team became even more tense now that we felt quite naked to the enemy's eyes and guns.

On the night of 29 January 1991, I was awakened by the voice of our combat engineer. I was to go on watch in another hour but, along with the rest of the team, I had to get up quickly. The enemy was observed fast approaching and I was needed, since I carried most of the firepower, the M-249 SAW. I put on my helmet, stowed my poncho-liner in my ruck, and went upstairs to see Jay. Sergeant Jestel pointed out more than fifteen enemy vehicles headed our way. Radio communications with our HQ section failed due to jamming by the enemy, and without guidance from higher headquarters, we prepared to engage the enemy.

Jay split the team into two groups with himself, Reuter, and the combat engineer on the north side of the building and Mike and myself on the southern side. Dykes would remain with the vehicle at the rear of the building, trying to establish communications with the HQ section.

Supported by Soviet-made BMPs, the enemy's T-62 and T-55 tanks moved to within one hundred meters of our position. The berm was an obstacle to their movement, and the only route the enemy could maneuver around went right through our position. As one of the enemy's vehicles moved into my machine gun sights, Sergeant Jestel and the other Marines let loose with an AT-4 and LAAW rockets. Mike attempted to fire his LAAW but it failed. He tried another and that, too, failed to fire. After hearing the volley let loose by the other Marines, I began to fire my SAW at the enemy vehicles to my direct front. Small-arms fire, tank fire, and rocket fire filled the night sky with brilliant flashes of light and a cacophony of sounds. A brief lull ensued after what seemed to be a few minutes of firing. The Iraqis had begun to withdraw. Jay yelled for us to move forward, and we did. Our team reached a group of small sand mounds in front of the building, where Jay organized us into a small defensive perimeter in preparation for the expected Iraqi counterattack. Then a red pop-up flare went up.

The flare signaled the team to move back to a small horseshoe-shaped berm located well behind the OP building. When the team got there we found the lieutenant trying desperately to get air and ground support. Navy air support was the first to arrive and it came in the form of a Navy A-6 Intruder. The big jet came in low and dropped its bombs, but failed to stop the Iraqi counterattack. By that time the Iraqis had located our platoon's position and placed us under heavy tank fire. The lieutenant was now arguing over the radio with the light armored vehicle (LAV) company commander, trying urgently to get the LAV commander to move his LAVs forward to our position to provide fire support for the platoon, but the LAV commander refused. The commander seemed to feel that he did not have enough armor to take on Iraqi tanks. I will never forget our lieutenant shouting into his radio handset, asking the LAV commander if he thought we really had a lot of armor!

In the meantime our platoon sergeant, S.Sgt. Gregory Gilliespie, put together an assault team to go forward with the sole intention of killing enemy tanks with rockets and small arms while we waited for ground support. Our recon team formed the core of this hastily assembled assault group. As we began to move forward the lieutenant asked the platoon sergeant what the hell he was doing. Sergeant Gilliespie's reply was short: "We're going to kill tanks, sir." The lieutenant told us we were crazy and to forget it. He had worked out a linkup plan with the LAV platoon located about a klick (one thousand meters) behind our position. All the teams then moved out together, with our team's vehicle bringing up the rear of a small motorized column.

The linkup with the LAVs was a little scary. Initially thinking us to be the enemy, the LAVs took our platoon under 25mm fire until a scream over the radio by our lieutenant halted the shooting. As we linked up with the forward elements of the LAVs, a fiery explosion to the north caught our attention. Later we learned that an LAV had been hit and destroyed by one of its own.

As we watched the first spectacle, another unfolded before our unbelieving eyes. An illumination flare came out of the sky and landed virtually on top of one of the LAVs to our front. The LAV commander jumped down beside it and tried to extinguish the bright-burning flare by kicking sand over it. The last thing I saw was a brilliant explosive flash as the vehicle was struck by a missile fired from an Air Force A-10 Warthog flying overhead. We moved away from the LAVs as quickly as possible, just in case word didn't get to the A-10 pilot that he had just fired on a friendly vehicle. Luckily, no other U.S. casualties were sustained then by that particular aircraft.

Our platoon remained with the LAV HQ section through the night and into the early morning hours. The coming of dawn revealed that Marine forces had soundly defeated the Iraqis, and later in the day we moved back into our old positions at OP-4.

The area around OP-4 was littered with the debris of war, including numerous destroyed enemy tanks and dead enemy soldiers inside those tanks. The ground was charred black and pockmarked from shell fragments. Our team had survived its first taste of battle.

The platoon remained at OP-4 several more days, until we were ordered to the rear for a few days of rest. We eventually made it all the way back to the DSA, where the platoon was allowed to take hot showers and wash out cammies at a water purification point on Manifa Bay. We discovered that the purification point could provide us with unlimited hot water for showers, and we took advantage of that.

After showering, the platoon members found additional relief in hot chow and some much needed sleep. While the security around the DSA was considerable, no one in the team seemed to rest well when none of us were on watch. But after a quick stint at the DSA preparing ourselves to go back into action, the platoon was called to 1st Marine Division headquarters. Upon arrival we received a warning order to carry out a POW raid on the Iraqi OP across from OP-4. Reconnaissance work had now given way to direct action.

Over the next several days our platoon prepared for the raid. The platoon was briefed by the division commander, Brig. Gen. Mike Myatt, and his staff. After the planning began, I found myself in the role of support. I would be tasked with driving an emergency extract vehicle while the rest of the platoon went out on the raid. I didn't like it, but I did it.

When the time came, the raid was executed smoothly, but no Iraqis were in the position when the platoon arrived. For a few hours, an ambush was laid at the site in case any Iraqi force should return, but none did. Our men walked back across the Saudi border, where those of us driving extract vehicles picked them up and returned to the division headquarters for a debriefing. Following the debrief, the platoon was sent to a forward staging area where we were to make our final preparations for the coming ground offensive.

Much to our surprise, division headquarters was still toying with the idea of sending us into Kuwait to probe the minefield in advance of the assault forces. Headquarters even went so far as to attach "war dogs" to our reconnaissance platoon. These dogs were trained to sniff out explosives, and someone thought they might help us locate buried mines. But after consulting with the dogs' handlers, we learned that the Iraqi mines were virtually impossible for the dogs to detect because each mine's explosive charge was sealed airtight. Still, our team practiced moving and operating with the war dog team. After several days the plan was scrapped. Instead, certain teams were tasked with conducting conventional ground reconnaissance missions. In our platoon Sergeant Davis and his team drew the mission and soon left to walk into what one team member would later describe as "hell."

Sergeant Davis's recon team returned after a few days and passed on what information they had gathered. The minefields were thick, but the mines themselves were, amazingly, *above ground*. (We later learned that wind and rain had exposed them.) The Iraqi troops were by then located behind that defensive wall and, seemingly, could not move forward, and oil well fires had turned the sky, horizon to horizon, into a dark, ominous environment. Hell on earth had just arrived.

Just prior to the actual commencement of the ground assault, our platoon was moved into positions along the line separating the two Marine divisions. In order to insure that we could observe any Iraqi force trying to drive a wedge between the two Marine divisions, our team was placed just out of small-arms range of the enemy. As our team dug in we received word to move back and link up with the platoon HQ and Team 3. Our team was placed in a position that had an RFA (restricted fire area) to the north and, in addition to rendering us incapable of calling for fire support should the enemy attack the point we occupied, our position was too exposed.

All the recon teams were instructed to link up and jointly occupy the platoon HQ's position through the night. And this night would be short.

During the brief time we occupied the position, our platoon found itself surrounded by Marine artillery, which had moved forward during the night to fire in support of the Marine breaching operation. The team awoke to the sound of big guns firing the first volleys of the ground offensive. Later in the day the platoon managed to link up with our company headquarters. Our platoon was then ordered to report to Task Force Grizzly's headquarters, and upon our arrival we were assigned to link ourselves with a platoon from D Company, 1st Reconnaissance Battalion.

Our platoon moved out and headed for the Al Jabber Air Base inside Kuwait, where D Company platoon was supposed to be assigned to Task Force Ripper. Our motorized movement through the breach and to the Al Jabber Air Base went smoothly.

Once there we found that the task force had surrounded the air base, ready to open fire and level the place. Psych (psychological) operation units were using loudspeakers to try to get those Iraqi soldiers still inside the base to surrender. However, just when it seemed that the CO of Task Force Ripper had had enough of the waiting game and every tank, LAV, and crew-served weapon was going to let loose upon the hapless Iraqis, a huge white flag of surrender was paraded out from an air base building near the main gate, followed by a large formation of Iraqi troops.

As that small crisis ended, our platoon and D Company

platoon received a new tasking from Ripper's CO directing us to conduct a mobile reconnaissance north of the air base and see if we could locate an Iraqi armored column that was reported moving south. After a quick briefing our platoon moved out.

As all twelve vehicles that carried our platoon moved northward we suddenly found ourselves under artillery fire. As if this were not serious enough, these artillery shells were filled with gas. We knew the shells contained gas since they did not explode on impact; instead they merely burst with a flash of sparks and spray. Our recon teams immediately donned and cleared their gas masks. That episode was to be the first of many times that our teams would find themselves operating in MOPP-4 (nuclear/biological attack) during the ensuing night. Immediately our teams moved back to our starting positions.

As we headed back toward Al Jabber Air Base, nightfall descended. Coupled with the thick black smoke from the hundreds of oil well fires set by departing Iraqi troops, the day turned into the blackest night I have ever encountered. It was so dark, I couldn't see the Marine seated next to me inside the Hummer, and I was wearing night vision goggles! The MEF (Marine Expeditionary Force) ordered all units to remain in place to prevent friendly units from accidentally engaging one another during the night. Our two platoons halted until a murky daylight allowed us to make our way back to the airfield. Back at Al Jabber we were told that the ground war had ended. There was some celebration, but it did not last long because we knew there would still be work to do.

We received our final tasking, to insure that the Iraqi positions north of Al Jabber Airfield were unoccupied by the enemy and collect as many of their weapons, conveniently left behind on the ground, as we could carry.

Our platoon spent the remainder of that day gathering up dozens of weapons and turning them in at a collection point set up at the air base. Then, after spending the night at Al Jabber, our platoon was ordered to return to the DSA in Saudi Arabia as part of the overall movement of the 1st Marine

Division south. Our platoon and the forces around us moved first to Kuwait City and then down the coastal highway all the way back to the DSA.

At the DSA we were allowed to rest and relax while anticipating our return home. Home for us was Camp Schwab, Okinawa, and in late April, via C-5A aircraft, we returned there to a hearty welcome by our fellow Marines. Just as quickly as we had departed Okinawa for war, we settled in to perform the mundane duties that all Marines face in garrison. Nonetheless, Camp Schwab had never looked so good to this recon Marine.

=== 25 ===

In Conclusion . . .

Without doubt the Stingray concept proved to be a remarkably effective killing machine. Uncomplicated, highly mobile, and tremendously effective when properly employed, as a "force multiplier" Stingray was tailor-made for existing (and follow-on) Marine capabilities. It was not the only concept that worked effectively as a result of the Corps searching to refine its future warfighting capabilities. The concepts of forward deployment of artillery; an air-mobile approach to contact and patrolling; and the sea-basing approach to long-range logistical problems all served to enhance Marine Corps operational capabilities.

Credit is certainly due to those innovative men who helped develop these ideas—to General Davis for his use of artillery raids in northern I Corps in support of Stingray, to General Walt for his initial understanding of the Stingray concept, to Lt. Gen. Herman B. Nickerson for his devotion to the "proper employment" of both force and division reconnaissance assets, and to the loyalty of the men who executed those missions.

The refinement of those unique infantry, reconnaissance, artillery, air, and logistical concepts that originated in the mid-1960s and helped change the future of the Marine Corps are described in the 1996 edition of *America's Armed Forces: A Handbook of Current and Future Capabilities.**

---

*Edited by Sam C. Sarkesian and Robert E. Connor Jr. Chapter 5 is entitled "The Marine Corps," by Marine historian Allan R. Millet, assisted

In it, the authors write:

Strategy and Missions
The Immediate Post-Vietnam Period, 1975–80

As the Marines withdrew from South Vietnam during 1969–1971, the Corps refocused on the amphibious warfare mission as well as the reinforcing role in NATO. Headquarters Marine Corps watched with great interest the developments in the field of armored and maneuver warfare, highlighted by the 1973 Arab-Israeli War, and the massive Soviet conventional buildup of the mid to late 1970s. Commandant Robert E. Cushman, Jr., and his successor, General Louis H. Wilson, Jr., introduced a series of reforms and policies that reflected the most likely contingencies in which Marines might become involved. They sought improved armored vehicles such as the M60A1 and M60A3 tanks and an improved amphibious assault vehicle. They sought more sealift in order to enhance the Corps' amphibious readiness. These improvements set the stage for General Wilson's emphasis on preparing the Marine Corps for its rapid reinforcing role in NATO, especially on the northern flank, and later participation in the Rapid Deployment Joint Task Force (RDJTF).

The commandancy of General Louis H. Wilson (1976–1980) was marked by the adoption of better artillery (M198 155-millimeter howitzer), as well as by better infantry assault weapons such as the M203 grenade launcher, the shoulder launched multipurpose assault weapon (SMAW), and the Dragon antitank missile system, all of which greatly enhanced the fighting power of Marine infantry units. Commensurate with the addition of the increase in firepower was the reorganization of the Marine infantry battalion, the basic tactical element of the Marine Corps. Reflecting the shift from manpower to firepower (as did the Stingray concept),

by Maj. Larry Alexander, USMC, S.Sgt. Leo J. Daugherty III, USMCR, and Sgt. Mike Nelson, USMCR.

Marine infantry battalions were reduced in total strength but were provided with the addition of a weapons company. The three (down from four) rifle companies were likewise provided with the crew-served weapons of the deleted company in order to bolster their firepower. This increase in firepower enhanced the combat effectiveness of Marine units, thus strengthening the Corps' claim that it could preserve its warfighting capability with a relatively modest investment in modernization.

General Wilson's decision to turn Marine Corps Base, Twenty-nine Palms, California, into the Corps' mobile warfare center encouraged Marine tactical commanders to think in terms of mobile as well as amphibious warfare. The role of Twenty-nine Palms as "a combined-arms training center" at first met with some skepticism and institutional opposition from purists on both the ground and air sides. The Combined Arms Exercises (CAXs) soon found general approval. These exercises simulated battles against a Soviet-style enemy in the high desert, a good representation of the Middle East. General Wilson and his successor, General Robert H. Barrow, paved the way for the Marine Corps' participation in the Rapid Deployment Joint Task Force, commanded by Lieutenant General (later Commandant) P. X. Kelly. Wilson and Barrow also initiated improvements of the Marine Corps well into the 1980s.

Coinciding with the continued emphasis on mobile warfare and rapid deployment, the Marine Corps benefited from the increased defense spending in the last year of the Carter administration and the first five years of the Reagan administration. The material improvement of the Fleet Marine Force coincided with the movement away from the noninterventionist policies of the late 1970s toward the increased opposition to Soviet-Cuban activity in the Third World. The fall of the Shah of Iran, coupled with the Soviet invasion of Afghanistan in 1979, demonstrated the vulnerability of the U.S. geostrategic interests in Southwest Asia, as well as the need for a force that could respond to any crisis within a matter of days. The appointment of General Kelly to head the newly created Rapid Deployment Joint Task Force was recognition that the Marine Corps would be a key element in U.S. power projection in the Middle East and Southwest Asia.

Despite the buildup that began in 1980 and the increased infusion of dollars under the first Reagan administration, both the RDJTF and General Wilson's revamped Marine Corps remained untested. Studies concluded after the Vietnam War, notably Martin Binkin and Jeffrey Record, *Where Does the Marine Corps Go From Here?*, questioned the need for a Marine Corps. Binkin and Record reflected the views of many critics, who argued that the U.S. experience in Vietnam showed the futility of Third World intervention. The events of Iran and Afghanistan, coupled with the fall of Anastasio Somoza in 1979 and the election of a Marxist regime in Grenada, however, kept the issue of power projection alive.

The election of Ronald Reagan in 1980 and the continued Soviet involvement in Afghanistan and Central America signaled not only the rearming of the U.S. armed forces but a return to a maritime strategy. The construction of a 600-ship Navy, advocated by then Secretary of the Navy John Lehman, ended only in 1990. The 50 percent increase in spending permitted the Navy and the Marine Corps to acquire new weapons as well as expand their research programs. For the Marine Corps, this research and development effort concentrated on enhancing its mobile war-fighting capability with the eventual addition of the six-wheeled light armored vehicle (LAV) as well as the upgrading of the infantry battalion's small arms.

The new administration quickly set about dispelling the notion that Vietnam had crippled the U.S. ability to protect U.S. interests. A Marine peacekeeping force went to Lebanon (1982–1984), while a Marine amphibious unit participated in the combined operation that liberated the Caribbean nation of Grenada (October 1983). The operation in Grenada demonstrated shortcomings in joint training, organization, and tactics.

The Marine Corps emerged from Grenada with deficiencies to correct, which included the physical training of its men, inadequate equipment (the lack of a mobile assault vehicle), and the need for another restructuring of the infantry battalion. Operation Urgent Fury revealed that Marines were capable of operating for short periods of time without rest, but needed more physical fitness training. The training issue did not stop there. Combat in Grenada likewise suggested that Marines in non-infantry military occupational specialty (MOSs) had forgotten the basic Marine adage: "Every Marine a rifleman." These problems were addressed by Commandant P. X. Kelly, but more intensely by Commandant Alfred M. Gray. Gray, in fact, again revamped the Marine Corps infantry battalion and ordered that all new Marines would receive thirty days of specialized infantry training.

The eventual acquisition of the light armored vehicle (LAV) and the upgrading and increased firepower of the LVPT7 amphibious assault vehicle (AAV) corrected the deficiencies in fire support for Marine battalions. (The numerous vehicle designations show variations of a basic vehicle such as light armored vehicle [LAV], landing vehicle personnel track [LVPT], landing vehicle track [LVT], amphibious assault vehicle [AAV], and amphibious assault vehicle personnel [AAVP]. For accuracy, the numbers such as LVPT7, LVPT7A1, and AAVP7A1 indicate different model numbers for the same vehicle with modifications. For accuracy, the appropriate model numbers are indicated where applicable.) This was dramatically revealed during the subsequent operations in Panama in December 1989, when a joint U.S. force stormed ashore into Panama City in order to install the democratically elected government of Panama, which had been blocked by Panamanian strongman General Manuel Antonio Noriega. Marine light armored infantry teams (LAI) in Operation Just Cause (December 1989) seized all their objectives in minimum time with few casualties.

The United States demonstrated in Grenada and Panama that it could still selectively employ military force whenever it deemed this necessary. The barracks bombing in Beirut, Lebanon (October 1983), as well as the continuing Soviet-Cuban role in Africa and Central America, however, raised serious questions regarding the military's role in civil wars where U.S. interests seemed vague. These same questions renewed the debate over the roles and missions of the various branches of the military, as each service sought to shape its warfighting doctrine according to the newly ordained emphasis on "low-intensity conflict." When both the Soviet Union and the Warsaw Pact collapsed at the end of the 1980s, the missions of the U.S. military became even more debatable. For the Marine Corps, the answer was simple: it prepared for global expeditionary warfare with a continued emphasis on power projection from the sea.

Despite the collapse of Soviet military power, other countries—notably Iraq, Iran, North Korea, China, and the new Russia—have filled the void of potential threats vacated by the dismembered Soviet Union. The victory over Iraqi forces during Operation Desert Storm in 1991 came about largely due to the absence of Soviet intervention. For the Marine Corps, Desert Storm resulted in one of the quickest, least costly, and most visible victories in history, though it remains to be seen if a victory of Desert Storm's scale can be repeated. Despite President Clinton's pledge to retain American military strength, the shift from one major adversary to a host of regional threats calls into question traditional planning and force structure.

Organization

The Marine Air-Ground Task Force (MAGTF)

While the Fleet Marine Force remains the administrative and operational headquarters, the MAGTF serves as the actual combat power in the execution of a naval campaign. A MAGTF would, in fact, be the "task-organized" element of an FMF, "an integrated, balanced air-ground combined arms force organized for combat with its own combat service support element (CSSE) . . . [and] . . . employed to apply ground combat power supported by the MAGTF's own aviation combat element and CSSE."

MAGTFs may vary in size, but the organizational structure will always include a single Command Element (CE) with a Ground Combat Element (GCE), Aviation Combat Element (ACE), and a Combat Service Support Element (CSSE). Although there are always four major elements within a MAGTF, other temporary, separate task organizations may be required to perform combat service support (CSS) functions. The commanders of those separate organizations report directly to the MAGTF commander. These organizations may include, but are not limited to, landing support, engineer, *force reconnaissance,* artillery, and electronic warfare task organizations. The flexibility built into the MAGTF is deliberate, since the FMF serves as "the nation's primary hedge against strategic uncertainty, and their operational planning and task organization concepts have been developed to meet that role on short notice."

The successful defense of Saudi Arabia can be attributed to the rapid deployment of Army and Marine forces after the initial Iraqi invasion of Kuwait. Part of this success can be credited to the fleet of pre-positioned logistics shipping in the Indian and Pacific oceans. Another part was the rapid deployment of a Marine expeditionary brigade during the first two weeks of Operation Desert Shield. The Marine–Army response was, in fact, a primary example of how the rapid deployment force might have reacted to a Soviet invasion of Iran in a similar scenario. The ability of the Marine Corps and Army to deploy rapidly during the initial days of Desert Shield demonstrated the intrinsic value of such floating supply depots as an enhancement to expeditionary forces in general and amphibious forces in particular.

There are two basic types of Marine Air-Ground Task Forces that can be utilized to perform any number of missions. They are the Marine Expeditionary Unit (MEU) and the Marine Expeditionary Force (MEF). The MEU is the smallest MAGTF and is thus restricted in the missions it is capable of carrying out. The MEF provides the combat power necessary for any initial lodgment on a hostile shore and sufficient firepower to defend an area until reinforced by U.S. or allied forces. The MEF's warfighting capability is enhanced by its ability to employ both fixed- and rotary-wing aircraft for complex offensive air operations, all integrated with ground units' mobile warfare.

The Marine Expeditionary Unit (MEU)

The MEU is built around a Battalion Landing Team (BLT) and a composite aviation squadron. It is commanded by a colonel and is attached to a naval task force that patrols a major ocean or sea in support of U.S. geostrategic interests. Weaponry of a MEU includes standard infantry battalion weapons, an artillery battery, a company of amphibious assault vehicles, a platoon of light armored reconnaissance vehicles (LAVs), and a platoon or more of tanks. With its command and support elements, it numbers around 2,000 Marines. The MEU provides an immediate reaction capability to crisis situations and is capable of limited combat operations. The operations most associated with a MEU are the following:

    Humanitarian and disaster assistance
    Noncombatant evacuation operations
    Tactical recovery of aircraft and personnel (TRAP)
    Counter-drug operations
    Amphibious raids
    Embassy security and protection
    Show-of-force operations

Each MEU that leaves Camp Lejeune, North Carolina, California, or Okinawa is required to be trained and certified as "special operations capable" and receives the designation MEU (SOC). This force is capable of performing limited special operations without additional reinforcements. The MEU receives sustainment from the accompanying fleet and is not self-sufficient in combat operations beyond fifteen days.

In the event of major commitments, a MEU will be reinforced with other Marine units and placed under the control of the next higher echelon, the Marine Expeditionary Force. The

Marine Expeditionary Force is built around at least a Regimental Landing Team, a composite Marine Aircraft Group, and a combat service support group (strength 5,000–6,000) and is commanded by a general officer. The MEF may be deployed afloat or dispatched to a crisis area by air to join maritime or land pre-positioned supplies and equipment. The advance elements of a MEF can be forward deployed for extended periods, receiving fly-in echelons, an amphibious assault echelon, and an assault follow-on echelon. The MEF's organic Combat Service Support Element enables the force to move rapidly into a hostile environment until reinforced or withdrawn. Aviation support for the MEF is either carrier based or shore based advanced airfields. The MEF will also be capable of participating in joint operations ashore with Army and other allied forces in time of war. A MEF, besides the standard infantry weapons organic to one or more Marine infantry regiments, has artillery battalions, tank companies, light armored reconnaissance companies, and antitank (TOW) companies. In short, the MEF can carry out a wide range of combat operations from low to mid-intensity levels. These include the following:

1. A follow-on reinforcement for a committed MEU or other forces.
2. Amphibious operations, that is, assaults, raids, demonstrations, or withdrawals.
3. Operations in support of a maritime campaign such as the seizure or defense of an advanced naval or air base.
4. Low-intensity conflict operations, such as counterinsurgency, counterterrorism, counterdrug actions, peacekeeping, or peacetime operations.
5. Humanitarian assistance/disaster relief.
6. Evacuation operations/protection of U.S. government property or individuals.

A MEF may be organized with variable task organizations and structure, tailored for any intensity of combat and capable of deploying to any geographic region of the world. Forming a

MEF can include combining existing forward-afloat forces, land-based forces, mission-deployed forces, maritime and pre-positioned equipment and supplies, additional forces from another MEF, and units of Selected Marine Corps Reserve (SMCR) or the members of the Individual Ready Reserve (IRR).

Into the Future

The U.S. Marine Corps of the post–World War II era was forged from its World War II experience in the Central Pacific campaigns, which created the integrated Marine Air-Ground Task Force. Refined and modernized through trial and error during the Korean and Vietnam Wars, the MAGTF emerged during the 1970s and 1980s as a preeminent assault force-in-readiness that successfully integrates new concepts in doctrine and weapons. Although Marines in Operation Desert Storm conducted only a minor amphibious linkup with I MEF during the third day of the ground war, the presence of an amphibious task force off the coast of Kuwait prevented the Iraqis from reinforcing their inland positions against General Schwarzkopf's main effort.

The MAGTF will have to be trained and tailored to respond rapidly and effectively to any threat from any quarter of the globe that threatens vital U.S. interests. This "tailoring" will require the addition of a new medium-lift helicopter and a new generation of amphibious assault vehicles able to meet the Navy's over-the-horizon requirements and retain the Marine Corps' ability to introduce sufficient combat power ashore at the outset of a naval campaign. Marine Colonel Patrick Collins [a career reconnaissance Marine] best summed it up when he wrote:

"Helicopter-borne infantry operating from over-the-horizon amphibious shipping, combined in a single command with attack helicopters and vertical short-take-off and landing Harriers, affords a revolutionary maneuver potential to a force projected from the sea. Such a force could maneuver at three or four times the speed of the fastest mechanized forces ashore."

The Marine Corps' claim as an expeditionary force-in-readiness will be effective only if it can develop an operational war-fighting doctrine that is compatible with its structure for amphibious operations.

While the MAGTF is structured to meet regional contingencies, its overall focus must not shift from its primary mission, which is to project ashore a sufficient level of combat power in the shortest possible amount of time. Given the absence of a major threat comparable with the Soviet Union, the Marine Corps, like the other branches of the U.S. military, will be operating within the framework of reduced budgets and manpower for the foreseeable future. The MAGTF commander will be required to fight, hold, and to win with a unit as small as a reinforced infantry battalion in some situations. The Marine infantry battalion landing team, even if provided with superior and overwhelming firepower, is capable of supplying only a limited amount of sustained combat power until relieved or reinforced.

The MAGTF, in short, is capable of providing a force that can be rapidly deployed to a regional crisis within a relatively short period, that is armed with sufficient firepower to accomplish military missions, and that is able to offer maximum flexibility in the achievement of specific geostrategic goals. Moreover, the MAGTF can float offshore for months, out of sight until it is needed in a crisis. This will become a key advantage in any future post–Cold War crisis like Somalia or Bosnia where it is diplomacy and global politics that count.

The demise of the Soviet Union and the U.S.-led coalition against Saddam Hussein have not made all of the world a safer place to live. The world has witnessed the deepening of ethnic and tribal conflicts that were either suppressed or redefined while the Cold War defined foreign policy. These problems have now emerged as the flashpoints that could destroy the stability many believed would follow the end of the Cold War. Moreover, as the nations of sub-Saharan Africa, Asia, Southwest Asia, and South and Central America emerge to take their places in the post–Cold War world, old tensions will place even greater demands on the ability of the U.S. armed forces to project military power into areas of the world that would have been unthinkable or technologically unfeasible until the 1990s. Hence the Marine Corps' adoption of the "From the Sea" strategy simply redefines an expeditionary operational concept within the uncertainty of world events.

Epilogue

It is now February 2000, and a full thirty years since I was a recon team member in 3d Force Recon Company in Vietnam. Over these many years many changes have been made within the reconnaissance community to assist the recon Marines and corpsmen of today in successfully carrying out their multiple missions. So, it was not surprising to recently read that Marine higher-headquarters is "once again" re-inventing the reconnaissance wheel. In an article written in November 1999, which appeared on page 8 of *Marine Corps Times*, a staff writer for the *Times* states that the new commandant, General James L. Jones, is reviewing both fire support and reconnaissance doctrines.

"Fearing that the capabilities of each group have been degraded seriously during the past decade, General Jones ordered reviews of each group's current capabilities and structure immediately after becoming commandant July 1."

The article goes on to say that in August 1999, Lt. Gen. Raymond P. Ayres Jr., deputy chief of staff for plans, policies, and operations (PP&O), was charged with completing each review and providing the commandant with proposed fixes.

In August, Ayres's group solicited input from the operating forces, Marine Corps Headquarters departments, Marine Corps Combat Development Command, and the training establishment regarding the identification of specific issues for correction and preliminary solutions.

"Specifically, PP&O requested input on the role, mission, organization, structure, and training of ground reconnaissance and artillery," said a spokesman at Marine Corps Headquarters. "The intent was to tap into the collective knowledge and experience throughout the Marine Corps, quickly frame the issues, and offer the commandant solutions.

"What General Jones did not want was another study that became drawn out over time."

Marine officials said Ayers's group is validating the information it gathered and preparing to turn over the results to Jones. The reports will include two sets of recommendations for Jones to consider—recommendations that can be enacted immediately as well as those that can be enacted during the course of his tenure.

During his first Corps-wide trip, made shortly after he became commandant, Jones asked Marines for their thoughts on reconnaissance.

"I personally think that we have atrophied and done damage to our reconnaissance mission in the Marine Corps, which is historically one of the things we have prided ourselves in since World War II," Jones said in a July interview.

Some areas under review and possible fixes included:

Reorganization: Marine officials are wrestling with the idea of providing each Marine Expeditionary Force with a force reconnaissance company and each division with a reconnaissance battalion. The new structure, if approved, would clarify command relationships and mission and provide each group with organic ground reconnaissance.

Currently, only I MEF has separate units, Marine officials said. Both II MEF and III MEF have combined units under the force reconnaissance company, which must support both the MEF and division.

One fear Marine officials have is that combined units blur command relationships between the MEF, the division, and the subordinate reconnaissance unit. The perceived blur leaves questions about the recon unit's proper chain of command, what the priority of its training is, who provides administrative and logistical support, and who gets priority reconnaissance support.

The MEF and division do not necessarily have the same reconnaissance needs. MEF focuses on deep reconnaissance, the commander's area of interest. Division focuses on distant reconnaissance, the commander's area of influence.

Refocusing: Marine officials also are trying to bring the focus of force recon back to providing the MEF commander with deep reconnaissance. While deep reconnaissance is supposed to be the group's primary mission, often it isn't.

"We must look at additional tasks that have been assigned to force units, perhaps degrading their primary function, serving as the commanders' 'eyes and ears.' It comes down to prioritizing tasks and focusing on those that are an enabler for the commander."

One area under review deals with providing recon capabilities to Marine Expeditionary Units. "We need to see if the way we train certain units within the MEU—like direct action missions, which are done by elite reconnaissance units—is worth the sacrifice of the recon capability."

Structure: Marine officials want to insure that the size of units and reconnaissance teams provides the capabilities needed for commanders at every level.

Marine officials also are reviewing the grade shape—how many sergeants or lieutenants are needed—and the training pipeline for the reconnaissance military occupational specialties (MOSs) to insure they meet the Marine Corps' needs.

While the Marine Corps wrestles with reinventing reconnaissance doctrine, concepts, and philosophy, it may do well to revisit its own history. A detailed examination of the III MAF Surveillance Reconnaissance Center of 1969, created by Lt. Col. Gerry Polakoff for Lt. Gen. Nickerson and his staff, and how it successfully addressed and improved upon many of the problems generated by joint operations, communications, and required support could prove to be invaluable. Additionally, Lt. Col. Alex Lee's book, *Force Recon Command: A Special Marine Unit in Vietnam, 1969–1970,* describes not only the creation of the SRC, but the inherent problems associated with coordination between the force recon company, the MAF, the U.S. Army, and all other supporting agencies. These problems may continue to plague future Marine "problem solvers" tasked with addressing changes to current reconnaissance capabilities and structure.

—Maj. Bruce H. Norton, USMC (Ret.)

Recommended Reading

Battalion Recon

First Recon—Second to None by Paul Young
Never Without Heroes by Lawrence C. Vetter Jr.
Reluctant Warrior by Michael C. Hodgins
Sergeant Major, U.S. Marines by Maj. Bruce H. Norton, USMC
    (Ret.) and Sgt. Maj. Maurice J. Jacques, USMC (Ret.)

Force Recon

Force Recon Command by Lt. Col. Alex Lee, USMC (Ret.)
Force Recon Diary, 1969 by Maj. Bruce H. Norton,
    USMC (Ret.)
Force Recon Diary, 1970 by Maj. Bruce H. Norton,
    USMC (Ret.)
Inside Force Recon by Michael Lee Lanning and Ray William Stubbe
One Tough Marine by First Sergeant Donald H. Hamblen, USMC (Ret.) and Maj. Bruce H. Norton,
    USMC (Ret.)

Index

347

Index